IMAGES
of America

DONNA TEXAS

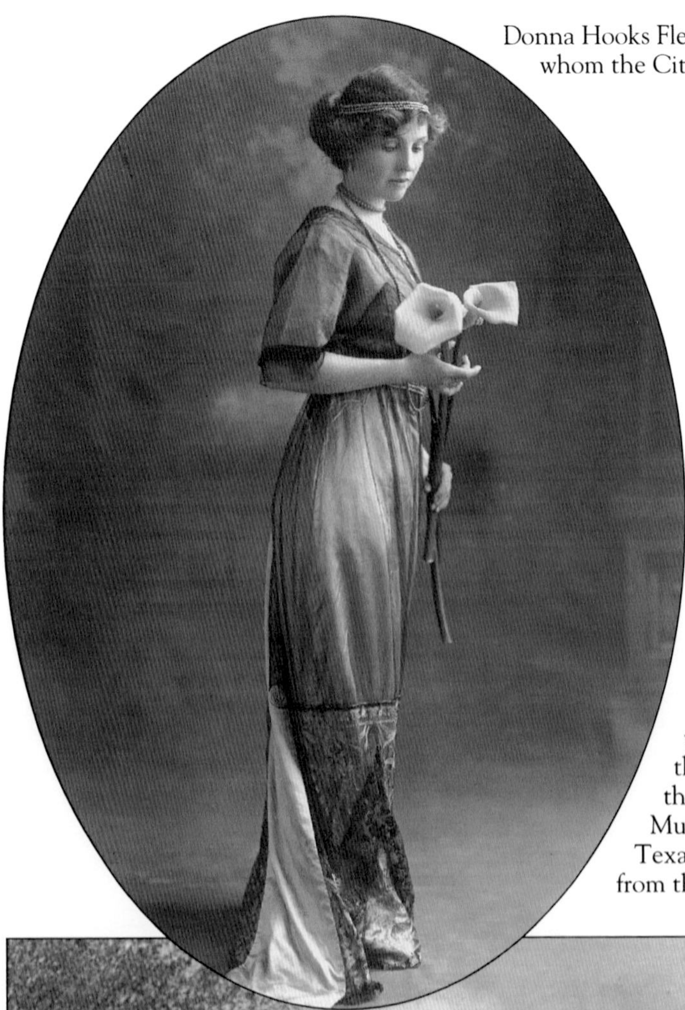

Donna Hooks Fletcher (1879–1969), for whom the City of Donna was named.

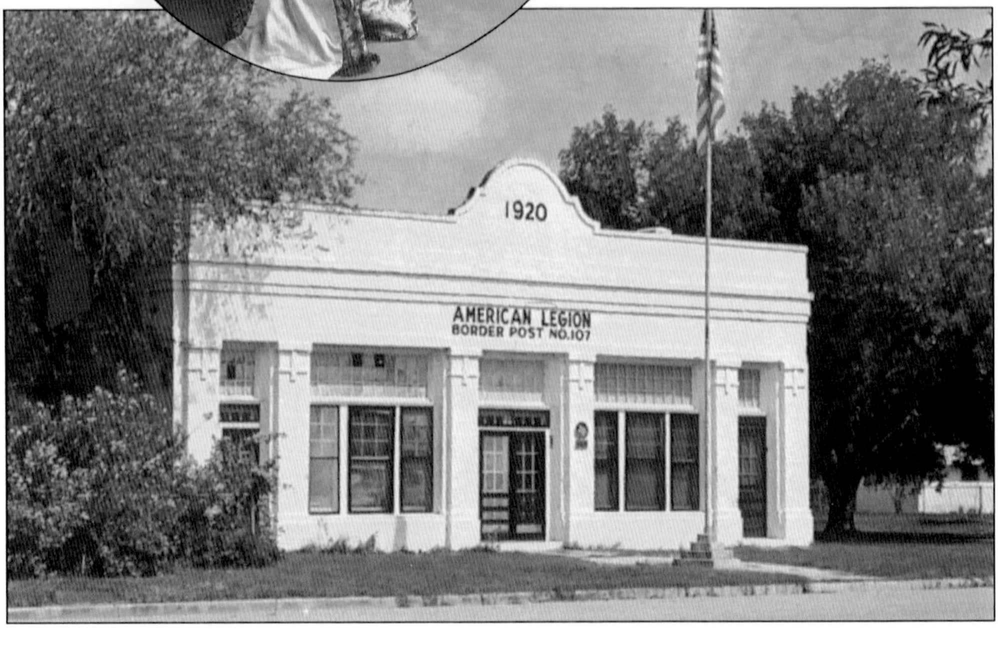

The American Legion Post No. 107, founded in Donna, built the first American Legion Hall in the world. Dedicated in 1920, the Post Hall, which contains the Donna Hooks Fletcher Museum, received this Recorded Texas Historic Landmark plaque from the State of Texas in 1964.

IMAGES
of America

DONNA
TEXAS

Karen Gerhardt and Laura Lincoln

ARCADIA
PUBLISHING

ISBN 978-0-7835-1943-2

Published by Arcadia Publishing
Charleston, South Carolina

Printed in the United States of America

Library of Congress Catalog Card Number: 2001095109

For all general information contact Arcadia Publishing at:
Telephone 843-853-2070
Fax 843-853-0044
E-mail sales@arcadiapublishing.com
For customer service and orders:
Toll-Free 1-888-313-2665

Visit us on the Internet at www.arcadiapublishing.com

This book is dedicated to Mr. Aaron Todd, for whom without his foresight in preserving photographs there would be no story to tell of an early Donna, Texas.

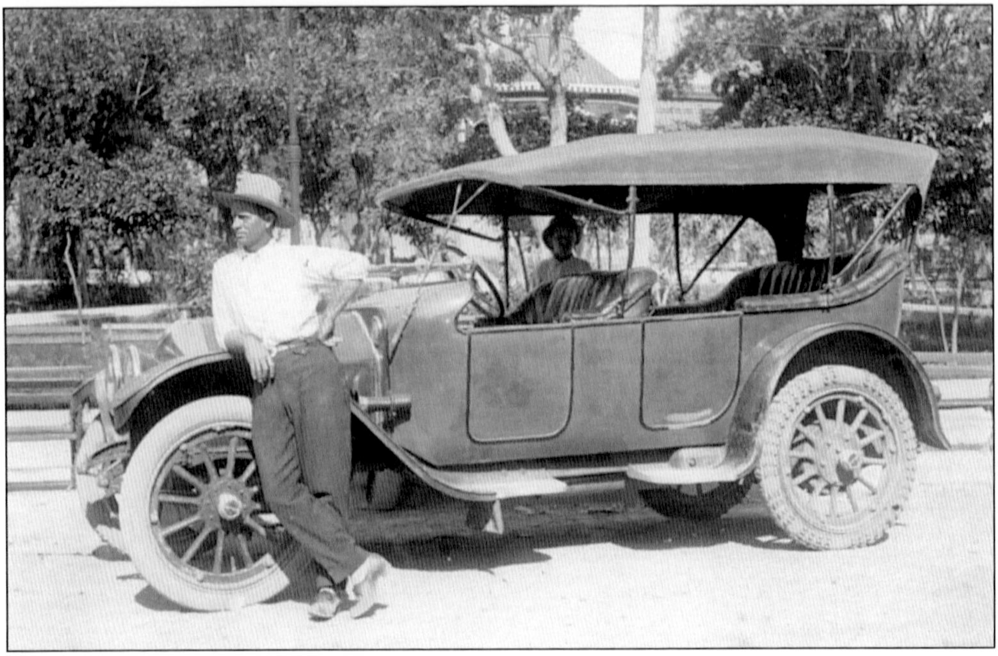

Donna's early years occurred during a time of rapid transition throughout the Valley. Here Deputy Sheriff Sam Barnard, equally at ease riding his horse through the brush country, leans against a roadster in front of the Donna City Park.

Contents

Acknowledgments

I wish to thank my co-author Laura Lincoln for her good spirit, good work, and good fun. It was a great joy to work with this great friend. I would also like to thank the Board of Directors of the Donna Hooks Fletcher Museum for their confidence in me and their generosity in the use of the museum's archives. Lastly, I want to thank Keith Ulrich of Arcadia Publishing for his patience, encouragement, and understanding. Great publishers are hard to find and a treasure to keep.

Karen Gerhardt

I would like to acknowledge an outstanding board of directors who oversee the Donna Hooks Fletcher Historical Museum for their wisdom, trust, support, and confidence in my work in addition to allowing me a treasured opportunity as a director of the museum. My friend and colleague Karen Gerhardt for sharing this project. My coworkers Amy Alejandro and Yolanda Ordonez for their professionalism and dedication. Thank you to the University of Texas at Pan American Intern program, especially Belen Tamez and Anabel Cantu. I am especially grateful to my parents Connie and Dan Lincoln; I appreciate everything you have done for me. I love you. Thank you both for sharing your knowledge of Rio Grande Valley history and all your wonderful stories. To my brother, Albert Lincoln, for your humor and great support. Finally I would like to thank the people and schools of Donna, Texas, for their tremendous support, and genuine interest in their museum, along with their cooperation in making it a success. To the City of Donna for believing in preserving all the historical and future merits of a great town.

Laura Lincoln

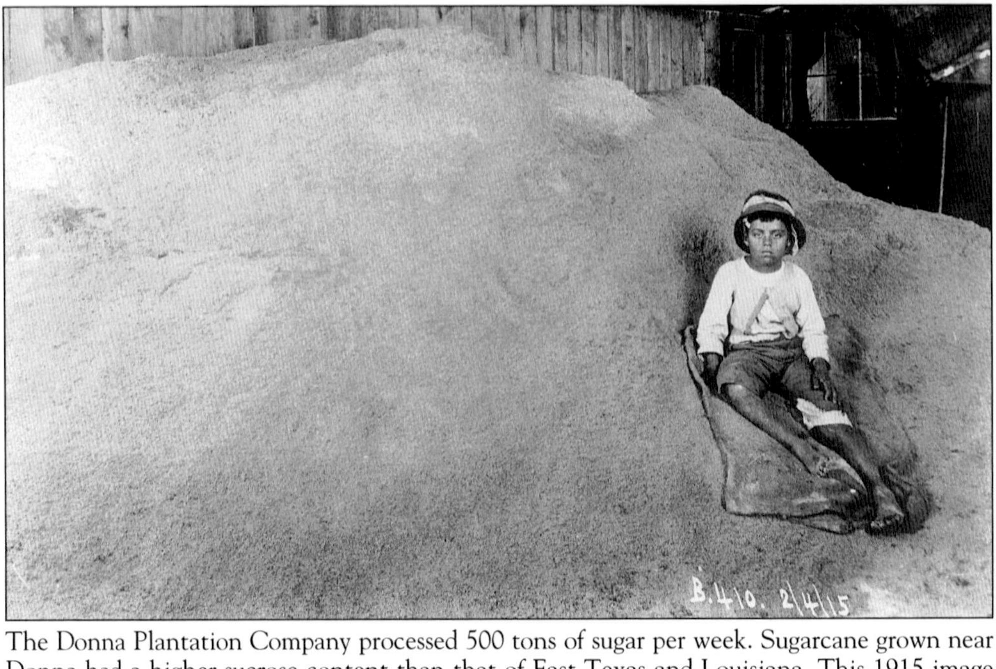

The Donna Plantation Company processed 500 tons of sugar per week. Sugarcane grown near Donna had a higher sucrose content than that of East Texas and Louisiana. This 1915 image shows a child, sitting on a bag, perched on a mound of unsacked sugar.

INTRODUCTION

The City of Donna, located on the Sam Fordyce extension of the St. Louis, Brownsville, and Mexico Railroad, lies in the heart of the Valley. On December 5, 1904, the Lott Town and Improvement Company incorporated with $100,000 in capital and named the City of Donna as its principal place of business. Railroad entrepreneur Uriah Lott named the town for Donna Hooks Fletcher, daughter of Thomas J. Hooks. The City of Donna incorporated in 1908.

The town grew slowly because of the lack of available potable water. *Portreros* brought water from as far away as Lyford and Mission to each home in Donna. A barrel of water cost 50 cents, and the water had to be boiled before it could be used for drinking or cooking. By 1908, a water tower and a filtration plant provided potable water for Donna residents. Electricity came in 1916.

Several of the founders of Donna lived south of town at Run, on the Military Highway. Ed Ruthven and then Andrew Champion operated the store and post office at Run. Children were first educated in private homes and then later at a small school. The struggle of man versus nature was a full-time job, and in the end, nature won. After the devastating flood of 1909, the Hooks and Hester families, as well as the Ruthvens, the Champions, the Holloways, the Vertrees, the Boeyes, the Norwoods, and others, left their farms and plantations and moved inland to Donna.

The following year, Donna began to build rapidly and continued its growth well into the 1920s. The bandit raids of 1914–1917 during the height of the 1910 Revolution in Mexico brought U.S. Cavalry, artillery, and infantry to Donna and the entire Valley, along with Texas militia and, beginning in 1916, the National Guard, to protect border citizens and restore peace. The National Guardsmen came from the Midwest, and they found the Valley climate a factor to be reckoned with. The influx of troops brought a prosperity that sped up the building boom. Many of the soldiers returned to Donna after World War I ended in 1918 and made it their permanent home. The world's first American Legion post was established in Donna in 1920.

The installation of pumps on the Rio Grande and the system of canals and laterals throughout the delta made large-scale agriculture highly profitable. Citrus fruit, cotton, sugar cane, and vegetables were grown all year long. Packing sheds and canning plants lined the railroad tracks. Rail cars were filled with vegetables and packed with ice. Refrigerator cars, a vast improvement over the open cars filled with ice, provided dependable temperature control and made possible nationwide markets for Donna (and Valley) produce.

Like its sister cities, Donna gave its heart and soul to the World War II effort, contributing its produce and its sons, until the enemy was vanquished in 1945. Donna citizens are proud of their heritage and traditions. They are also a warm people, welcoming strangers and prodigals alike. Donna is truly the heart of the Valley.

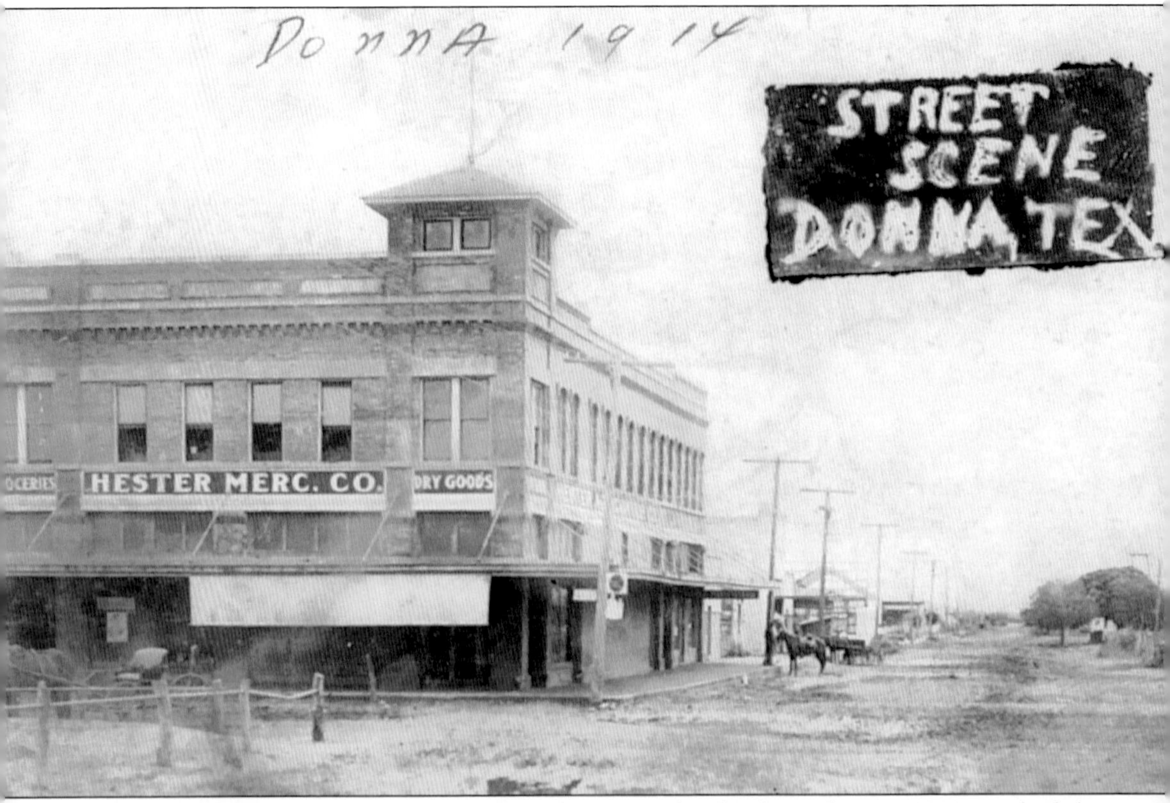

The Hester Mercantile Company with its distinctive facade, shown here in 1914, was built by A.F. Hester Sr., a business partner of Thomas J. Hooks. The Hester family played an integral part in the early development of Donna.

One

Life Along the Rio Bravo

At the turn of the 20th century, life on either side of the river, known as the Rio Bravo in Mexico and the Rio Grande in the U.S., had not changed a great deal from the days of its initial settlement by the Spanish in 1749. The land supported livestock such as cattle, sheep, goats, and pigs. Corn and melons thrived in the hard dry soil. Ranch workers and their families lived in small villages along the river.

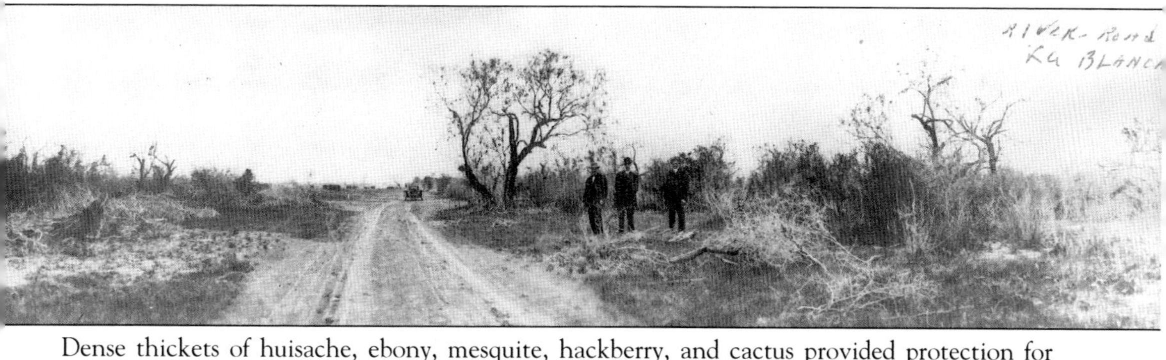

Dense thickets of huisache, ebony, mesquite, hackberry, and cactus provided protection for wildlife, but limited travel between ranches and ranch villages to the river and to hand-cleared trails, or *senderos*. The La Blanca Road, shown here as it was being cleared in 1908, brought a new way of life to ranch families and settlers alike.

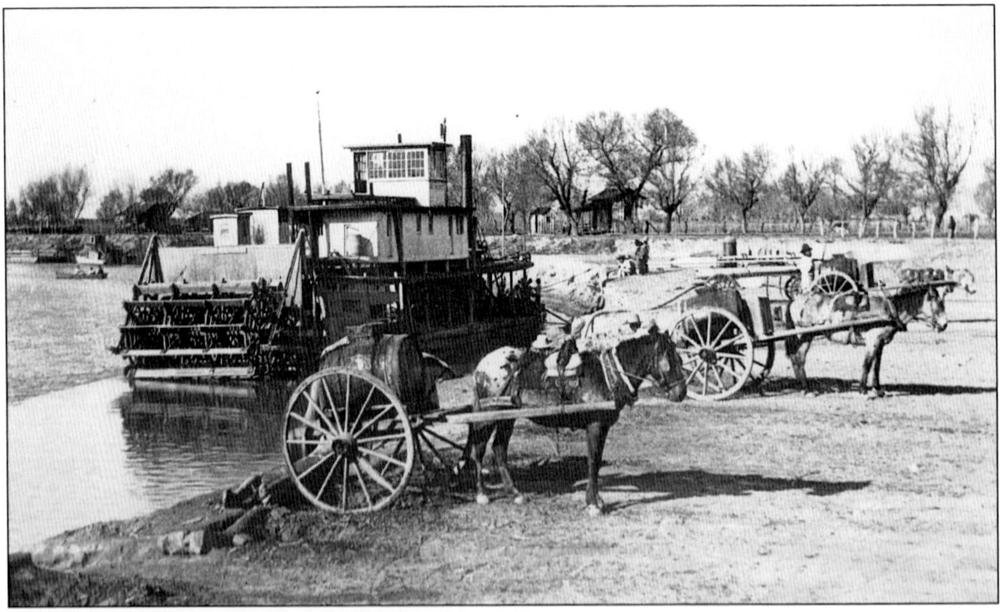

Steamboat travel on the Rio Grande began in 1847 during the Mexican War, when the U.S. Army brought steamboats to transport soldiers and military supplies up and down the river. After the war, partners Richard King and Mifflin Kenedy bought surplus steamboats and gained control of the river traffic, which they maintained until after the Civil War. The sternwheeler *Bessie*, built in 1876 and shown here around 1900, carried passengers and goods such as hides, tallow, and beeswax, which were traded at the ranch landings for beans, coffee, sugar, flour, and rice. The *Bessie* operated until 1902, when she was dry-docked.

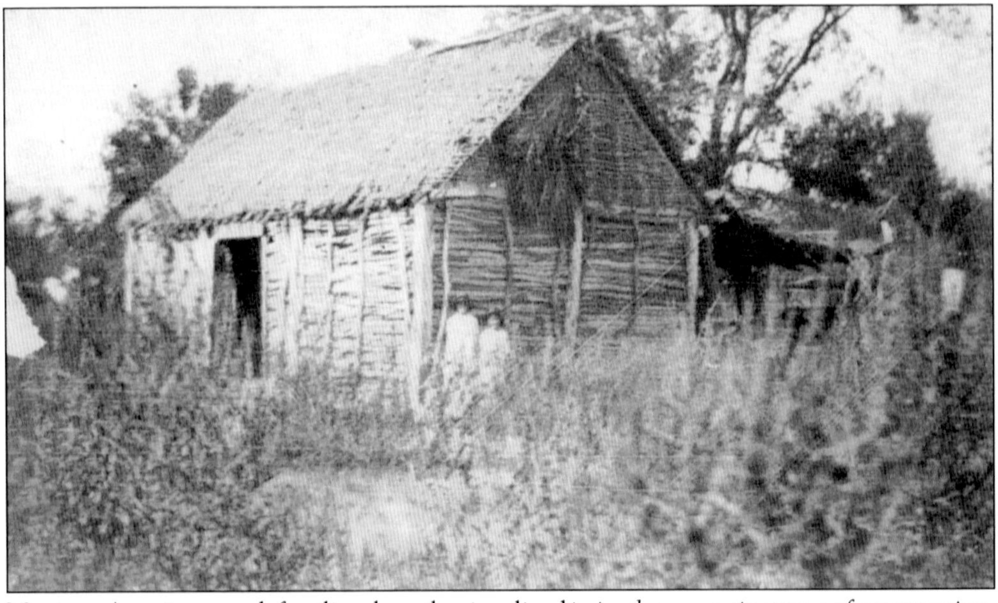

Mexican-American ranch families along the river lived in *jacales*, an ancient type of construction. Gardens grew close to the walls, and meals were cooked outdoors. Most of the *jacales* in the Lower Rio Grande Valley were destroyed in the storms of 1909 and 1933. Only two or three remain standing today.

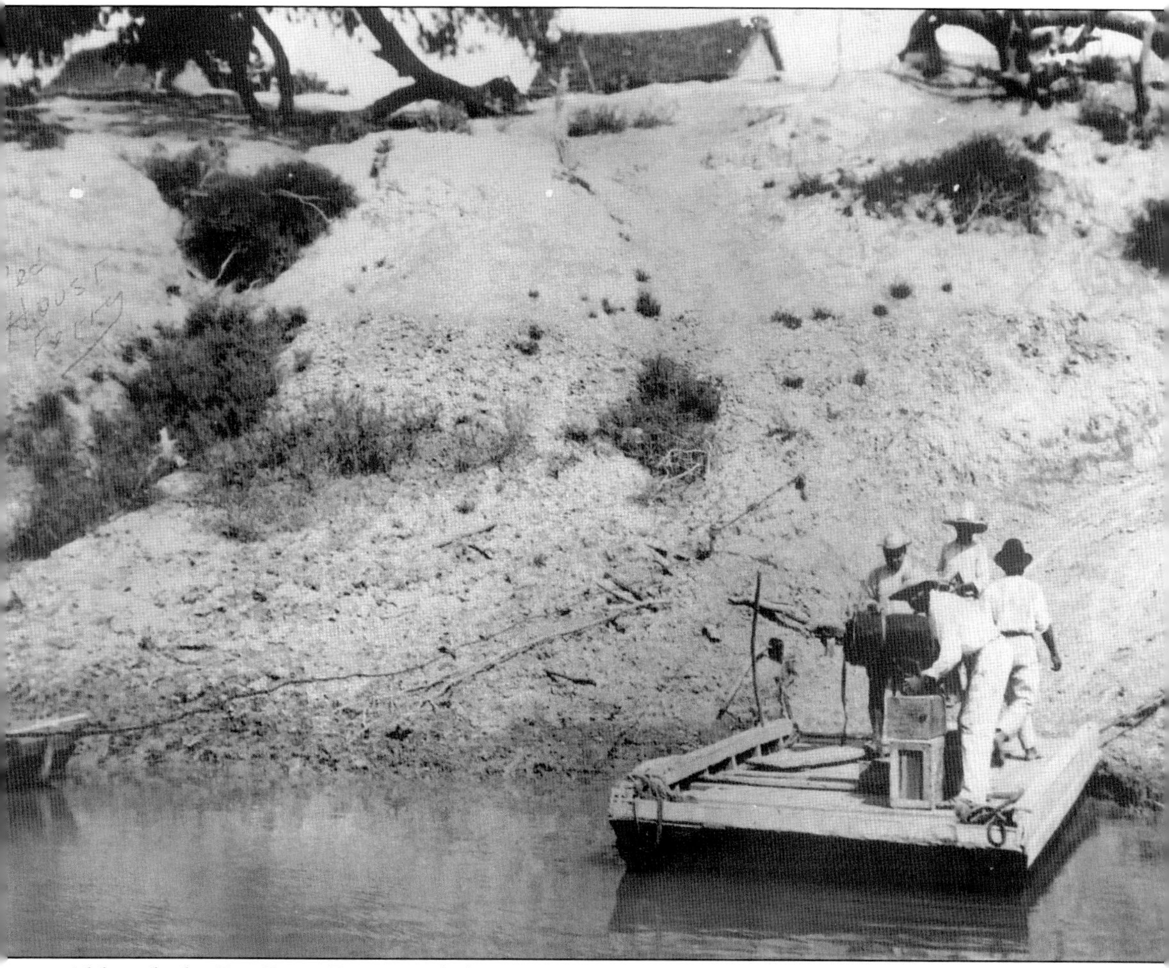

Although the Rio Bravo/Rio Grande became an international boundary between Mexico and the U.S. in 1848, families living on both sides of the river traveled freely back and forth. The hand-pulled ferry at *Casa Colorado* (Red House), south of Donna, was one of the best-known crossing sites. The family of Mr. Alonso Salinas received the charter to operate the ferry, which carried travelers and livestock across the river well into the 20th century.

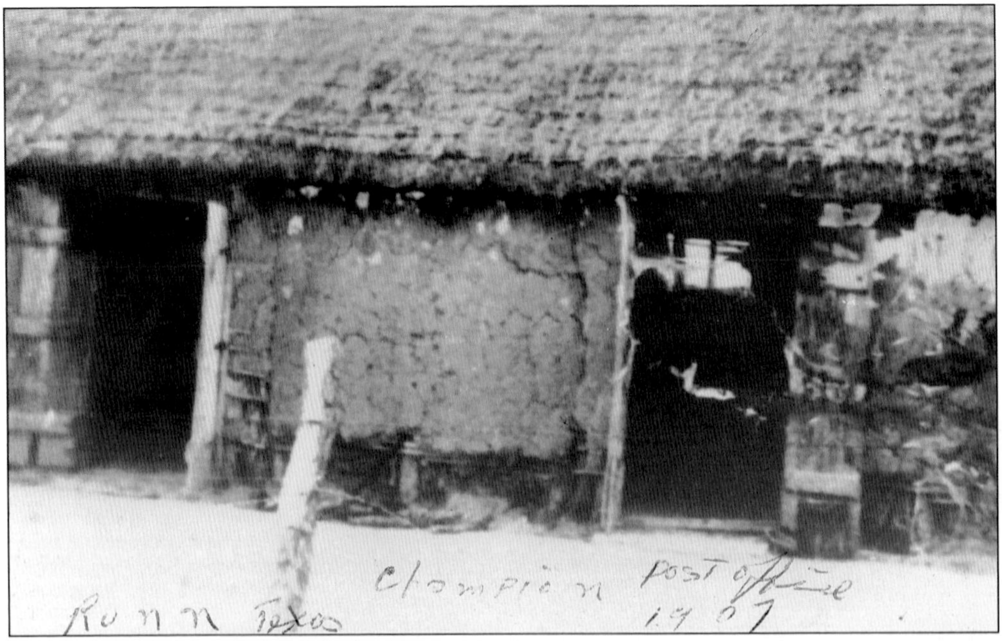

Ed Ruthven [also spelled "Ruthevan"] opened the first general store at Run, a contraction of the letters of his name, in 1904. He also became the first postmaster. When Ruthven moved to Donna, T.J. Hooks and A.F. Hester Sr. asked Andrew Champion Sr. to operate the post office and grocery store at Run. Born and raised in Point Isabel, Champion had been a farmer, general store owner, and mounted customs inspector before moving to Hidalgo County to farm in 1900. In 1906, he left his farm in the former Llano Grande land grant and moved to Run. This is the building in 1907.

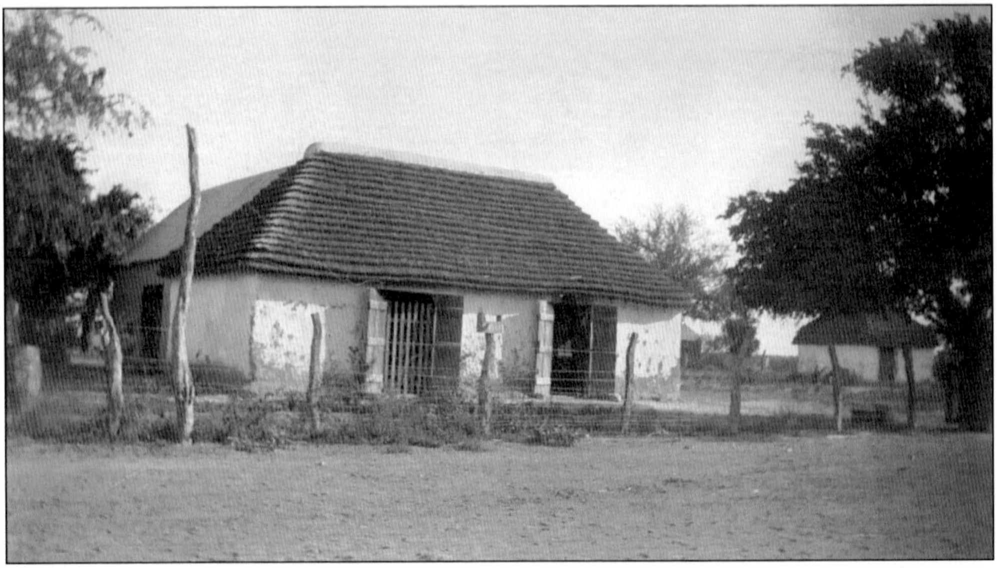

The store and post office building at Run was constructed in the manner of a *jacal*, or hut, made of local materials. The photograph dated 1907 shows such typical construction features as willow stake walls plastered with mud, plank doors, and a thatched roof. The same building, shown here in 1909, illustrates improvements, such as whitewashed walls and a neat, sod roof.

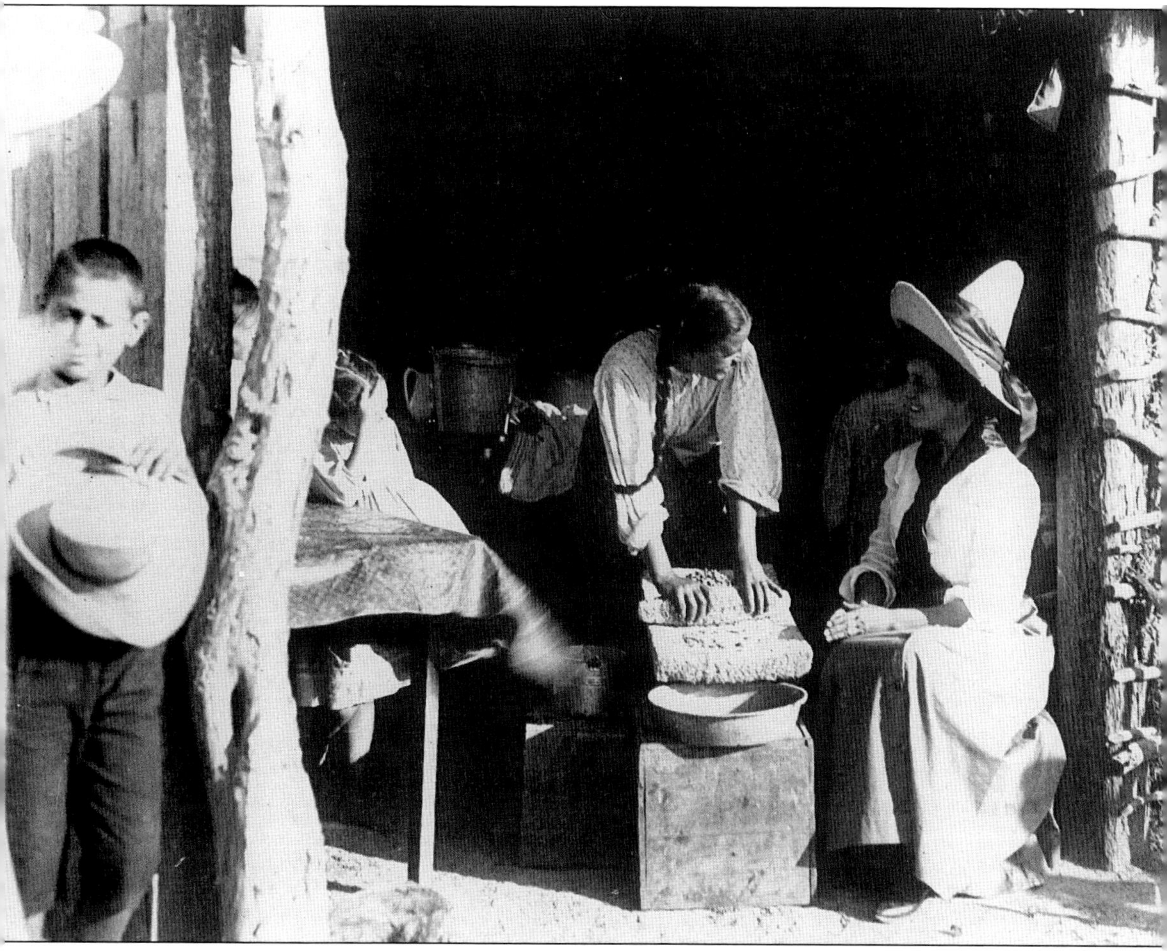

The woman bending over the *metate* is grinding corn with a *mano* to make cornmeal, which is collected in the metal pan. She will add water to the cornmeal to make a paste and will shape the paste into a ball. Next she will pat the ball between her hands until it becomes a flat, round tortilla and will cook the tortilla on a griddle.

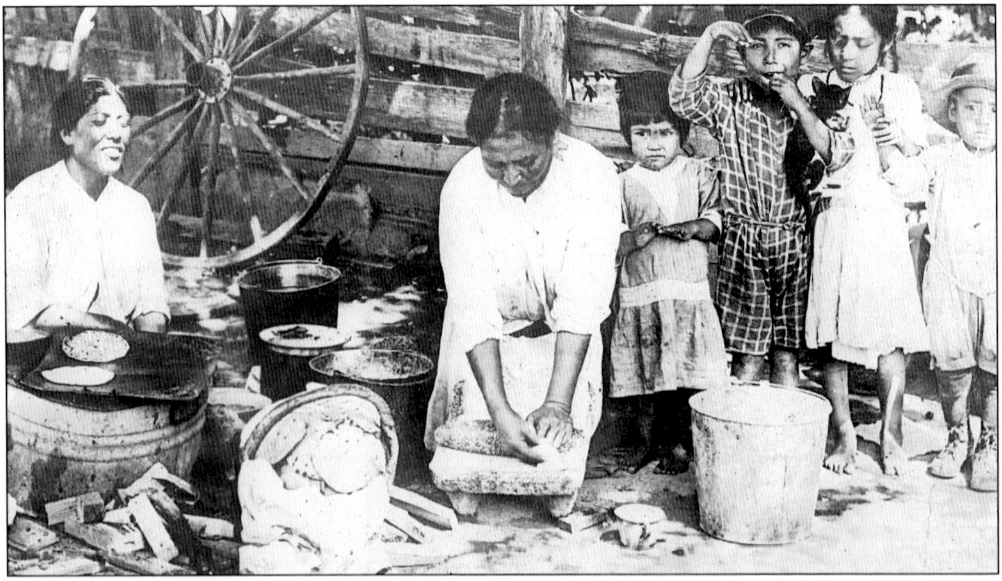

Women often made and cooked tortillas outdoors. The wagon in the background suggests that this may have been a campsite.

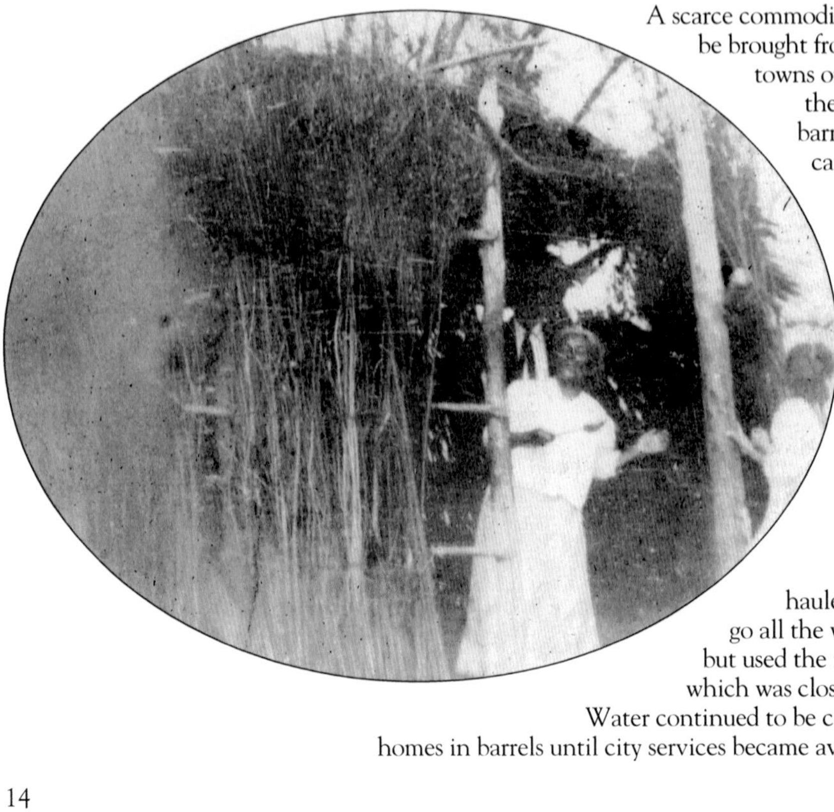

A scarce commodity, water had to be brought from other Valley towns or siphoned from the river into large barrels mounted on carts. Barrels were then delivered to homes, where the water had to be boiled and strained before use. After the systems of canals and laterals were developed, the men who collected and hauled water did not go all the way to the river, but used the irrigation water, which was closer to the towns. Water continued to be carried to Donna homes in barrels until city services became available in 1908.

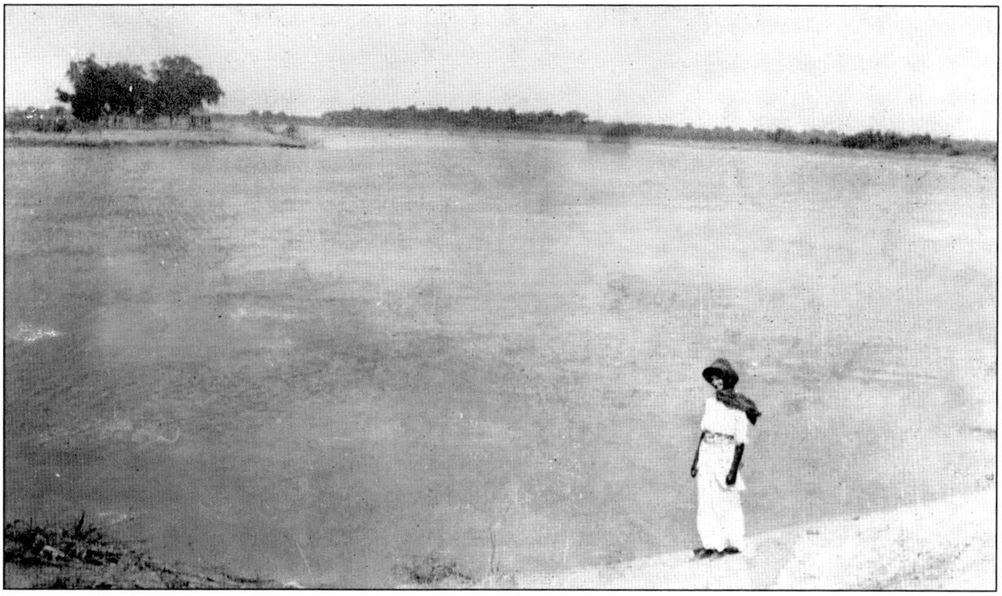

Despite the hardships of life along the river, ranch families and newcomers alike found time for recreation. Shown here about 1915, a woman walks along the river near the town of Hidalgo, the county seat of Hidalgo County before it was moved to Edinburg in 1908.

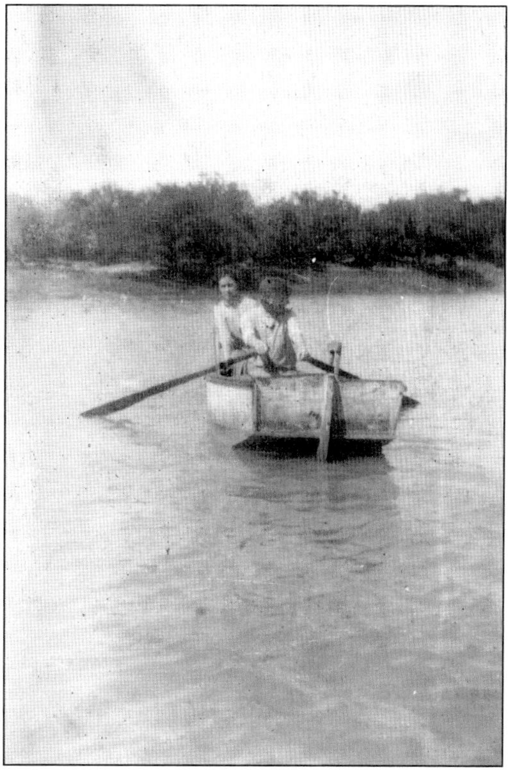

Boating on Llano Grande Lake, another form of recreation, was also popular. The Llano Grande tract was located near Mercedes, downriver from Donna. The lake was fed by water channeled from the Rio Grande.

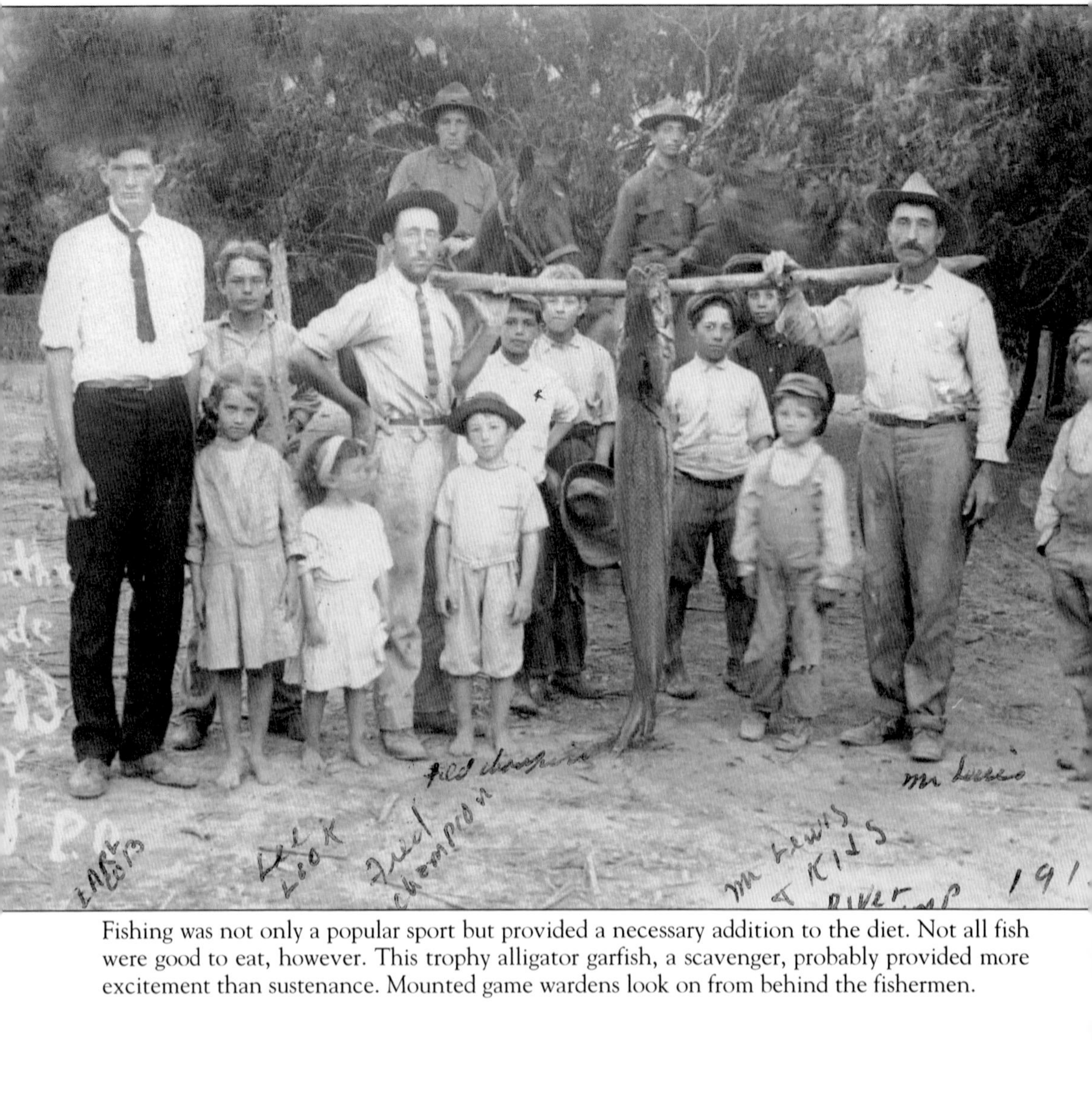

Fishing was not only a popular sport but provided a necessary addition to the diet. Not all fish were good to eat, however. This trophy alligator garfish, a scavenger, probably provided more excitement than sustenance. Mounted game wardens look on from behind the fishermen.

Two

FOUNDING HISPANIC FAMILIES

From the beginning, Hispanic families played an important role in the history of Donna. Some founding families came from the Valley, while others came from different parts of South Texas. These families created the nucleus of a socioeconomic middle class of businessmen and their employees, teachers, photographers, and other professionals. The descendants of these pioneers continue to define much of the social, economic, and cultural character of Donna and the Rio Grande Valley.

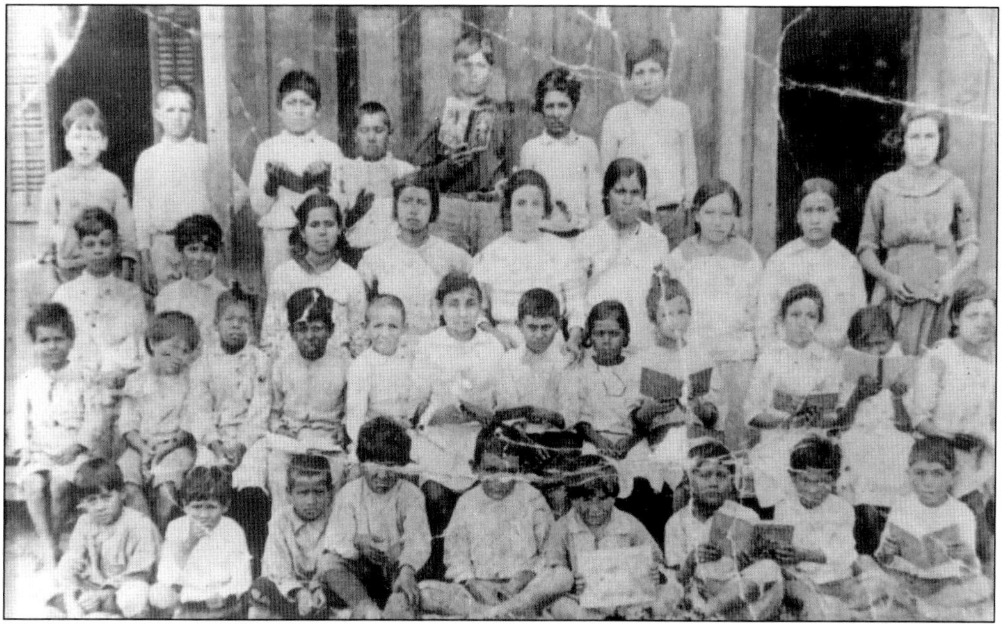

The first Hispanic teacher in Donna was Paciana Guerra of Mier, Tamaulipas, hired in 1911 by Severiano Avila, Apolonio Balli, and Bentura Bentiz to teach their children. In East Donna Spanish-speaking children attended classes at the Escuela Mexicana (Mexican School) to receive their education. The school building was a two-story wooden house.

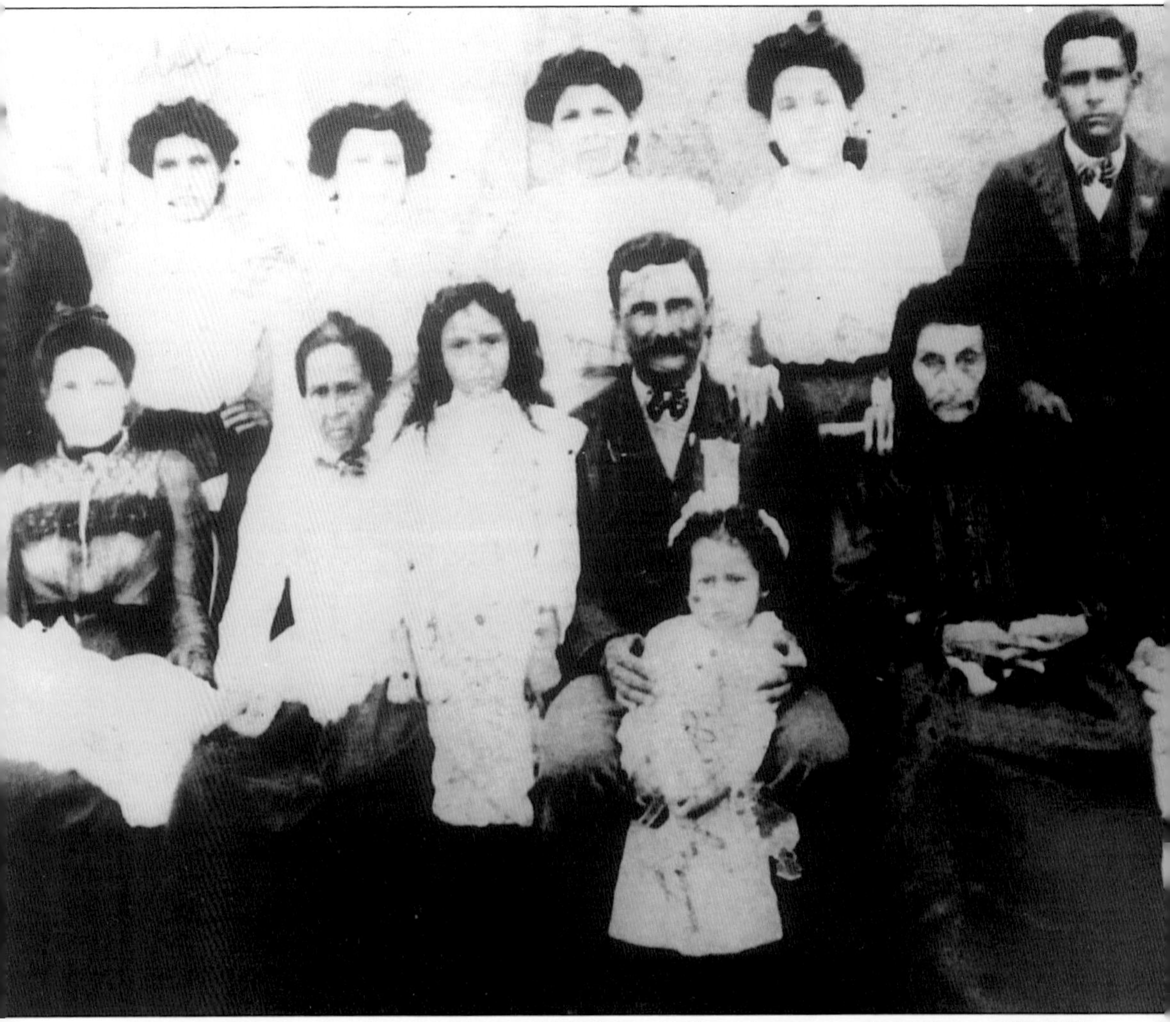

The Muñoz family, one of the first Hispanic families to settle in this area, is shown here c. 1906. The family arrived about 1850, when Dionicio Muñoz was eight months old. The Muñoz family later established the Azadores Ranch, now the location of Run. Pictured are, left to right: (front row) Antonia Muñoz Uresti and Francisca Flores Muñoz; (middle row) Andrea Muñoz, Dionicio Muñoz with Preciliana Cavazos Muñoz, and Guadalupe Uresti; (back row) Tranquilino (Quiron) Avila, Adela Muñoz Avila, Natalia, Victoria, Maria, and Candelario Muñoz. Unseen at the far right is Jesús Muñoz with child (partial image) Roberto Uresti.

This is a marriage portrait of Daniel Muñoz and Maria Eloisa Handy, center. The best man was Albert Handy (far left), and the maid of honor was Adela Muñoz (far right). Daniel and Adela were brother and sister, as were Albert and Eloisa. The young couple was married on June 16, 1903, at the Esperanza Ranch on the Handy family tract located off the Military Highway, south of Alamo.

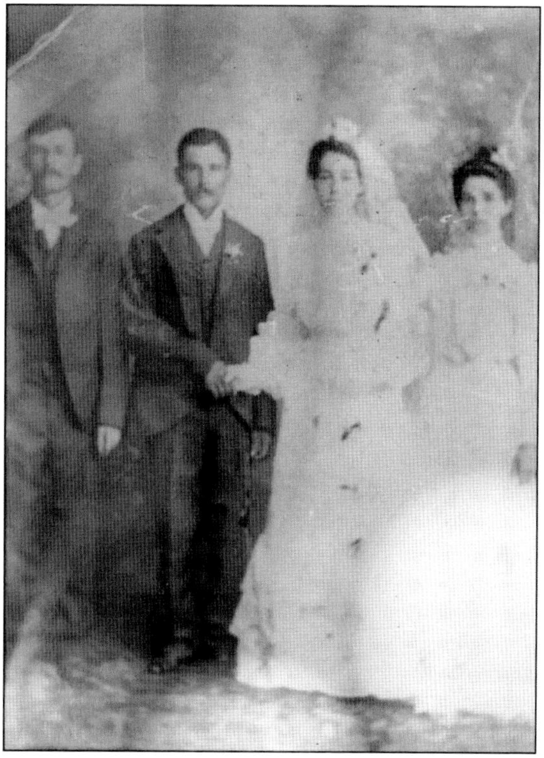

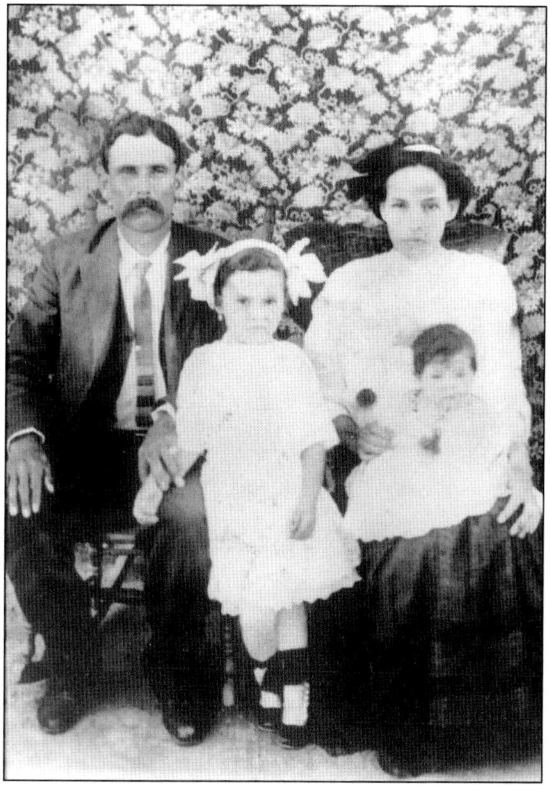

This is a family portrait of Daniel and Eloisa Muñoz with daughters Anita (left) and Victoria (right) in 1912. Note the floral quilted backdrop. The Hispanic founders of Donna were proud to have photographers capture special moments to later serve as reminders of times and faces.

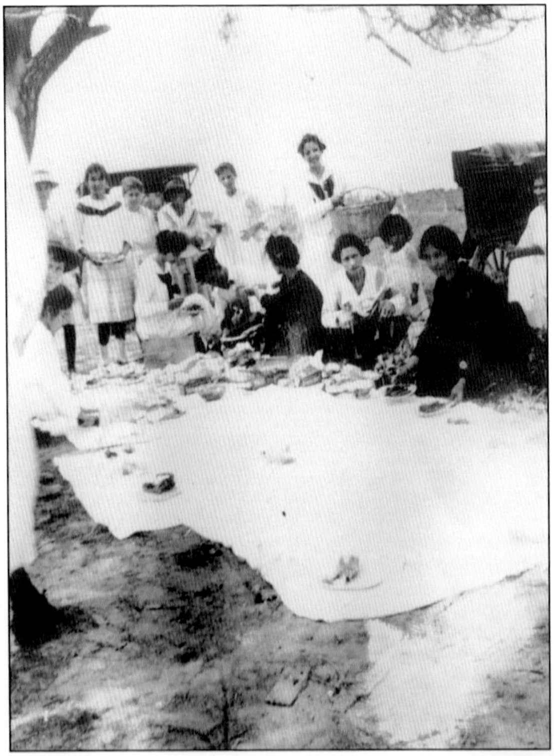

The Muñoz and Yanez families gather near the Rio Grande for a picnic (*c.* 1925–1927). Here, the women of both families place crisp linens on the ground and set out a great variety of food.

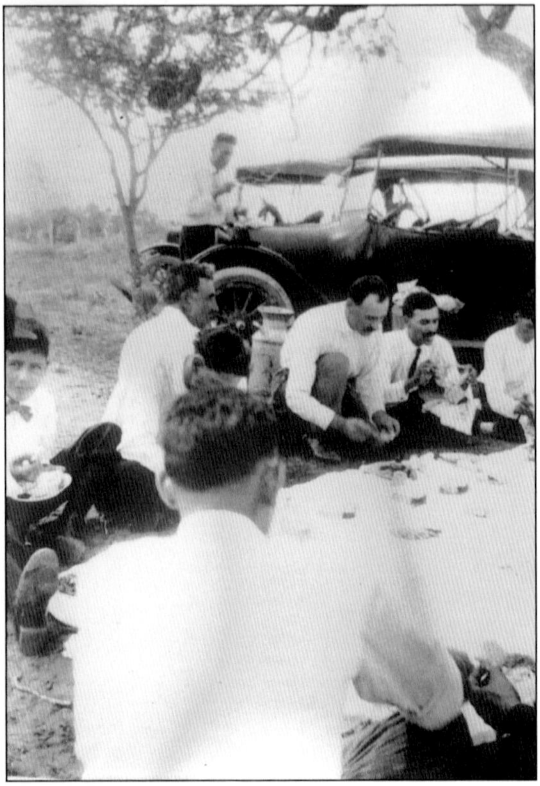

Family members enjoy the cool breezes off the river while they share food and conversation on Sunday afternoons.

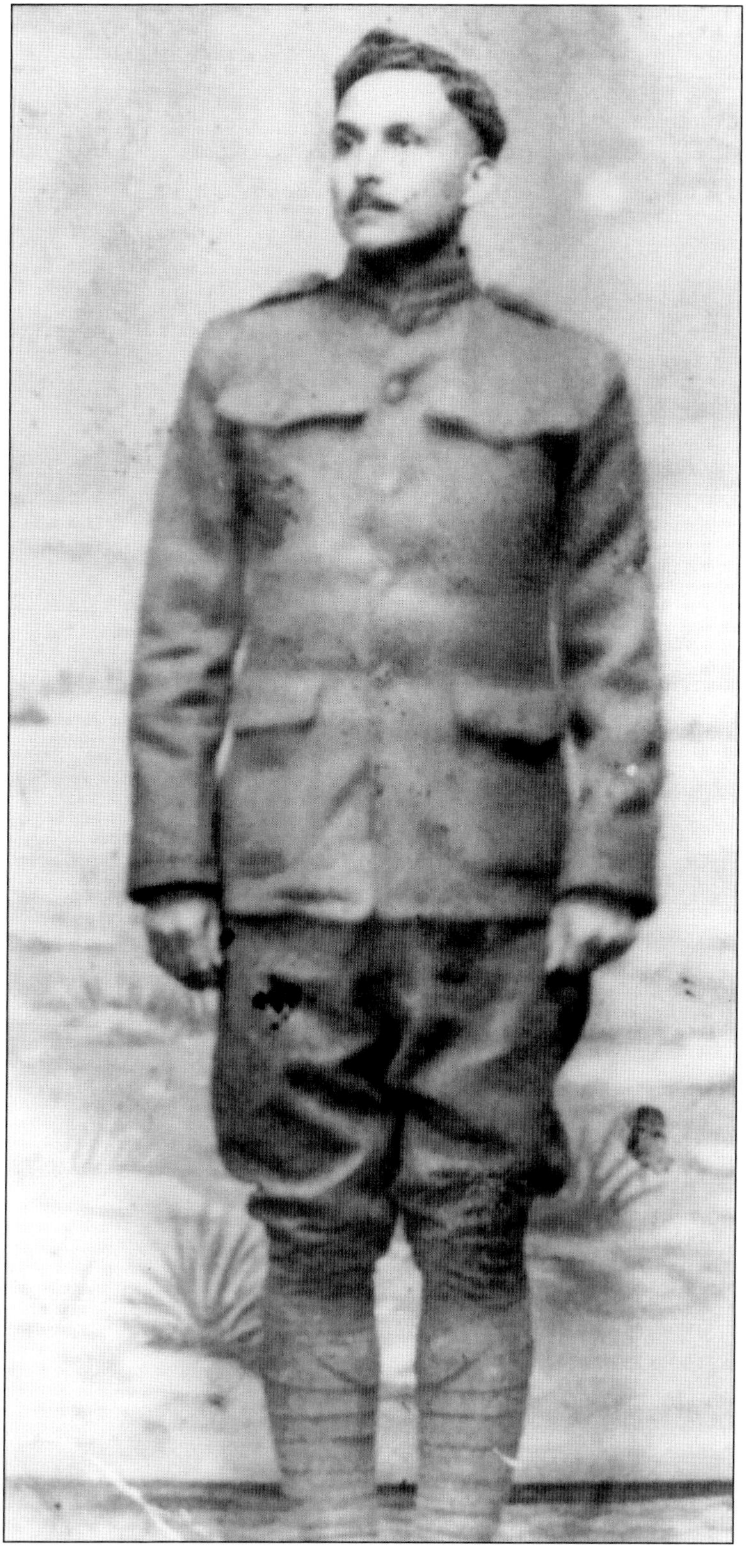

Candelario Muñoz, son of Dionicio and Francisca Flores Muñoz, is pictured in his World War I uniform. Candelario Muñoz was the proprietor of the first silent movie theater in Donna (other sources state that Donna Hooks Fletcher owned the first movie theater.) He delivered mail for his father, who was postmaster for the town of East Donna (also known as Beatrice or Beatriz). Candelario usually delivered mail on horseback, but during inclement weather he used a buggy. A founding member of the American Legion Border Post 107, he was the only veteran of Mexican-American descent to be included in the 1920 charter.

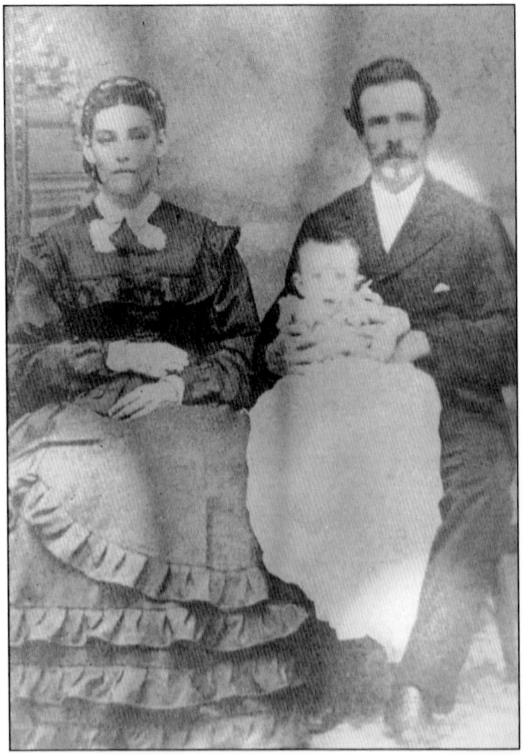

Originally from Wisconsin, Thomas James Handy came to the Valley as a serviceman with the Federal occupation forces immediately after the Civil War. A mail carrier, his route probably included the Azadores Ranch, where he met Angelita Cavazos. Her father, Salvador Cavazos Gallegos Sr., owned the ranch. Thomas J. Handy married Angelita Cavazos on April 25, 1866. They are shown here with their first child, son Chauncey.

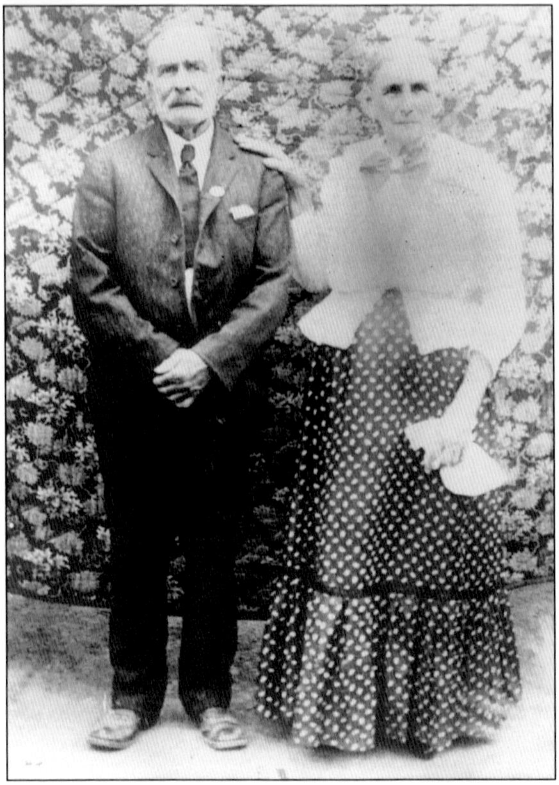

Around 1880, Thomas J. Handy bought 3,300 acres at 50¢ per acre from Juan Jose Treviño, owner of the Agostadero del Gato land grant. Handy called his new ranch La Esperanza ("hope"). By 1902, land values had risen to $2.00 per acre, indicating a significant increase in land values. This portrait of Thomas J. and Angelita Cavazos Handy shows the couple in 1912.

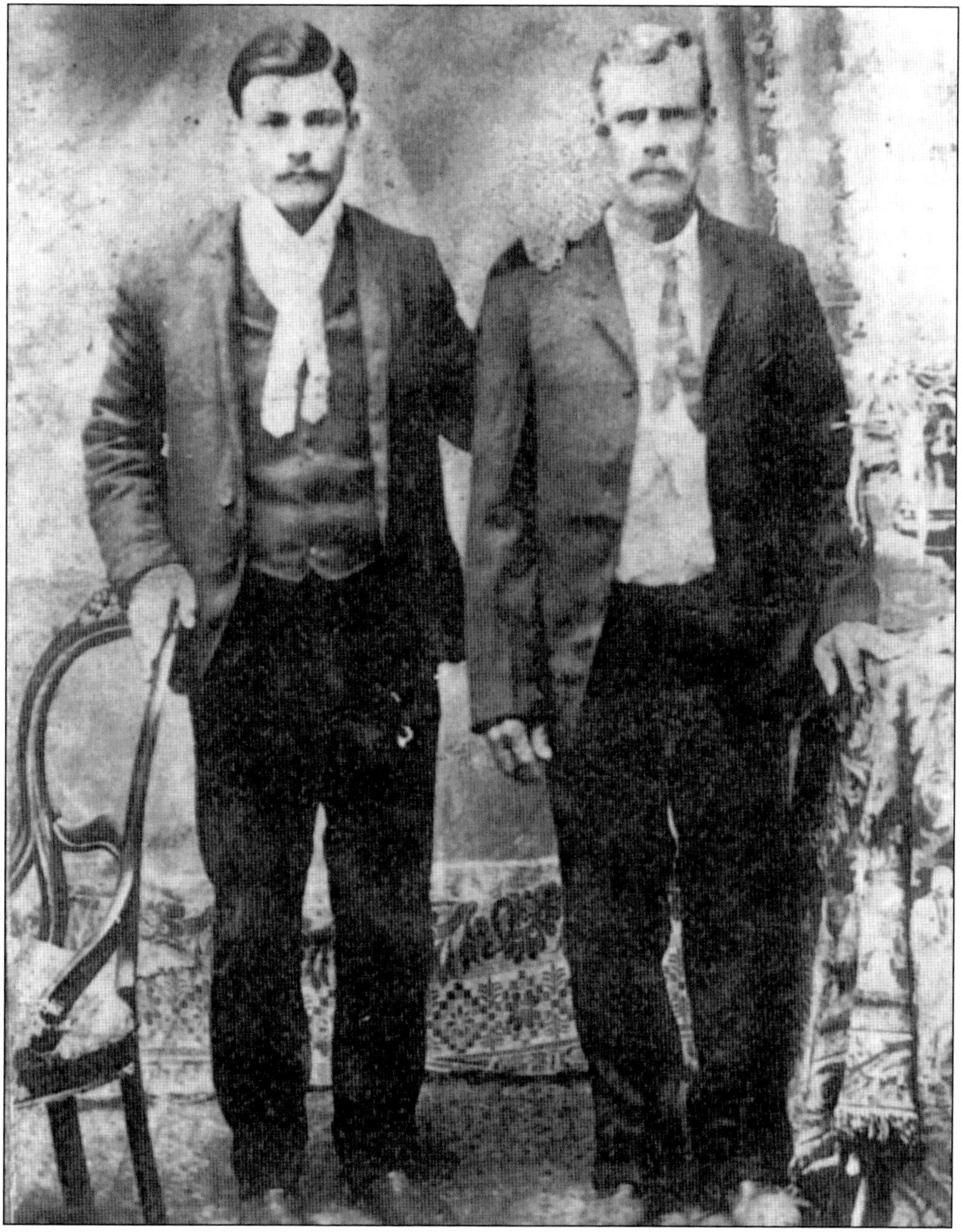

Abelardo Rubalcaba (left) stands beside his father, Antonio Ballí Rubalcaba (right). Born in 1857, Antonio Ballí Rubalcaba established a land tract along the Military Highway and named it the Ballí Ranch. This area was originally part of the 1731 land grant given by King Philip V of Spain to Padre Nicolas Ballí, his confessor (the grant included what we know today as Padre Island). The land passed to family members Juan Jose Hinojosa de Ballí and his daughter Rosa Maria Hinojosa de Ballí. The La Blanca land grant had been awarded to Lino Cavazos of Reynosa by the governor of Tamaulipas, Mexico, in 1834, but Cavazos did not file for transfer of title until 1849, when Texas was no longer part of Mexico. Overlapping Spanish and Mexican surveys and unclear titles delayed the purchase of many sections of land.

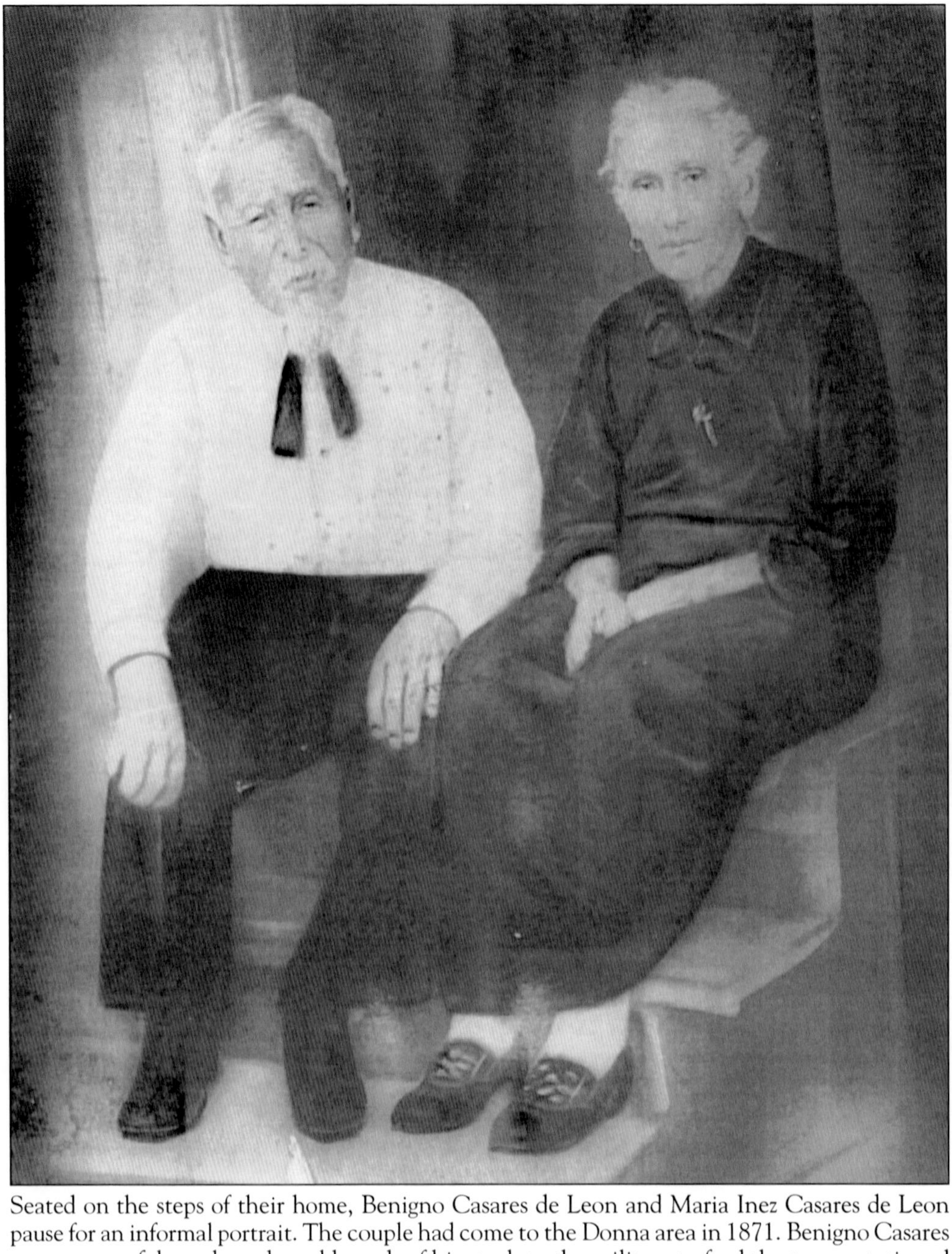

Seated on the steps of their home, Benigno Casares de Leon and Maria Inez Casares de Leon pause for an informal portrait. The couple had come to the Donna area in 1871. Benigno Casares was a successful rancher who sold much of his stock to the military to feed the troops stationed near Donna between 1914 and 1917. (Courtesy of Tomás Krummel.)

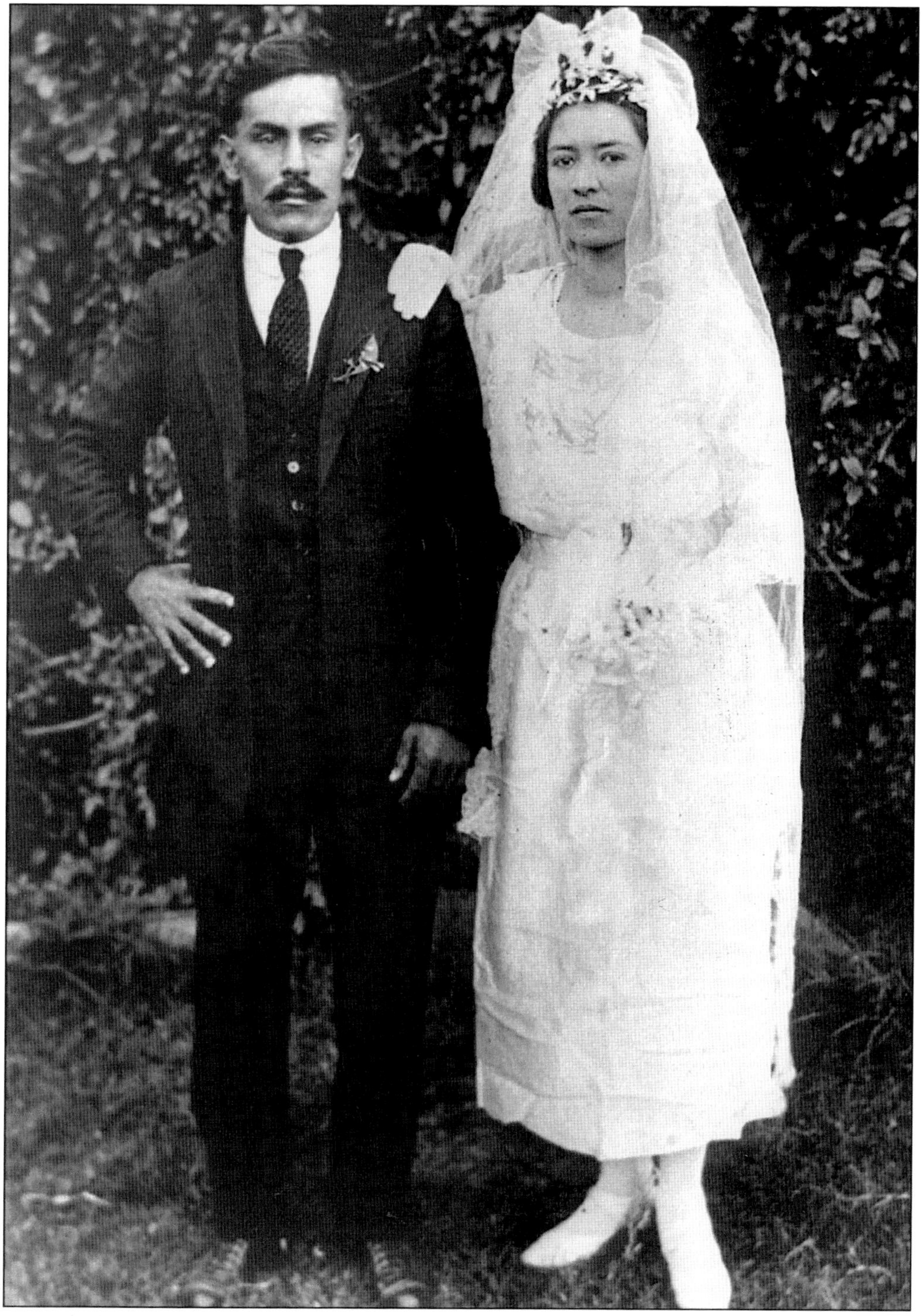

Mr. Telesforo Mendoza and Miss Inez Nava are shown on their wedding day in 1922. The parents of Inez Nava, Tranquilino and Magdalena arrived in East Donna from Irapuato, Guanajuato, Mexico, between 1908 and 1910. They had three children: Inez (pictured here), Paula, and Florentino. Tranquilino Nava owned a leather shop. (Courtesy of Julian Mendoza.)

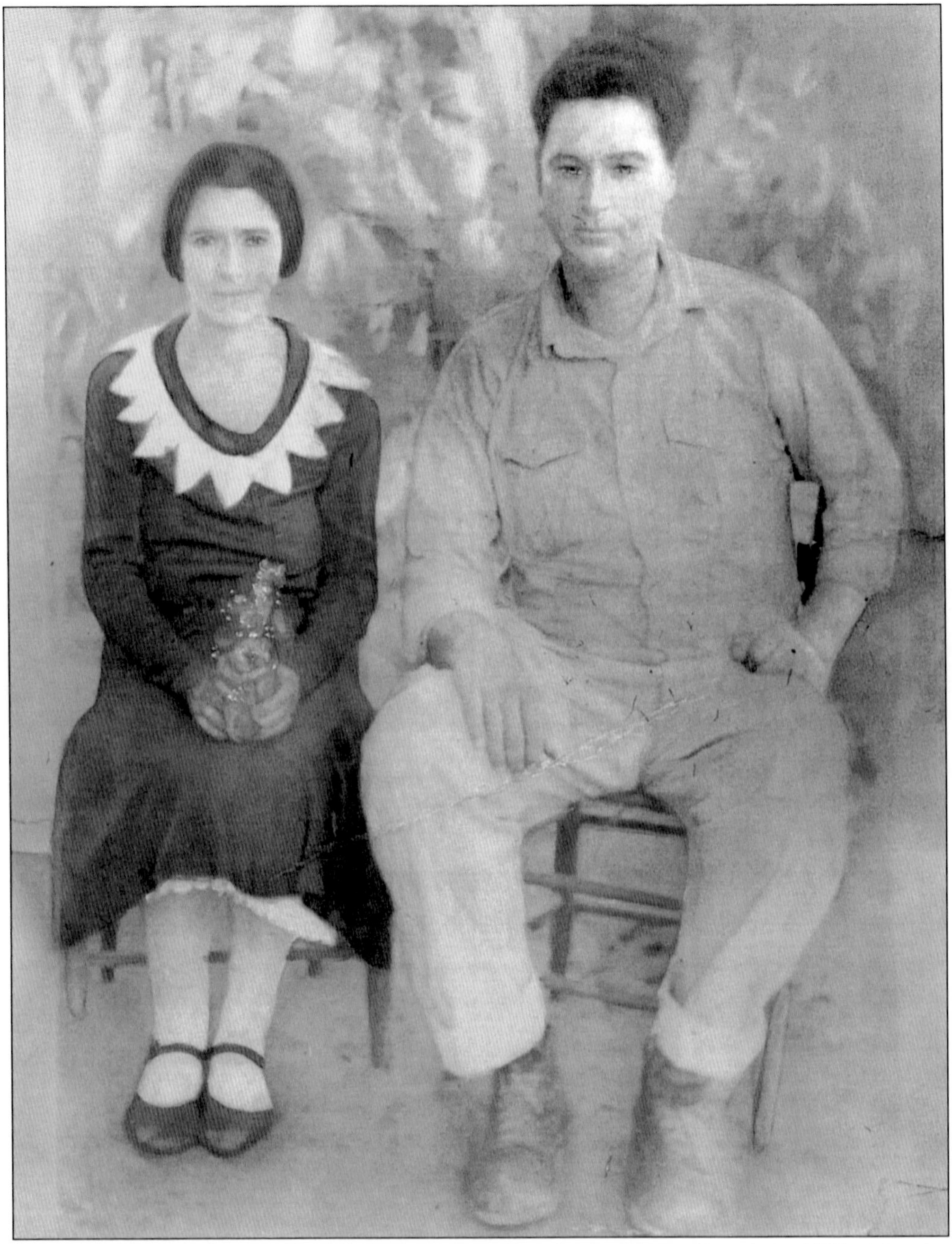

Daniel Singleterry, born in Kenedy, Texas, moved to the La Blanca Ranch in 1895. Here he met and married Norberta, and they had nine children. Daughter Pilar stated in an oral history interview that her mother was often sought after as a faith healer. Daniel was a farmer and rancher, who also provided wood for the boilers at the irrigation pump houses. He served on the Run school board for almost 40 years.

In 1920, 19-year-old Benigno Escobar arrived in East Donna from his home in Escobares, a small town near Roma, Texas. Later that year, at the age of 20, without any prior experience in running a business, he opened a *botica*, or pharmacy, with the help of an uncle. Since he was not trained as a pharmacist, he relied on the wholesale pharmaceutical companies to explain the uses for the medical supplies and drugs he purchased from them.

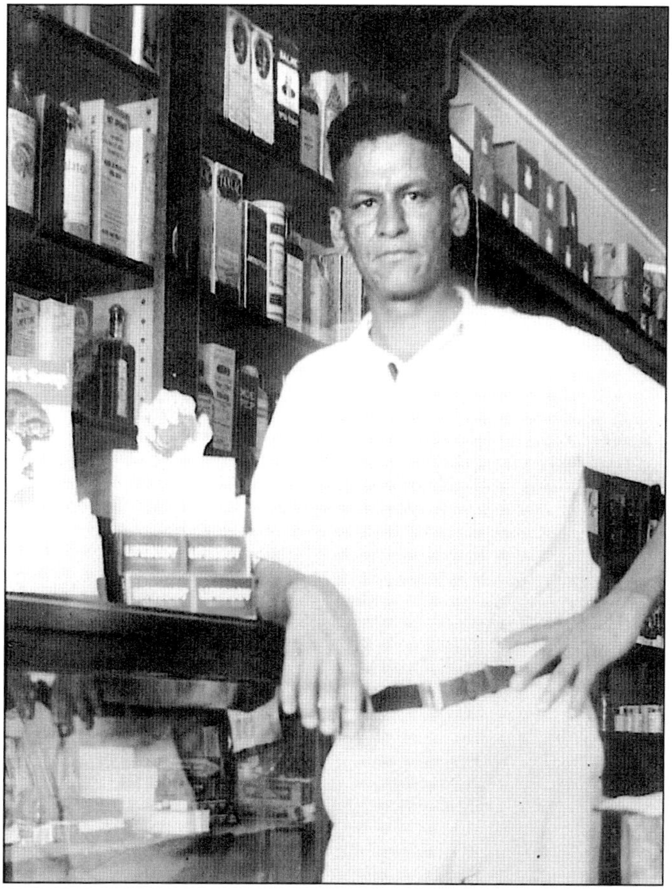

From 1929 until 1948, Benigno Escobar's pharmacy occupied the bottom floor of this building. His wife worked alongside him in the store, and he and his family lived on the second floor. Escobar was also a notary public, and his services were in great demand during the *bracero* movement.

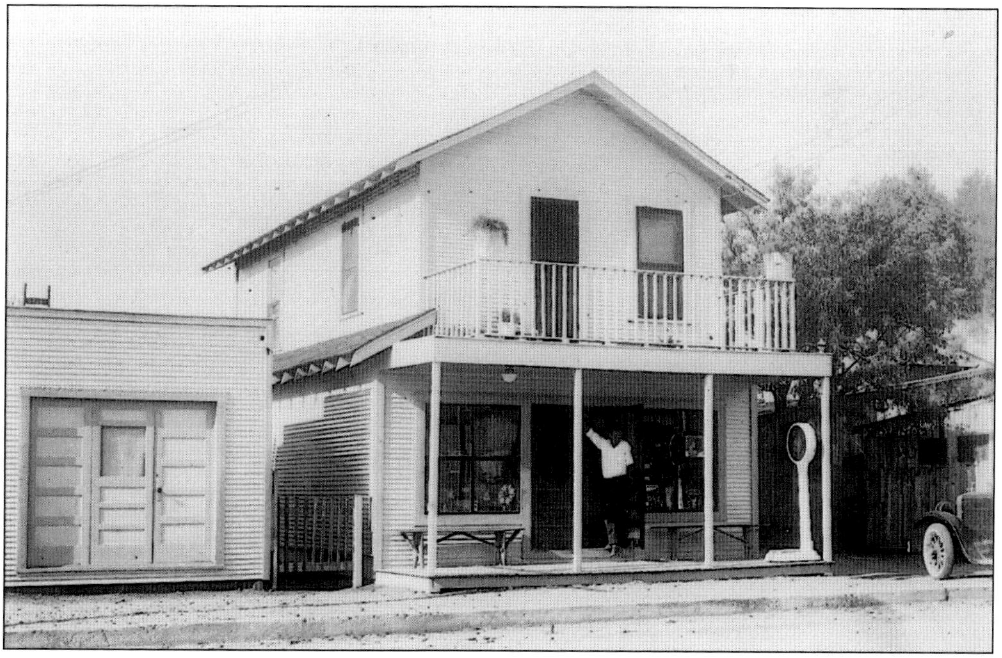

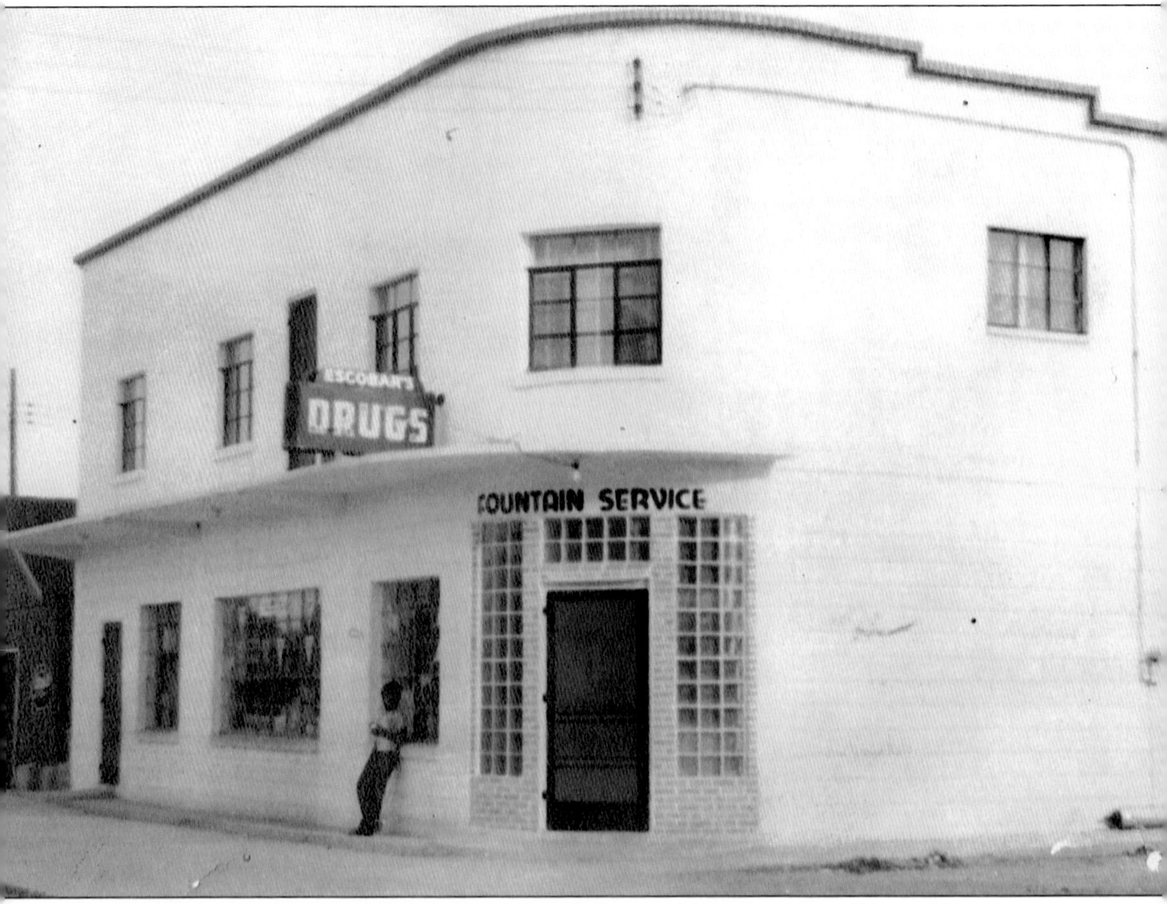

In 1948, as the town of Donna prospered, so did many business owners. Benigno Escobar moved from the two-story frame building to this handsome new structure, where he sold prescriptions and fountain drinks to his customers until 1989.

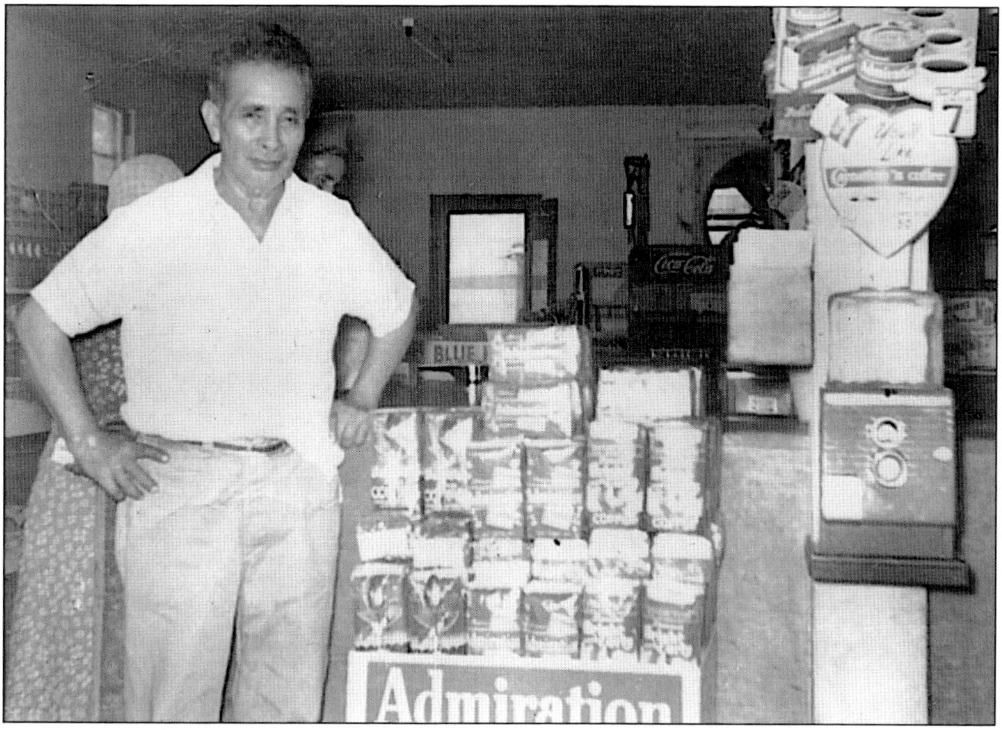

Margarito Cardenas was another successful Donna businessman. For 75 years, he owned and operated the first grocery store in East Donna. He is shown here next to a display of Admiration Coffee, which was ground fresh at the store. (Courtesy of Rosalinda Zamora.)

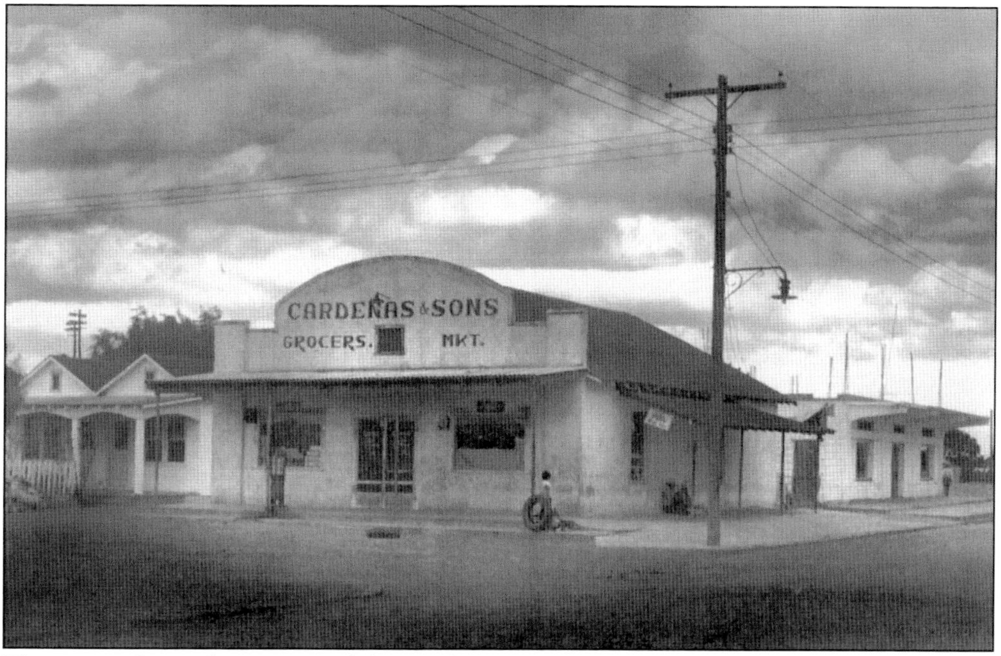

This image shows the exterior of the Cardenas Grocery Store in East Donna. Note the small child with the large inner tube from a tire. (Courtesy of Rosalinda Zamora.)

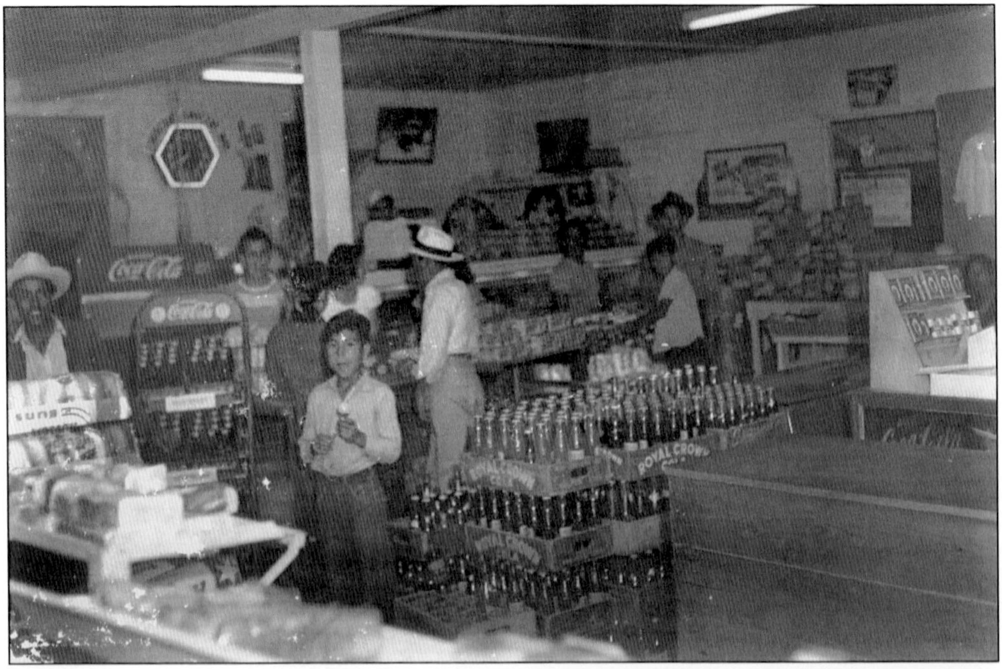

The interior of Cardenas Grocery Store contained many kinds of merchandise for sale, much like older style mercantile stores. Sodas, ice cream, bread and baked goods, hats, and tobacco could be purchased here. The store also provided a gathering place for friends and neighbors. (Courtesy of Rosalinda Zamora.)

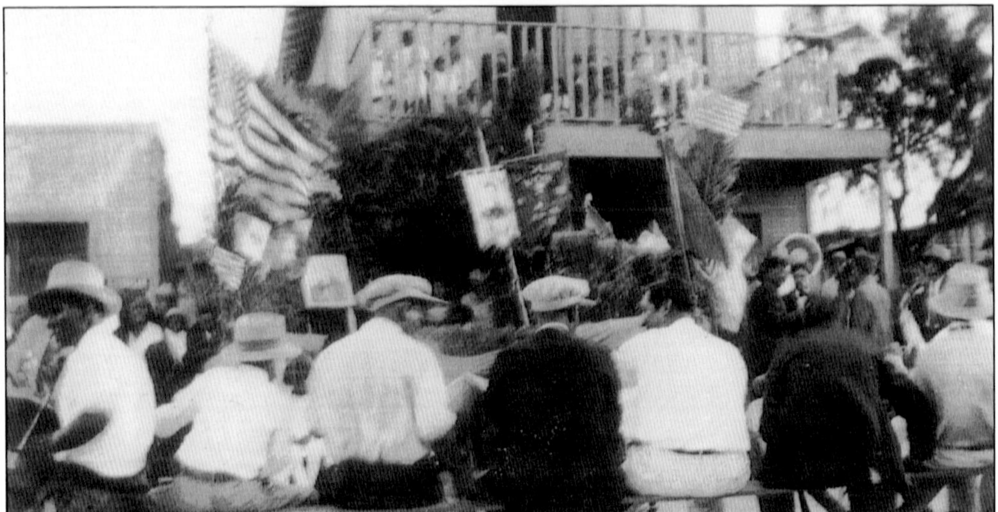

This crowd has gathered in front of Benigno Escobar's pharmacy for a Hispanic Woodmen of the World rally for health insurance. Farm and ranch workers, as well as employees of small businesses, did not have health insurance and often could not afford to call in a doctor or go to a clinic or hospital for medical care. For generations, the infant mortality rate among Hispanics was exceptionally high. Many relied on home remedies and the services of *curanderas* (faith healers who were also experts in herbal medicine). Fraternal organizations such as Woodmen of the World provided a voice and an opportunity for employees' needs to be heard.

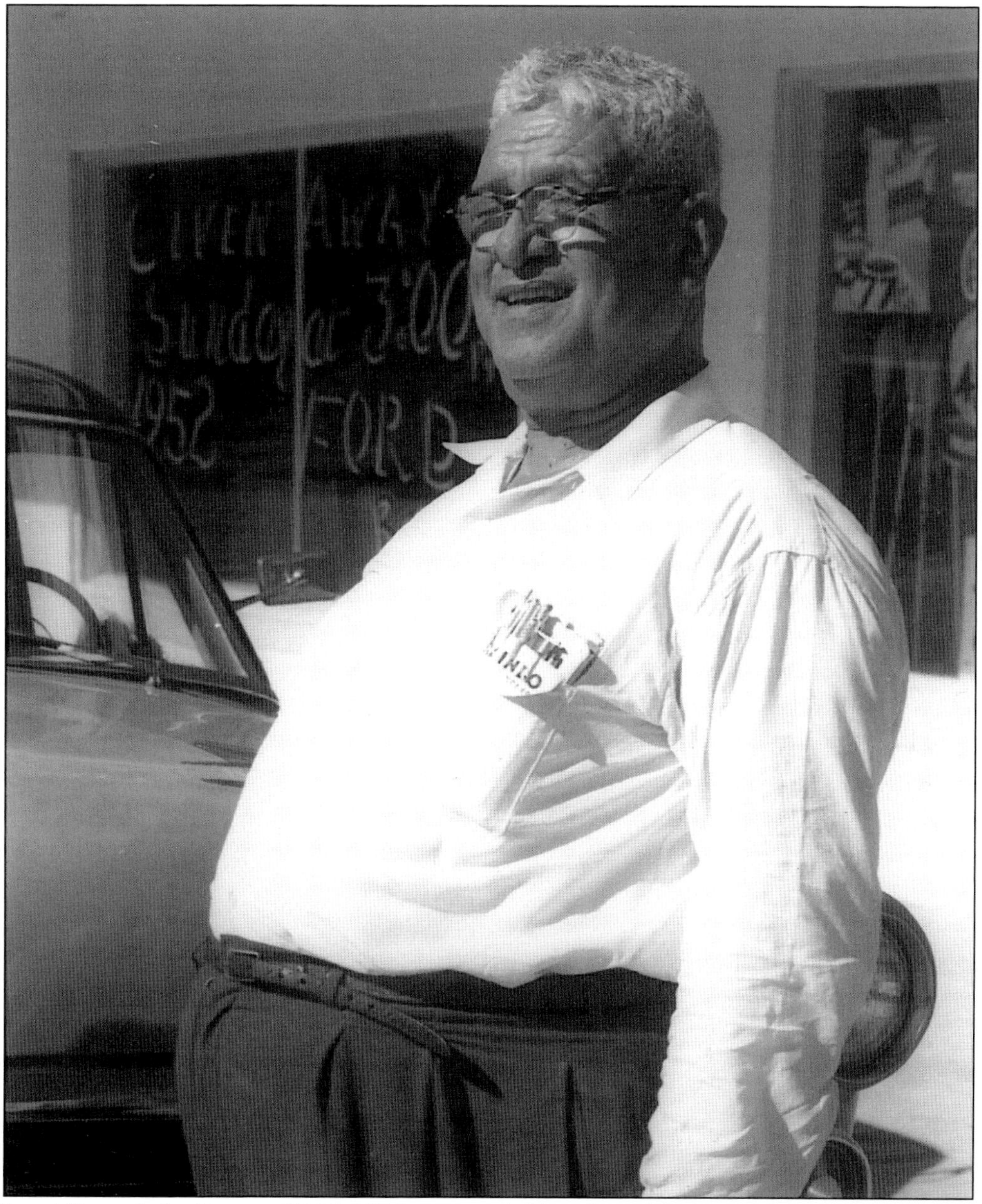

Juan Wenceslado Caceres (1896–1976), a remarkably talented businessman, was born on the Ballí Ranch. His parents were Lazaro Ballí Caceres and Claudina Uresti de Caceres. He married Carlota Zuniga on December 10, 1919, and in time they became the parents of 15 children. With the encouragement of his father-in-law, Enrique Zuniga, he opened his first store in Weslaco in 1920. Eventually he closed that store and opened several businesses in Donna, among them a pool hall, a dry goods store, and a grocery store. He also operated a department store and a meat market. In 1939 he opened stores in La Villa and Elsa, and by 1945, he owned five grocery stores in Donna, Weslaco, Elsa, Pharr, and McAllen, which remained in operation for about 35 years. Additional business interests included a lumberyard, service station, slaughterhouse, auto dealership, and a movie theater. This energetic gentleman served the community as a member of the Donna school board for many years. (Courtesy of Julian Mendoza.)

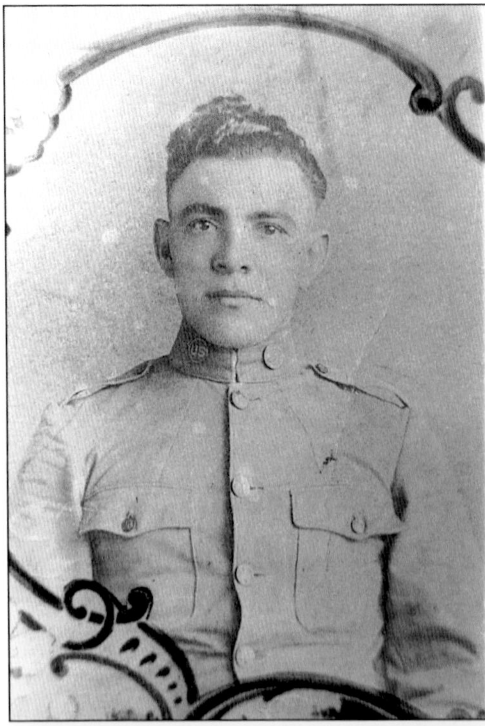

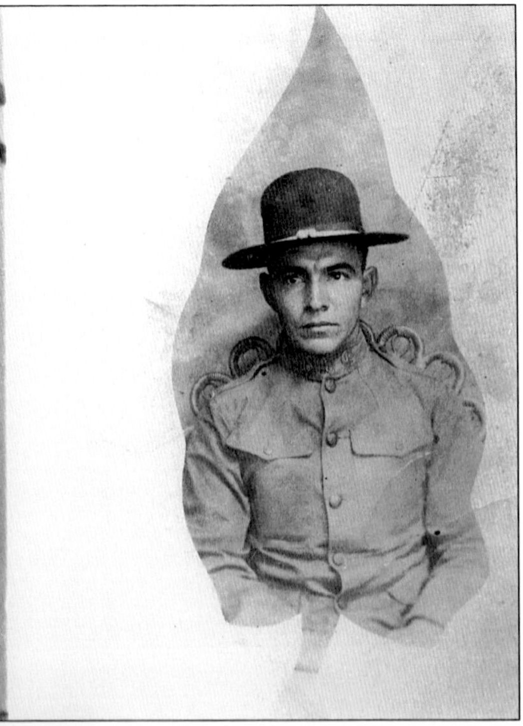

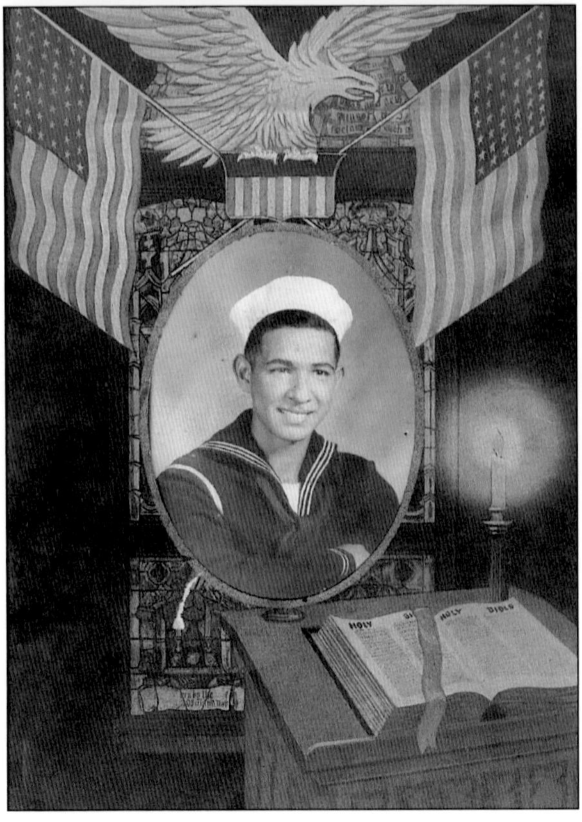

In 1908, Martin Ochoa Salazar left his home in Ojo de Agua (now Abram) and joined his siblings in East Donna. In 1917, at the age of 21, Martin Salazar joined the army and served throughout World War I. When he returned, he owned a butcher shop and provided ice deliveries to homes. (Courtesy of Eloy Salazar.)

Following in the tradition of his father, Martin Ochoa Salazar, Eloy Salazar joined the U.S. Navy and served aboard the USS *Iowa* during World War II. He returned to Donna after the war and became a teacher and an administrator in the Donna Independent School District. He is a member of American Legion Post 107.

Three

THE LURE OF THE MAGIC VALLEY

With the construction of the St. Louis, Brownsville, and Mexico Railroad in 1904, land companies purchased large tracts for development of towns and farms. They advertised in newspapers throughout the Midwest and provided excursion trains to bring potential settlers to the Lower Rio Grande Valley. The area became known as the "Magic Valley" because almost any type of fruit and vegetable, as well as cotton, could be grown in abundance all year long due to the temperate climate and extensive irrigation system. Railroad companies built packing sheds along the tracks and delivered fruits and vegetables, packed in ice, to distant states.

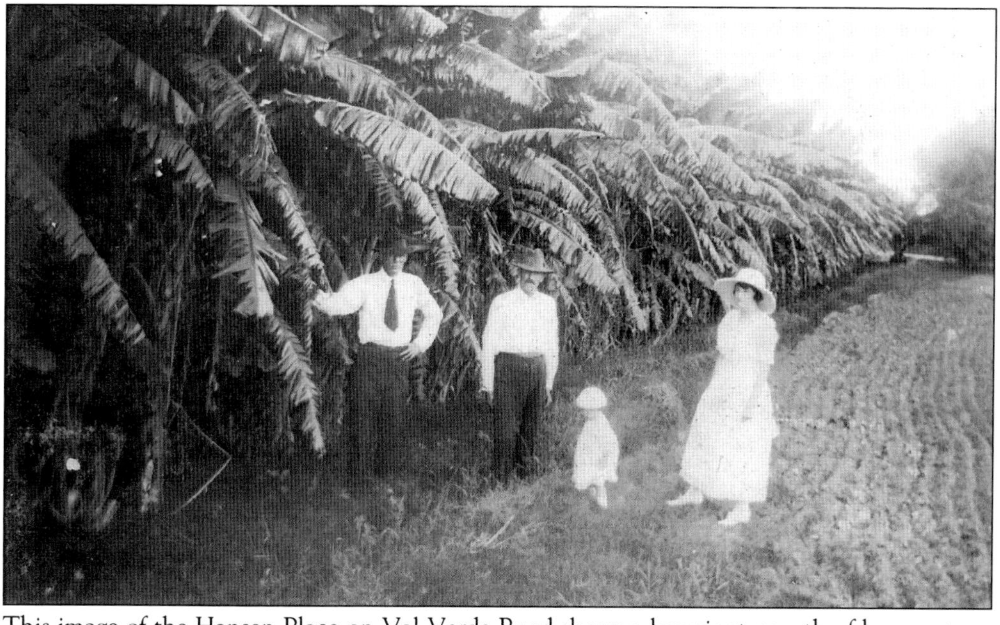

This image of the Hansen Place on Val Verde Road shows a luxuriant growth of banana trees and cultivated crops. H.P. Hansen developed the Val Verde area west of Donna. Once a hotel for land excursion parties, Hansen's famous Val Verde Country Club featured an Olympic-sized pool, a recreation hall, and a three-story tower, which contained an apartment for guests such as movie stars and gangsters, who wintered in the valley during the 1920s and 1930s.

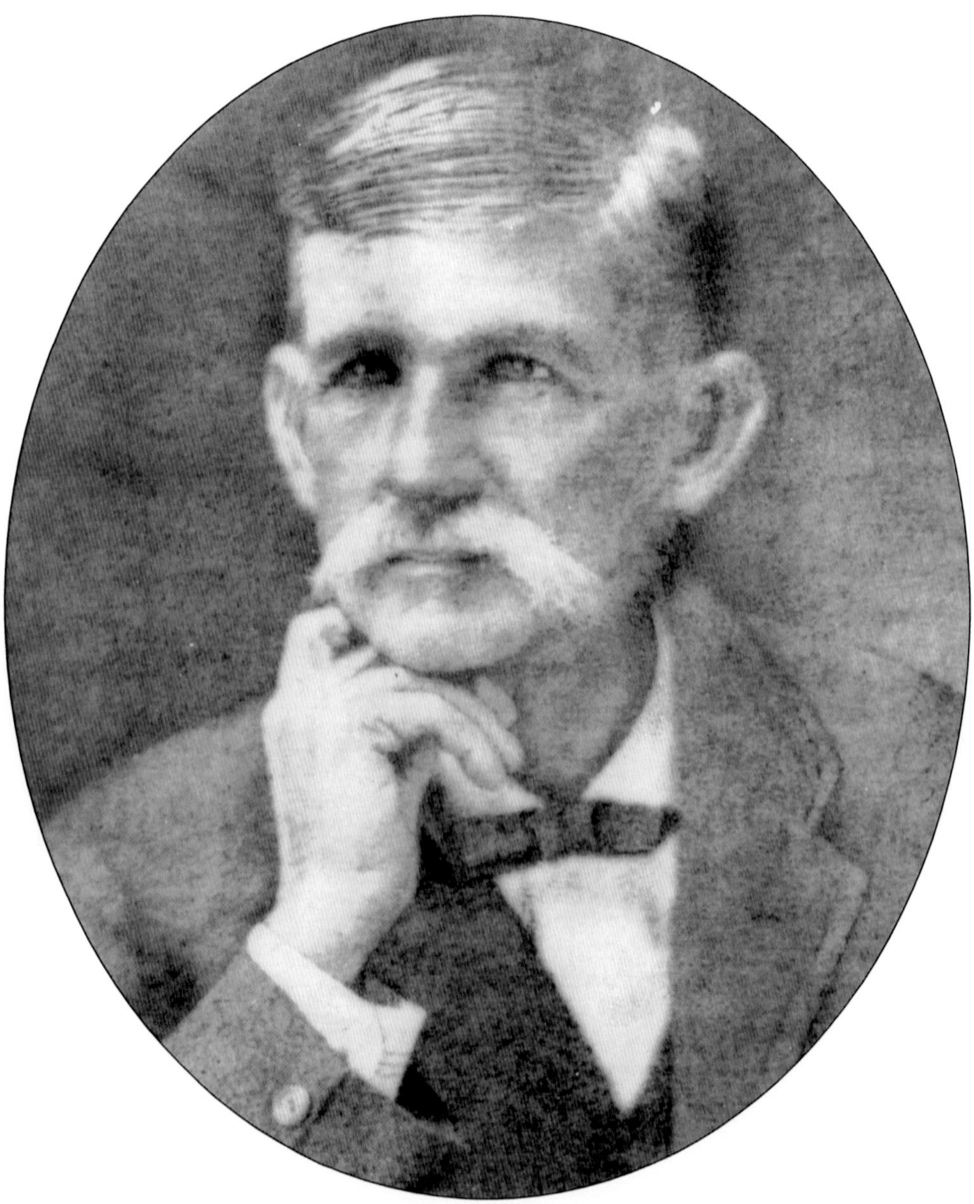

Thomas Jackson Hooks (1850–1922), father of Donna Hooks Fletcher, was born and raised in East Texas. A Hardin County merchant, he and a group of friends wanted to expand into large-scale rice farming. Accompanied by Albert Franklin Hester Sr., Hooks traveled to Brownsville in 1898 to scout for land. The high salt content of the water made it unsuitable for rice, and the two men, led by Harlingen founder Lon C. Hill, traveled along the Military Highway (now U.S. 281) to John Closner's plantation, where they met Closner's manager, Ed Ruthven. Hooks and Hester, joined by four partners, selected land from the Llano Grande and La Blanca land grants. Hooks moved his family to the Valley in 1901, and upon receiving a clear title to the land in 1902, he and his partners established the La Blanca Agricultural Company. Construction of a pumping plant and irrigation canals began in 1902, and hundreds of acres were placed under cultivation.

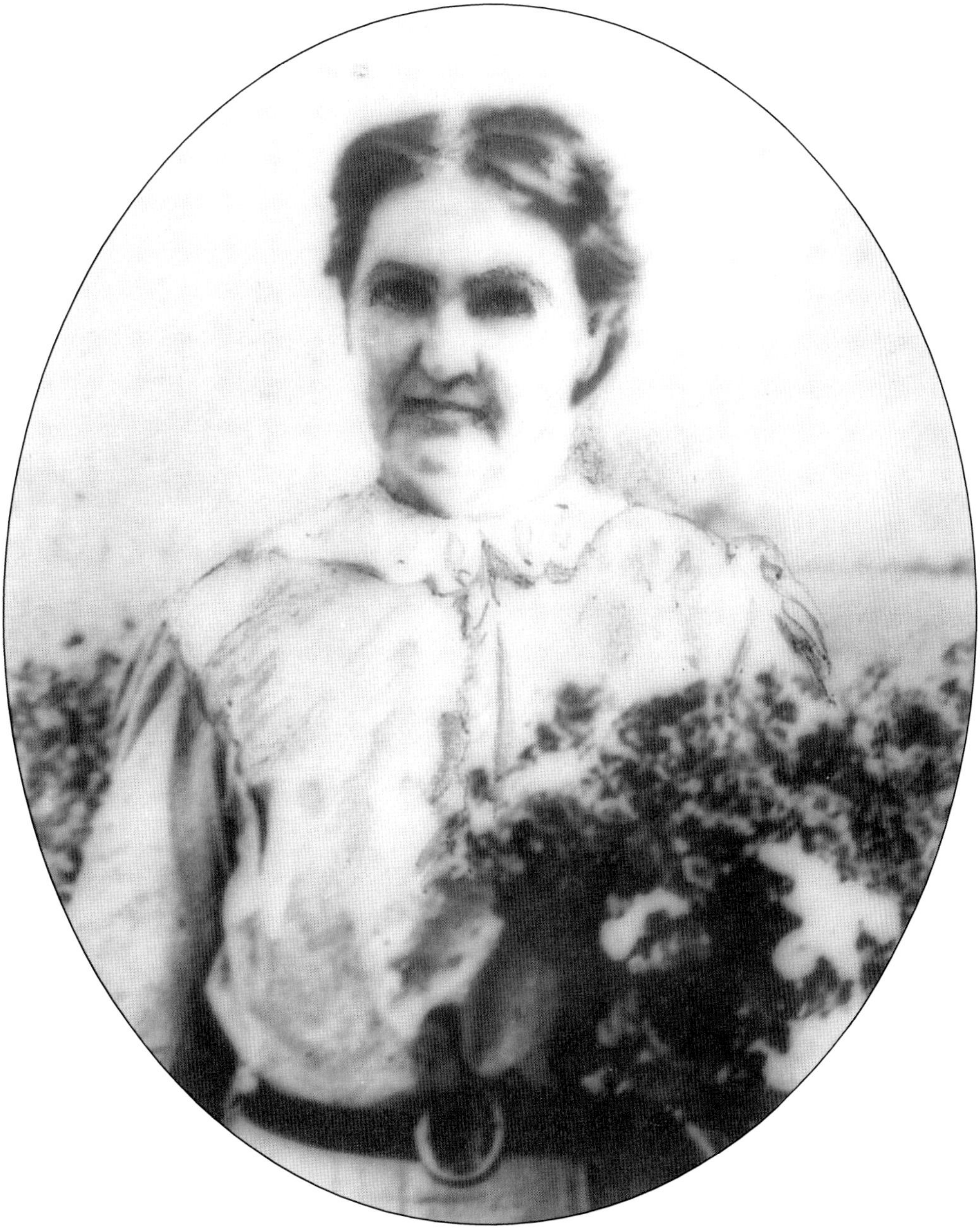

Virginia Tarver (1854–1933) was born in Louisiana but grew up in East Texas. Her father was a merchant and a talented violinist. On a trip to New Orleans, her father heard the Swedish singer, Jenny Lind. His description of the singer's performance made such an impression on young Virginia, who loved to sing, that the family nicknamed her "Jenny." In 1873 she married Thomas J. Hooks, a union that lasted 49 years, and they became the parents of five sons and five daughters. Donna, born in 1879, was their third child.

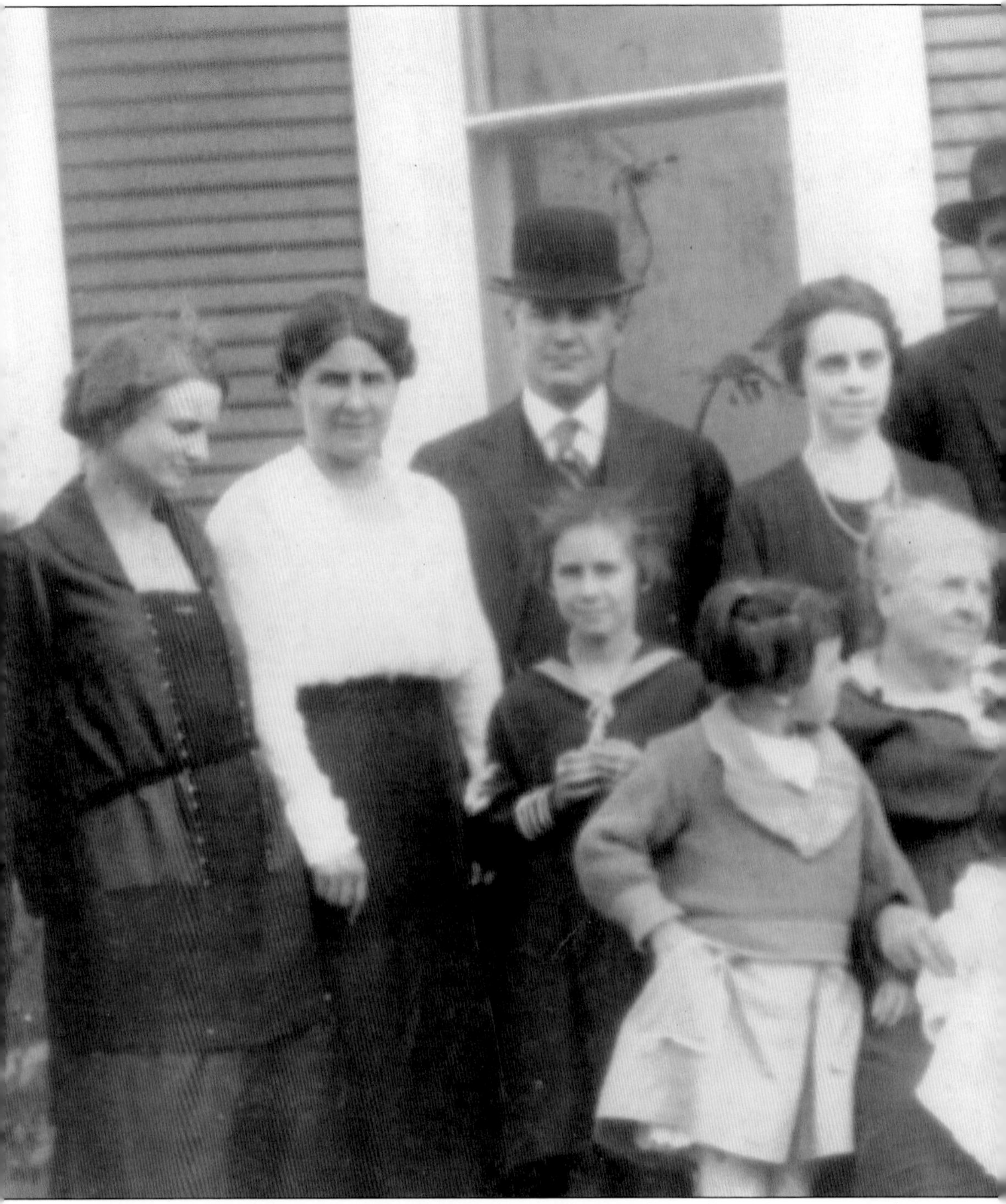

Albert Franklin Hester Sr. (1847–1944), who was born and raised in Mississippi, settled in Houston, Texas, in 1870, where he worked for a lumber mill. He moved to Village Mills, near Beaumont, two and a half years later. There he continued in the lumber business and engaged in rice farming. He married Mary Jane Richardson in 1883, and they became the parents of five children. Hester brought his family to Run in 1902, where he built the second permanent home

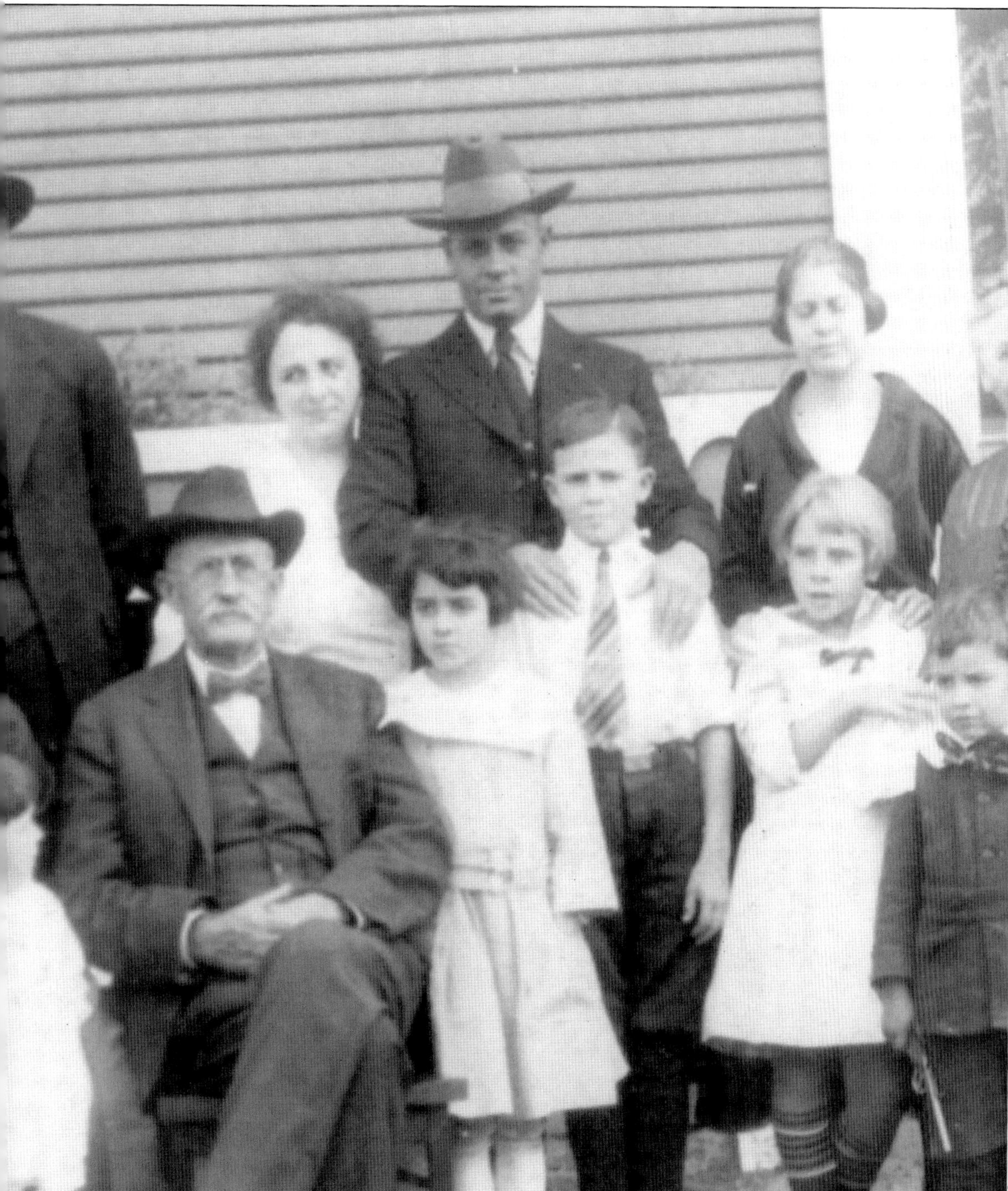

in the area. In 1911, he built a new home and moved to Donna. A.F. Hester was president of the First State Bank and the school board, commissioner for Donna and for Hidalgo County, and an elder in the First Christian Church. With his sons, he owned a mercantile business, a hotel, and a drug store. In this family photograph, Mr. and Mrs. A.F. Hester Sr. are seated in the center.

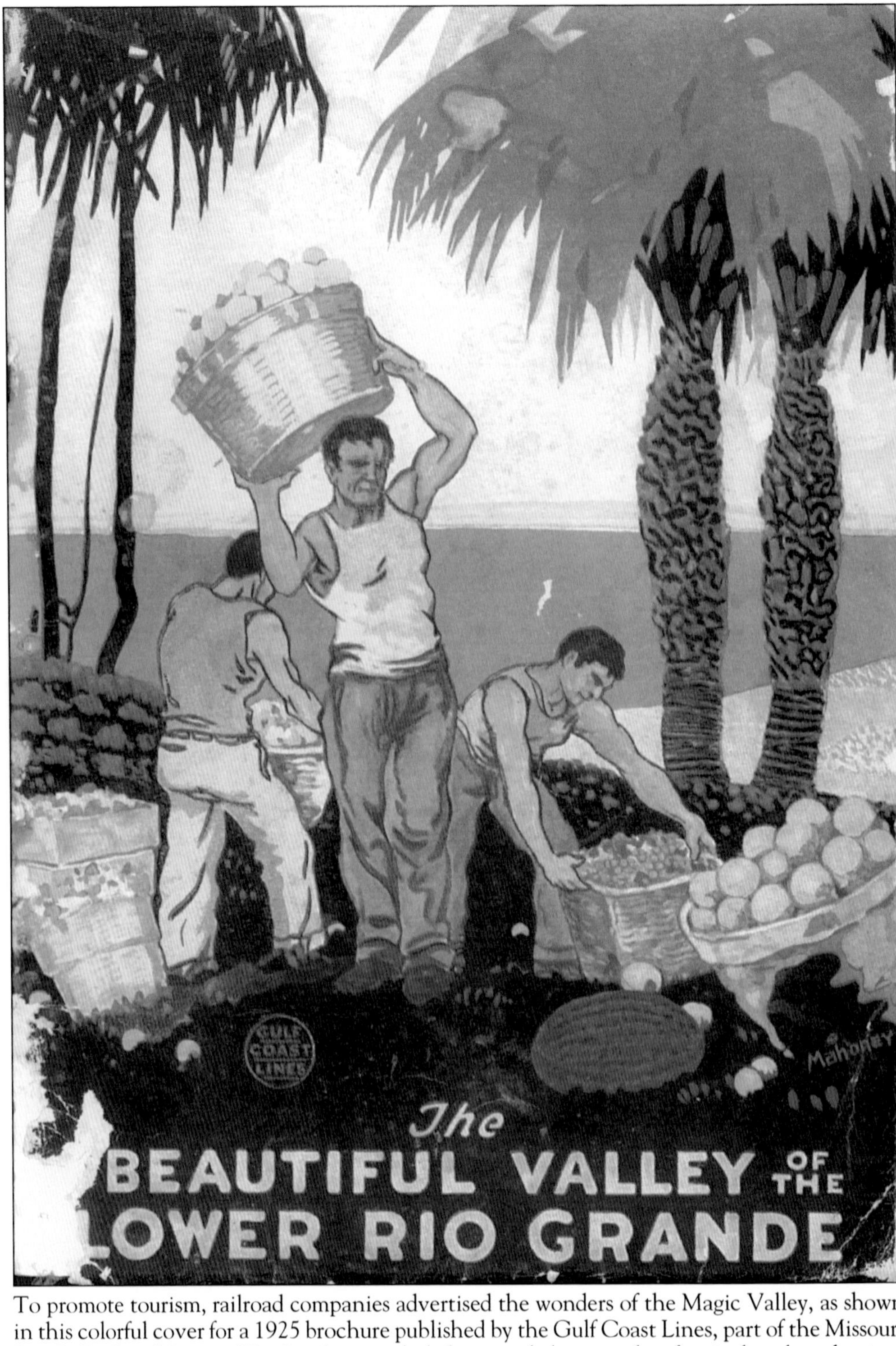

To promote tourism, railroad companies advertised the wonders of the Magic Valley, as shown in this colorful cover for a 1925 brochure published by the Gulf Coast Lines, part of the Missouri Pacific Railroad System. The brochure included text and photographs of agricultural production, residences, and significant public buildings.

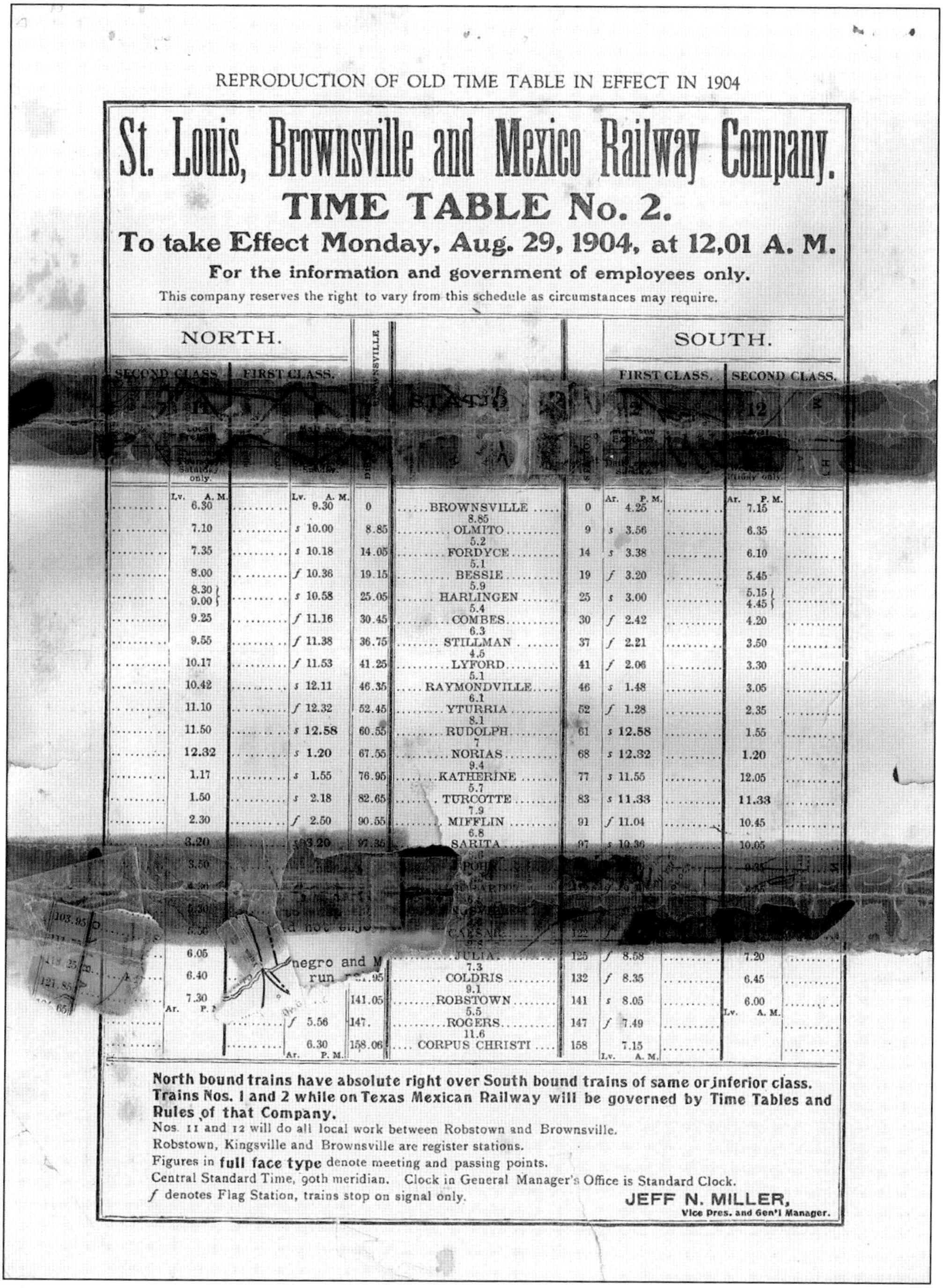

REPRODUCTION OF OLD TIME TABLE IN EFFECT IN 1904

St. Louis, Brownsville and Mexico Railway Company.

TIME TABLE No. 2.

To take Effect Monday, Aug. 29, 1904, at 12,01 A. M.

For the information and government of employees only.

This company reserves the right to vary from this schedule as circumstances may require.

NORTH. SECOND CLASS. 11	NORTH. FIRST CLASS. 1	Distance from Brownsville	STATIONS	[illegible]	SOUTH. FIRST CLASS. 2	SOUTH. SECOND CLASS. 12
Local Freight [illegible] only.	Mail and [illegible]				Mail and Express [illegible]	[illegible] only.
Lv. A. M. 6.30	Lv. A. M. 9.30	0	BROWNSVILLE	0	Ar. P. M. 4.25	Ar. P. M. 7.15
			8.85			
7.10	s 10.00	8.85	OLMITO	9	s 3.56	6.35
			5.2			
7.35	s 10.18	14.05	FORDYCE	14	s 3.38	6.10
			5.1			
8.00	f 10.36	19.15	BESSIE	19	f 3.20	5.45
			5.9			
8.30 } 9.00 }	s 10.58	25.05	HARLINGEN	25	s 3.00	5.15 } 4.45 }
			5.4			
9.25	f 11.16	30.45	COMBES	30	f 2.42	4.20
			6.3			
9.55	f 11.38	36.75	STILLMAN	37	f 2.21	3.50
			4.5			
10.17	f 11.53	41.25	LYFORD	41	f 2.06	3.30
			5.1			
10.42	s 12.11	46.35	RAYMONDVILLE	46	s 1.48	3.05
			6.1			
11.10	f 12.32	52.45	YTURRIA	52	f 1.28	2.35
			8.1			
11.50	s **12.58**	60.55	RUDOLPH	61	s **12.58**	1.55
			7			
12.32	s 1.20	67.55	NORIAS	68	s **12.32**	**1.20**
			9.4			
1.17	s 1.55	76.95	KATHERINE	77	s 11.55	12.05
			5.7			
1.50	s 2.18	82.65	TURCOTTE	83	s **11.33**	**11.33**
			7.9			
2.30	f 2.50	90.55	MIFFLIN	91	f 11.04	10.45
			6.8			
3.20	s 3.20	97.35	SARITA	97	s 10.36	10.05
			[illegible]			
3.50	[illegible]	[illegible]	[illegible]	[illegible]	[illegible]	9.35
[illegible]	[illegible]	[illegible]	[illegible]	[illegible]	[illegible]	[illegible]
5.30	[illegible]	[illegible]	[illegible]	[illegible]	[illegible]	[illegible]
[illegible]	[illegible]	[illegible]	CAESAR	122	[illegible]	[illegible]
			[illegible]			
6.05	[illegible]	[illegible]	JULIA	125	f 8.58	7.20
			7.3			
6.40	[illegible]	[illegible]	COLDRIS	132	f 8.35	6.45
			9.1			
7.30 Ar. P. M.	[illegible]	141.05	ROBSTOWN	141	s 8.05	6.00 Lv. A. M.
			5.5			
	f 5.56	147.	ROGERS	147	f 7.49	
			11.6			
	6.30 Ar. P. M.	158.06	CORPUS CHRISTI	158	7.15 Lv. A. M.	

North bound trains have absolute right over South bound trains of same or inferior class.
Trains Nos. 1 and 2 while on Texas Mexican Railway will be governed by Time Tables and Rules of that Company.

Nos. 11 and 12 will do all local work between Robstown and Brownsville.
Robstown, Kingsville and Brownsville are register stations.
Figures in **full face type** denote meeting and passing points.
Central Standard Time, 90th meridian. Clock in General Manager's Office is Standard Clock.
f denotes Flag Station, trains stop on signal only.

JEFF N. MILLER,
Vice Pres. and Gen'l Manager.

This St. Louis, Brownsville, and Mexico Railway Company timetable for 1904 shows the schedule from Harlingen and Brownsville to Corpus Christi. The La Blanca Agricultural Co. offered 1,600 acres of land as a bonus to bring the railroad west from Harlingen. The state issued a charter to the Lott Town and Improvement Company on December 3, 1904, for the formation of a town site. Railroad president Uriah Lott named the town for Thomas J. Hooks' daughter, Donna. The town incorporated in 1908.

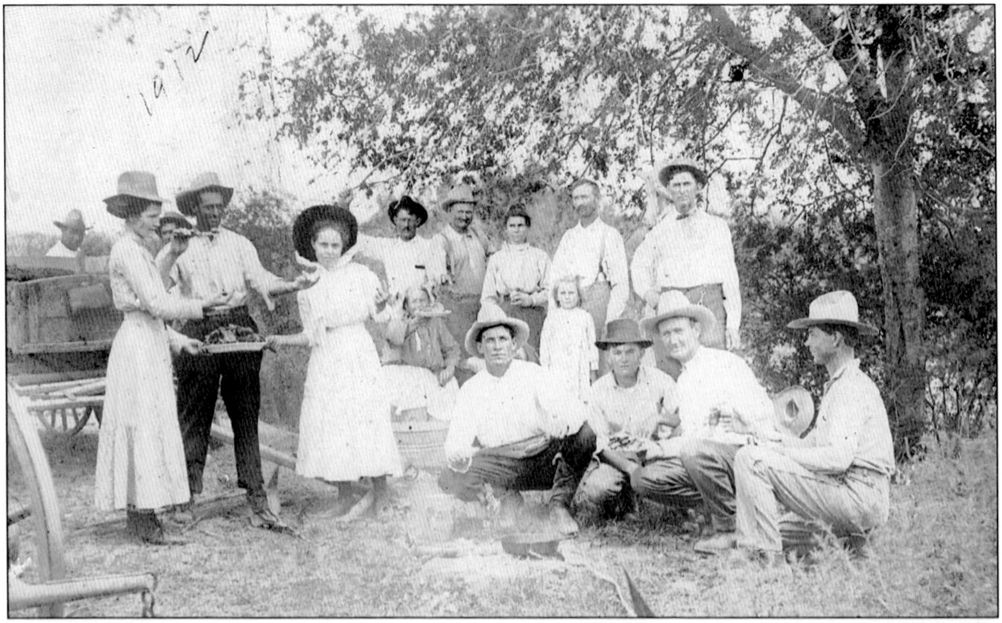

Establishing homes, farms, and businesses in Donna and throughout the Valley was a challenging process that required concentration and hard work for six days of every week. Leisure activities were reserved for Sunday afternoons. This 1912 image shows a fish fry held at Run.

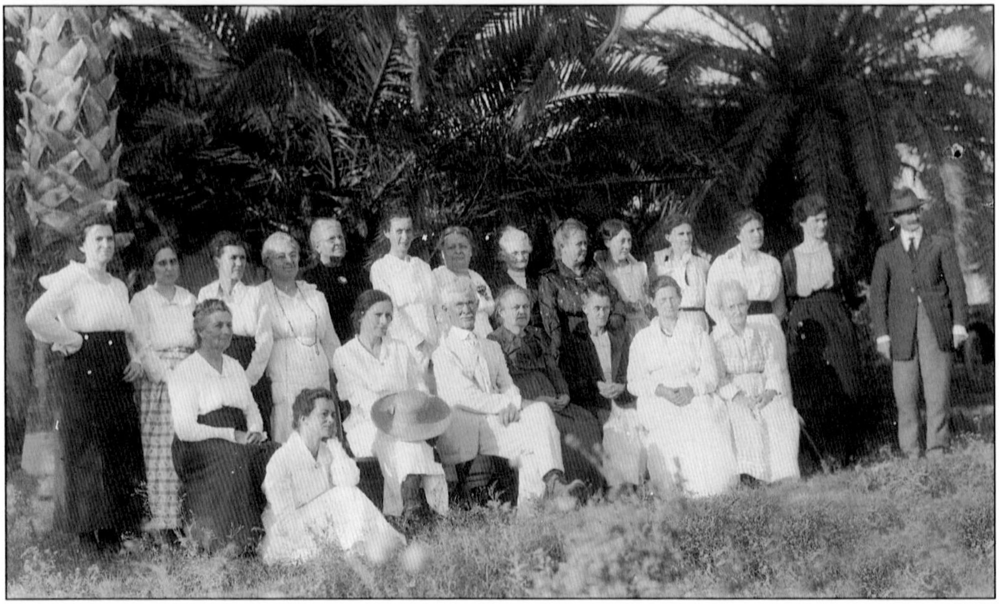

As the town of Donna grew, so did businesses, schools, and churches. This Sunday school class of the First Christian Church, organized in 1911, is shown in 1920. W.H. Snow, a charter member of the church, was the Sunday school teacher. Pictured are, left to right: (standing) Mrs. Stone, Mrs.E.E.Schwertfager,Mrs.BudNewland,Mrs.Furman,Mrs.N.T.(Nick)Hester,Mrs.O.L.Anderston, Mrs. Gerye Stevens, unidentified, Mrs. J.B. Moye, Mrs. T.W. Mudd, Mrs. Eubanks, Mrs. Elmer Hodges, Mrs. A.C. Baily, and Reverend Swan; (seated) Mrs. Macy, Mrs. Seargent, Mrs. Gibson, Mr. W.H. Snow, Mrs. Stevens, Mrs. George Davis, and Mrs. W.H. Snow.

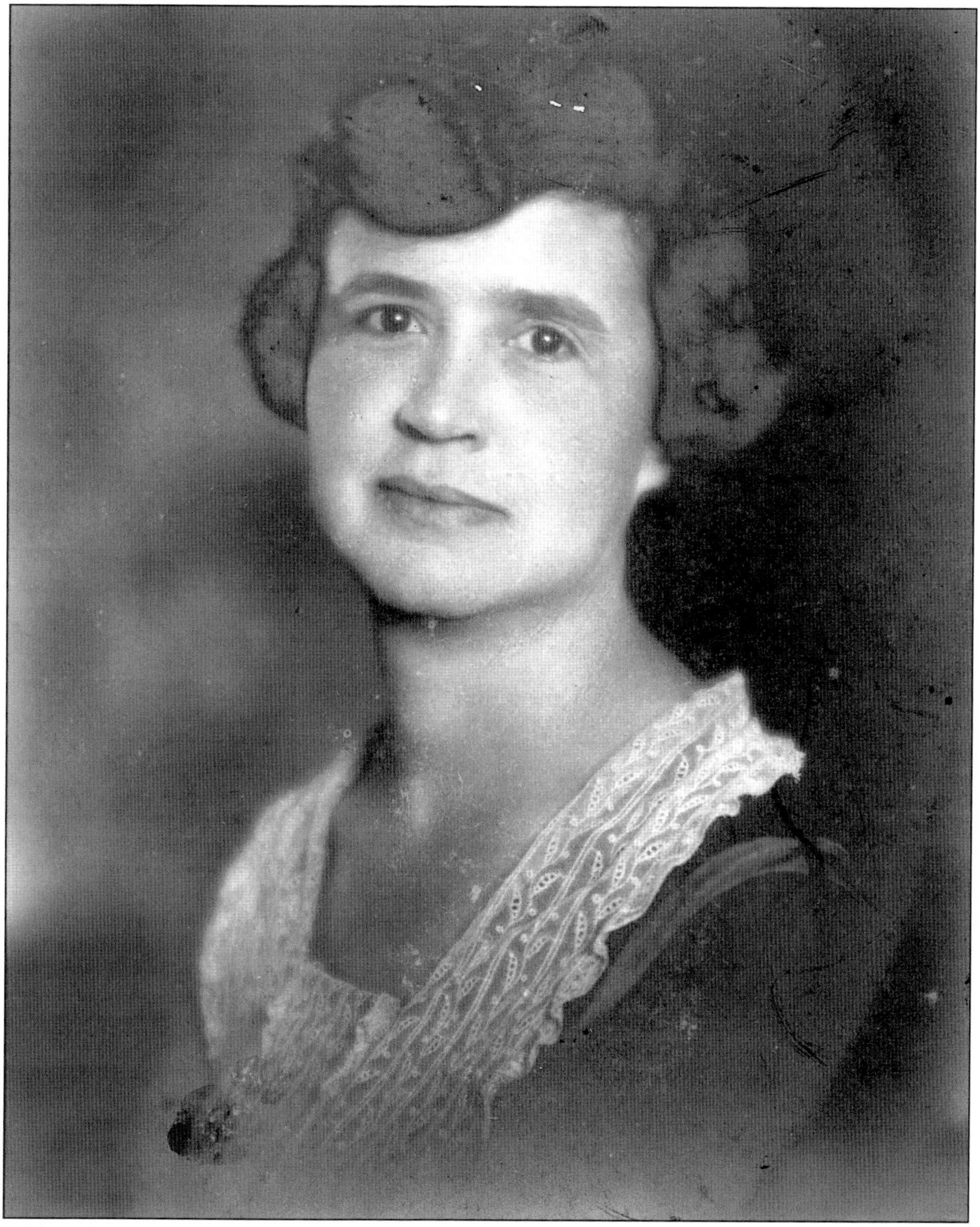

Although her parents and siblings moved to Donna in 1908, Beulah Moye did not arrive until 1911. Her father, J.B. Moye Sr., was a close friend of A.F. Hester Sr. when they all lived at Village Mills. Miss Moye attended Sam Houston Normal College (Sam Houston University) in Huntsville. A.F. Hester, who was president of the school board, asked her to teach at the Run school. Her salary was $50 per month. She boarded with the Hesters and paid for her room and board at a cost of $3 per week. When the Hesters moved into Donna, she found a place to live about two miles from the school. She walked, or rode a burro when the weather was cold or wet. She later moved to Donna, where she served as a classroom teacher, then a principal at the East Donna Elementary School. The Beulah Moye Junior High School was named for her. She remained an educator throughout her long life.

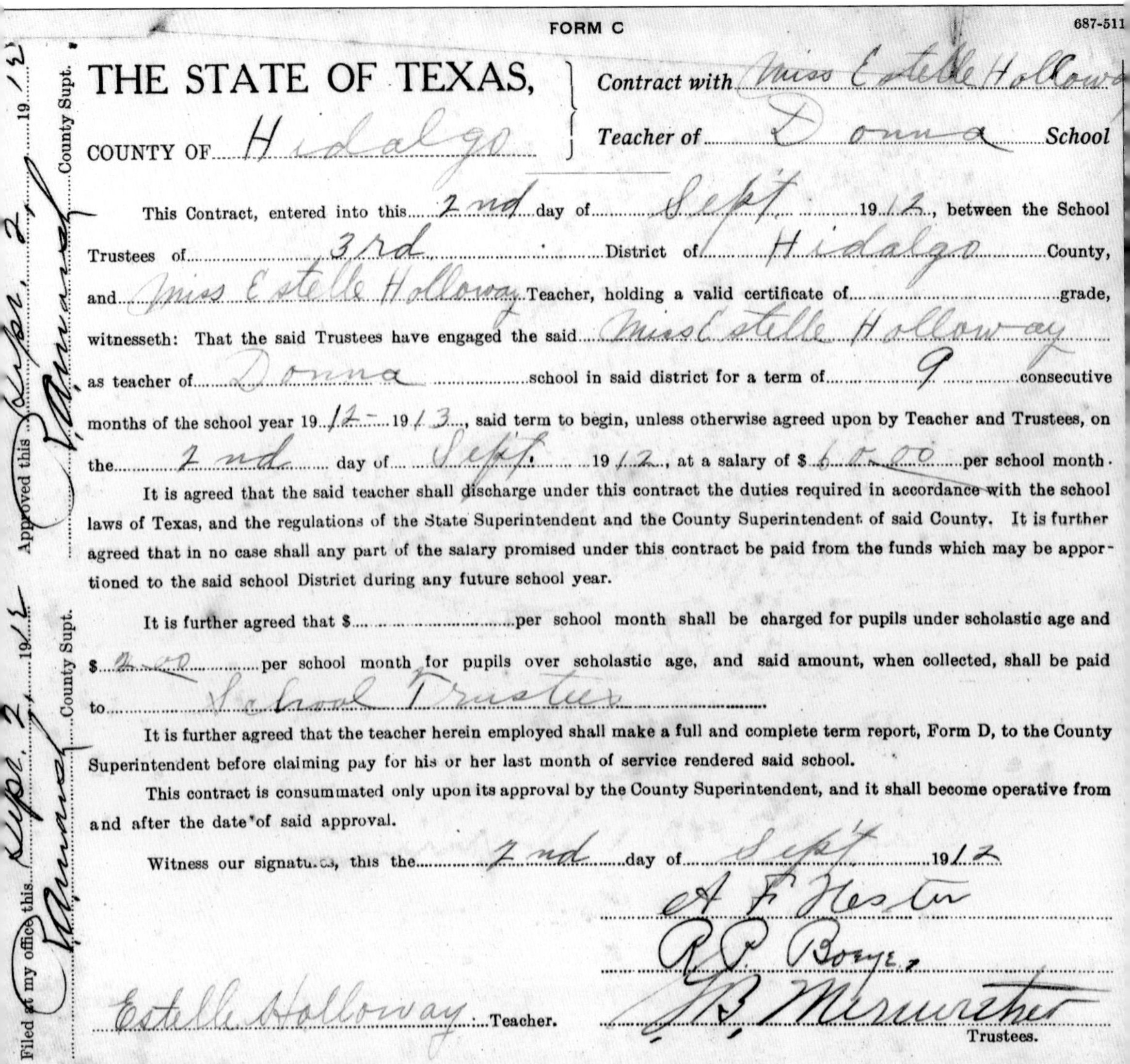

FORM C 687-511

THE STATE OF TEXAS, COUNTY OF Hidalgo

Contract with Miss Estelle Holloway *Teacher of* Donna *School*

This Contract, entered into this 2nd day of Sept 1912, between the School Trustees of 3rd District of Hidalgo County, and Miss Estelle Holloway Teacher, holding a valid certificate of .... grade, witnesseth: That the said Trustees have engaged the said Miss Estelle Holloway as teacher of Donna school in said district for a term of 9 consecutive months of the school year 1912–1913, said term to begin, unless otherwise agreed upon by Teacher and Trustees, on the 2nd day of Sept. 1912, at a salary of $60.00 per school month.

It is agreed that the said teacher shall discharge under this contract the duties required in accordance with the school laws of Texas, and the regulations of the State Superintendent and the County Superintendent of said County. It is further agreed that in no case shall any part of the salary promised under this contract be paid from the funds which may be apportioned to the said school District during any future school year.

It is further agreed that $........ per school month shall be charged for pupils under scholastic age and $2.00 per school month for pupils over scholastic age, and said amount, when collected, shall be paid to School Trustees.

It is further agreed that the teacher herein employed shall make a full and complete term report, Form D, to the County Superintendent before claiming pay for his or her last month of service rendered said school.

This contract is consummated only upon its approval by the County Superintendent, and it shall become operative from and after the date of said approval.

Witness our signatures, this the 2nd day of Sept 1912.

A. F. Hester
R. P. Boyce
J. B. Meriwether
Trustees.

Estelle Holloway Teacher.

Approved this Sept. 2, 1912 [signature] County Supt.

Filed at my office this Sept. 2, 1912 [signature] County Supt.

This contract between Miss Estelle Holloway and 3rd District of Hidalgo County, dated September 2, 1912, permits her to teach at Donna during the 1912–1913 school year. She earned $60 "per school month." In 1902, the Milton H. Holloway family had left Louisiana and sailed to Brazos Santiago on the same ship carrying the Hester family. The Holloway, Hooks, and Hester families lived near each other in Brownsville and later at Run. Milton H. Holloway purchased ranch land adjacent to the tract belonging to the La Blanca Agricultural Land Company. The Holloway children attended a one-room school at Run, which was taught by Mr. Lowber Snow. When the children outgrew the one-room school, the family moved into Donna, where the children attended the new junior high school.

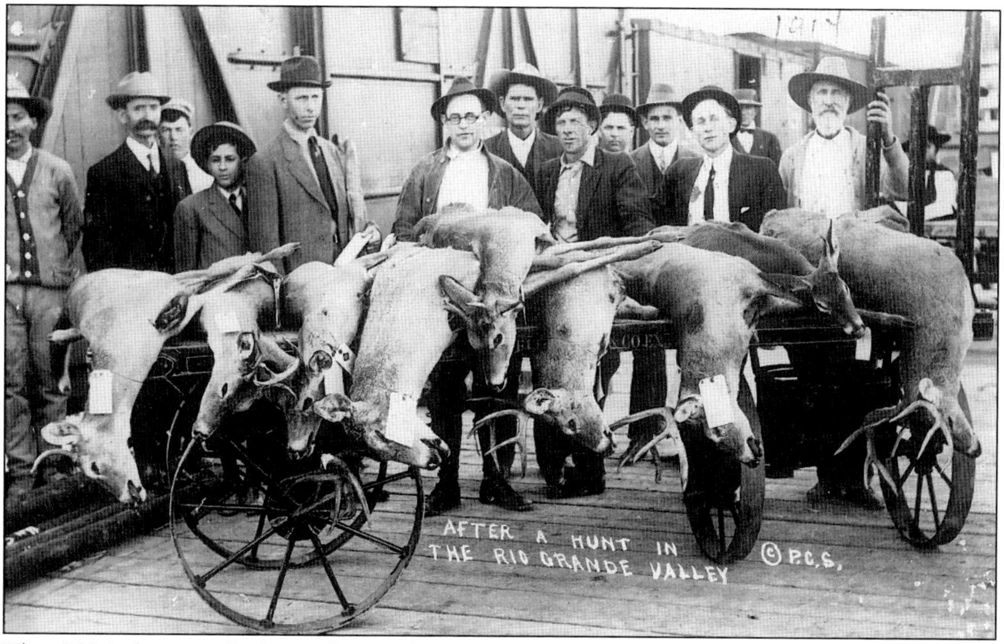

This 1914 photograph shows the results of a successful deer hunt. Nine deer have been laid across a railroad baggage cart. Plentiful wildlife, including many kinds of game birds, javelinas, ocelots, bobcats, and deer kept game wardens such as Charles G. Jones, with a three-county territory, busy enforcing the state's game laws.

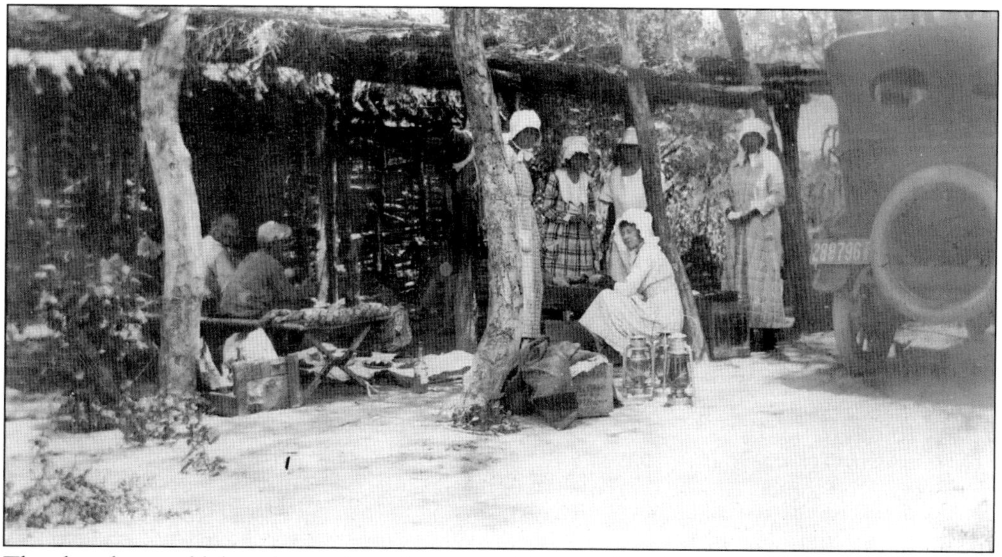

The abundance of fish and game brought many visitors and settlers to the Valley. Fishing camps were popular on both sides of the river. The fishing camp here, shown in 1920, consists mostly of a lean-to, built of local materials like a *jacal*.

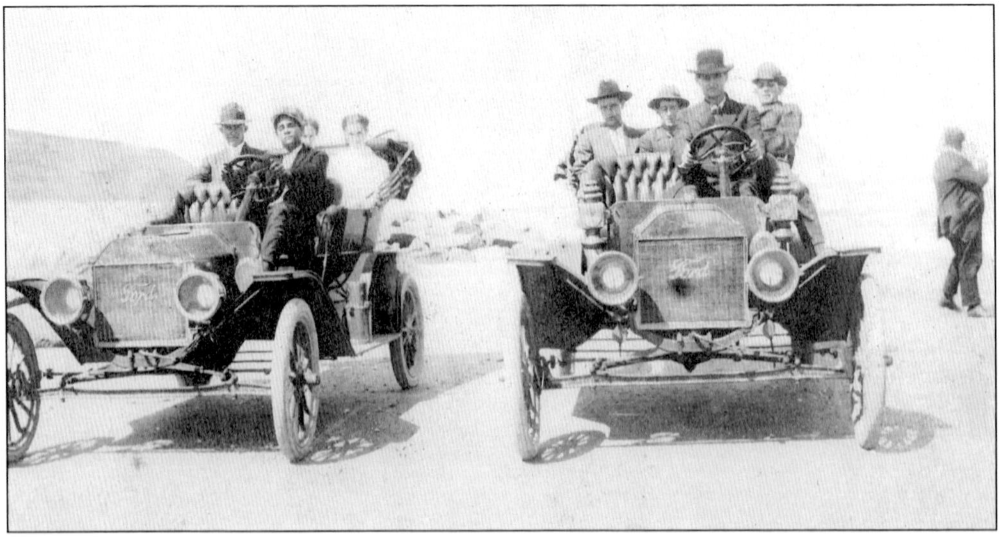

As more tourists and settlers came to the Valley, automobiles became more commonplace. The first automobiles in Donna, primarily Model T Fords and Maxwells, appeared during 1908 and 1909. Drivers speeding more than 12 miles per hour could be fined as much as $200. Here, sightseers travel along the Military Highway in July 1909. The road, originally cleared by General Zachary Taylor's troops during the war with Mexico (1846–1848), extended from Ft. Brown at Brownsville to Ft. Ringgold at Rio Grande City. Later known as the Military Telegraph Road because of the telegraph lines connecting Ft. Brown to Ft. Ringgold, it was eventually incorporated into the U.S. 281 highway system. Most Valley residents still call it the "military highway."

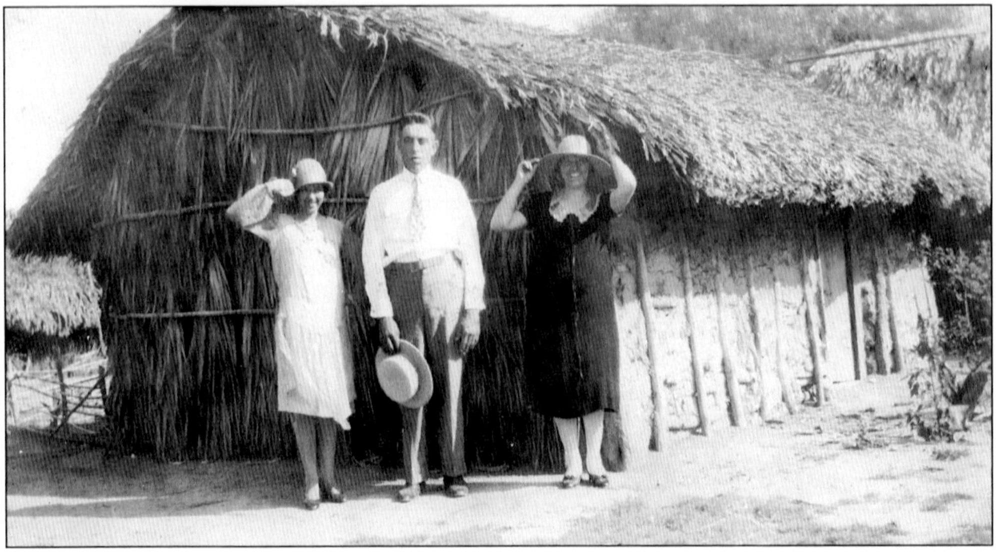

Newcomers to the area, including Donna founders T.J. Hooks and A.F. Hester Sr., lived in *jacales*. They supervised land-clearing crews from Mexico, preparations for planting crops, and construction of their homes. Their families lived in Brownsville until the new homes were ready. The Hooks and Hester plantations lay between the river and the Military Highway (U.S. 281). T.J. Hooks built the first permanent home of adobe brick formed and fired on site. A.F. Hester built the second permanent home with lumber brought from East Texas.

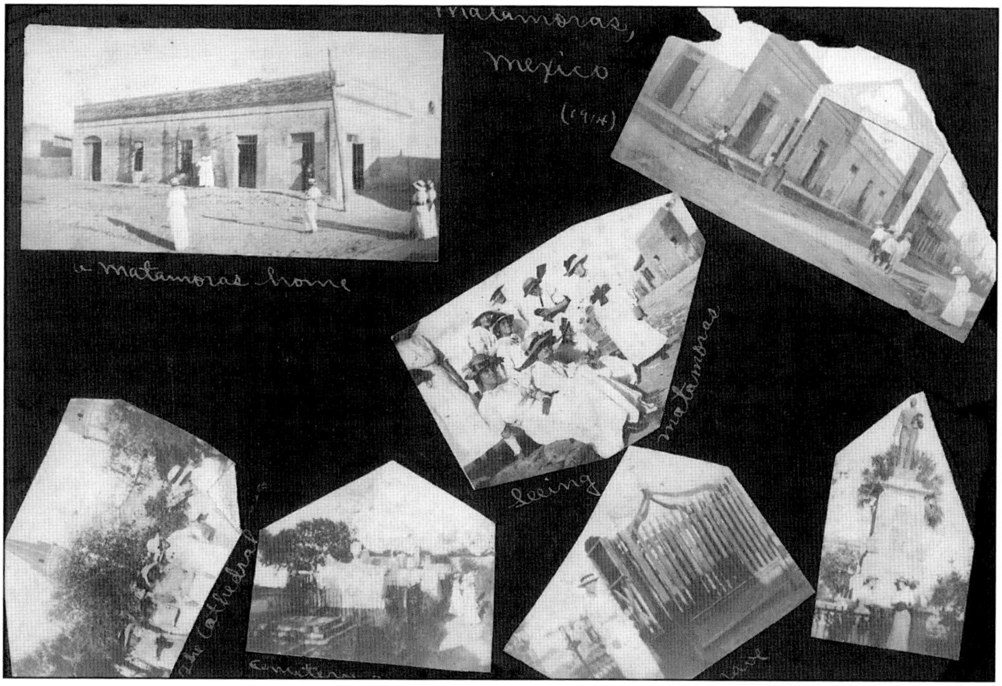

Matamoros, Mexico, was a popular place to visit. This building (top left), identified in the original photograph as a home, is dated 1914. Only a short ferry ride across the river from Brownsville, Matamoros provided a sense of adventure in a country perceived as exotic by U.S. citizens.

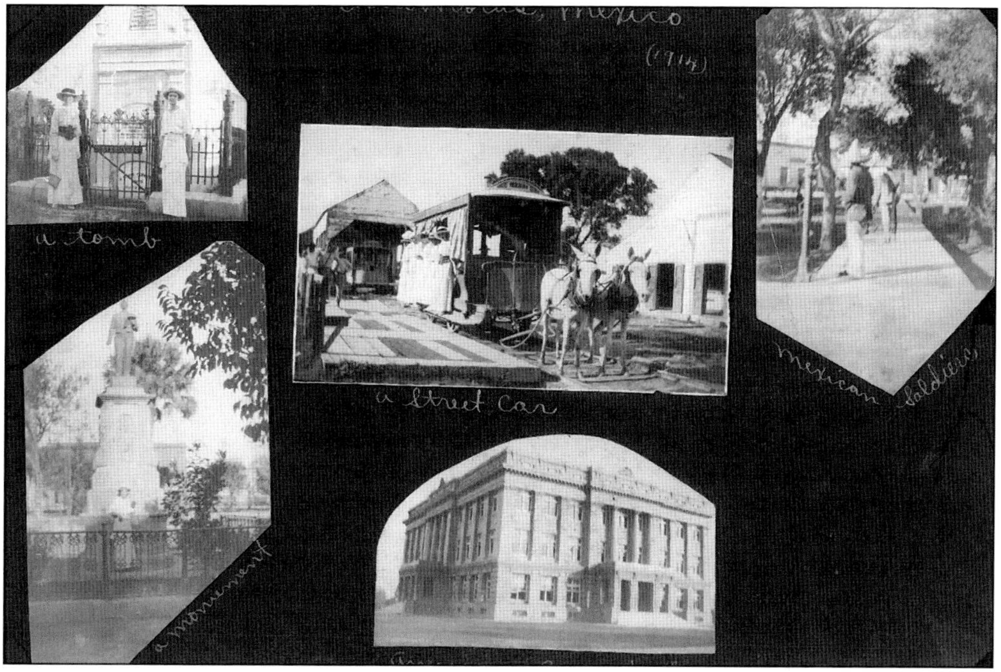

Visitors to Matamoros in 1914 would have found the mule-drawn streetcars curious and old-fashioned. Most U.S. citizens were accustomed to electric streetcars (center) with comfortable seats and handsome decorations.

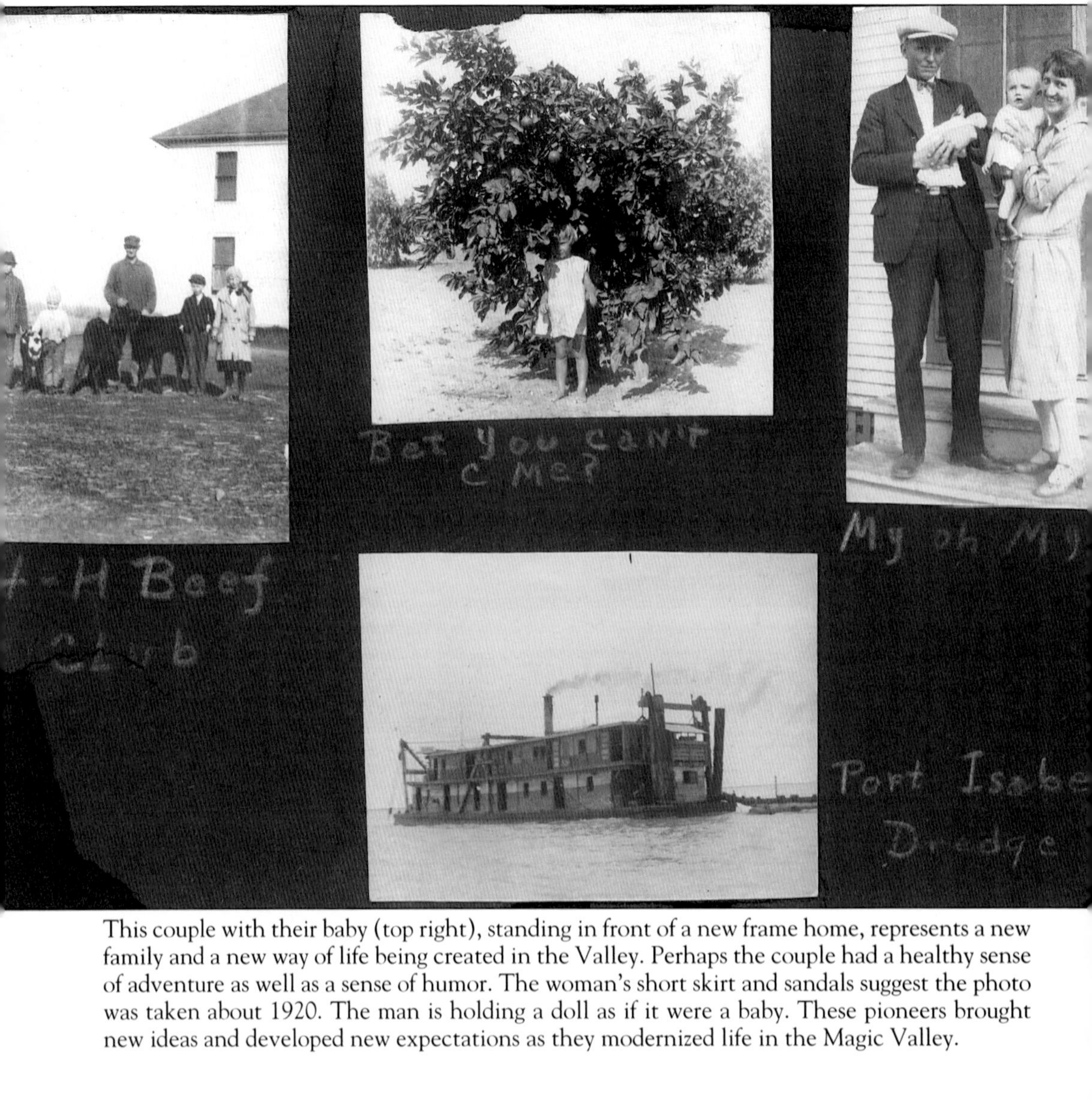

This couple with their baby (top right), standing in front of a new frame home, represents a new family and a new way of life being created in the Valley. Perhaps the couple had a healthy sense of adventure as well as a sense of humor. The woman's short skirt and sandals suggest the photo was taken about 1920. The man is holding a doll as if it were a baby. These pioneers brought new ideas and developed new expectations as they modernized life in the Magic Valley.

Four

NORTHERNERS COME SOUTH

The irrigation and railroad systems made large-scale production of citrus and vegetable crops highly successful. Advertisements from developers, railroads, and businessmen's organizations brought many Texans and Midwesterners to Donna, which was renowned for enormous crops of sugarcane, onions, alfalfa, corn, tomatoes, cabbages, celery, beans, cucumbers, and cotton. Often newcomers bought their farms on time and paid for them out of the first year's profits. After 1920, soldiers from the Midwest, who had been stationed in the Valley, returned to farm and operate businesses. They became permanent members of the community.

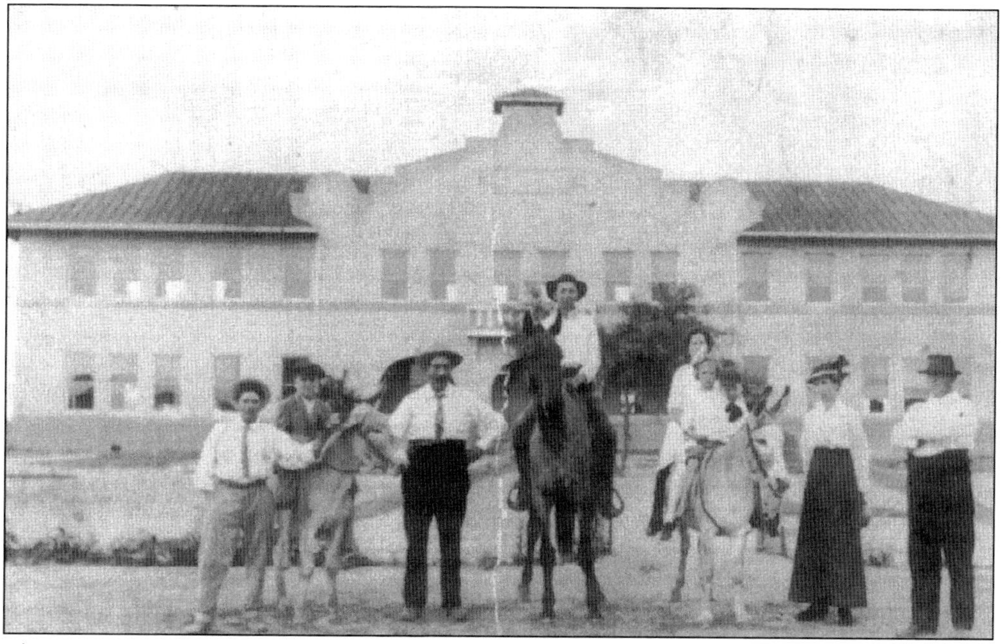

The Oscar John Anderson family and two friends are standing in front of the first Donna Junior High School in 1915. The Andersons came from Nebraska in February 1916 after an earlier reconnaissance trip, and lived and farmed south of Donna. The hurricane of 1933 destroyed the school building. (Courtesy of Hazel and Orin Anderson.)

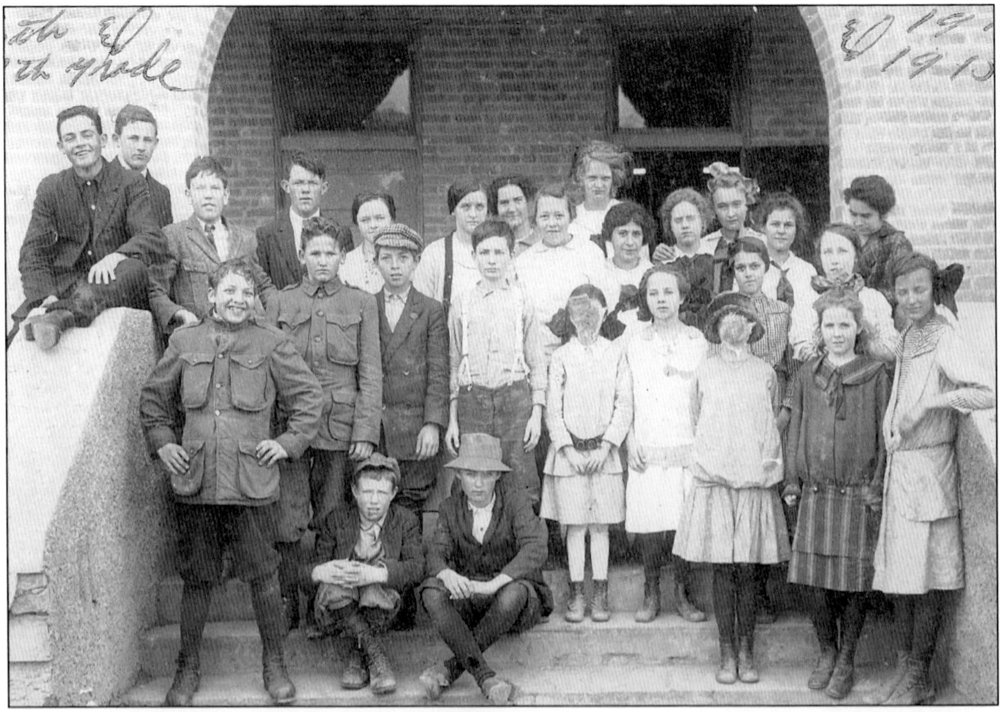

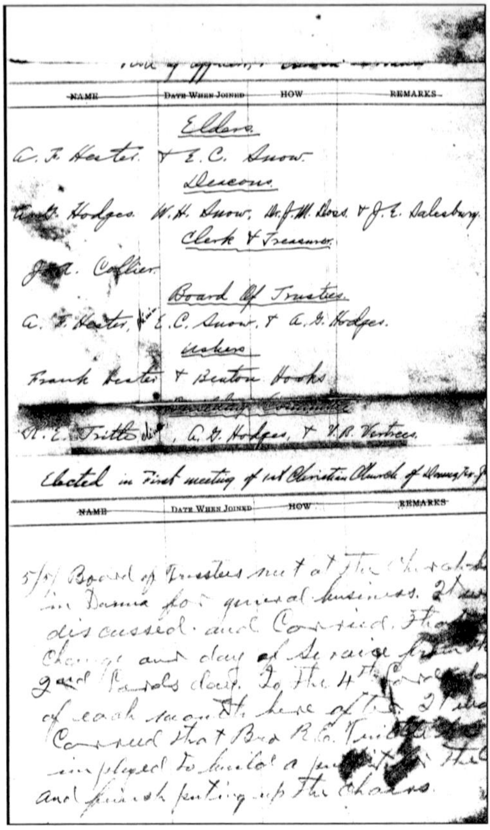

NAME	DATE WHEN JOINED	HOW	REMARKS

Elders
A. F. Hester & E.C. Snow
Deacons
A.D. Hodges W.H. Snow, Dr. J.M. Doss, & J.E. Salesbury
Clerk & Treasurer
J.A. Collier
Board of Trustees
A. F. Hester, Sr. E.C. Snow, & A. D. Hodges.
Ushers
Frank Hester & Benton Hooks
Building Committee
R.E. Tritt Sr., A.D. Hodges, & U.B. Vertrees.
Elected in First meeting of 1st Christian Church of Donna

NAME	DATE WHEN JOINED	HOW	REMARKS

5/5/ Board of Trustees met at the Church in Donna for general business. [illegible] discussed and Carried. [illegible] Change and day of Service [illegible] 2nd Sunday [illegible] to the 4th [illegible] of each month. [illegible] Carried that Bro R.E. Tritt [illegible] employed to build a [illegible] and finish putting up the Chairs.

The 6th and 7th grade class of 1914–1915 is standing at the entrance to the new junior high school. Mexican-American children attended schools in the homes of highly educated teachers from Mexico. After the flood of 1909, a school was built in Run, and another school was organized in Donna in a former store. The first graduating class of four graduated from Donna High School in 1913. At the time, the school district included what is now Weslaco and extended to the Mercedes corporate boundary.

In 1910, members of each of the Protestant congregations combined their funds to build a community church. The building was shared by all, who would gather to hear any available minister. The First Methodist Church was founded in 1909, followed by the First Presbyterian and First Baptist Churches in 1910, and the First Christian Church in 1911. This handwritten page lists members in attendance at the first meeting of the First Christian Church, who were elected by the 46 charter members to serve in different capacities: A.F. Hester Sr., elder; Dr. J.M. Doss, deacon; and U.B. Vertrees, building committee.

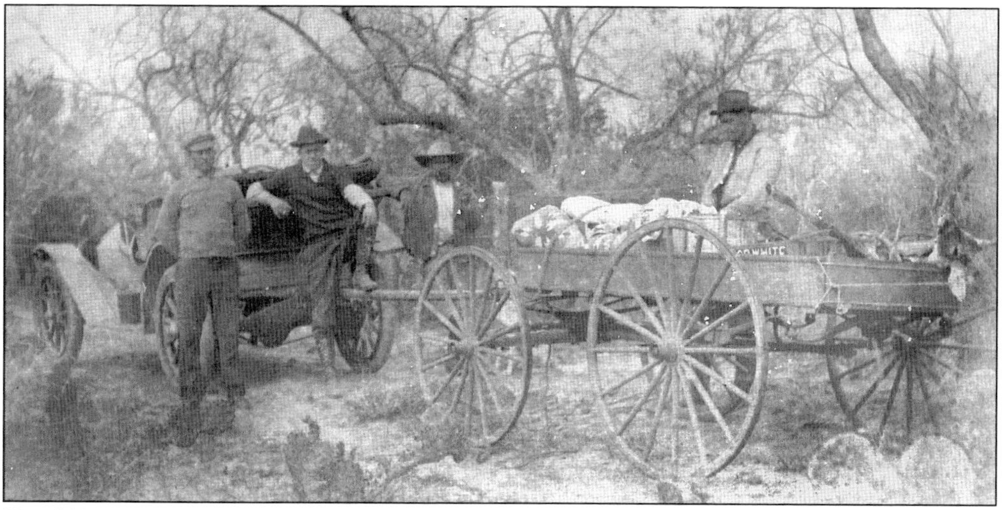

Harold Vertrees, Tom Hester, and Dr. J.M. Doss, the first physician in Donna, are shown at a deer hunt near Donna. The closest hospital was in Brownsville, and Dr. Doss, as well as other early physicians, traveled by buggy to a patient's home. Among his many interests, Thomas I. Hester (1889–1955) owned a pharmacy, established and operated the Donna [Cotton] Gin Company for over 30 years, owned two automobile dealerships (in Edinburg and Rio Grande City), was a bank president, built streets and roads in and around Donna (sometimes with Sam Barnard as co-contractor), and served as a county commissioner for 16 years. He was the son of A.F. Hester Sr.

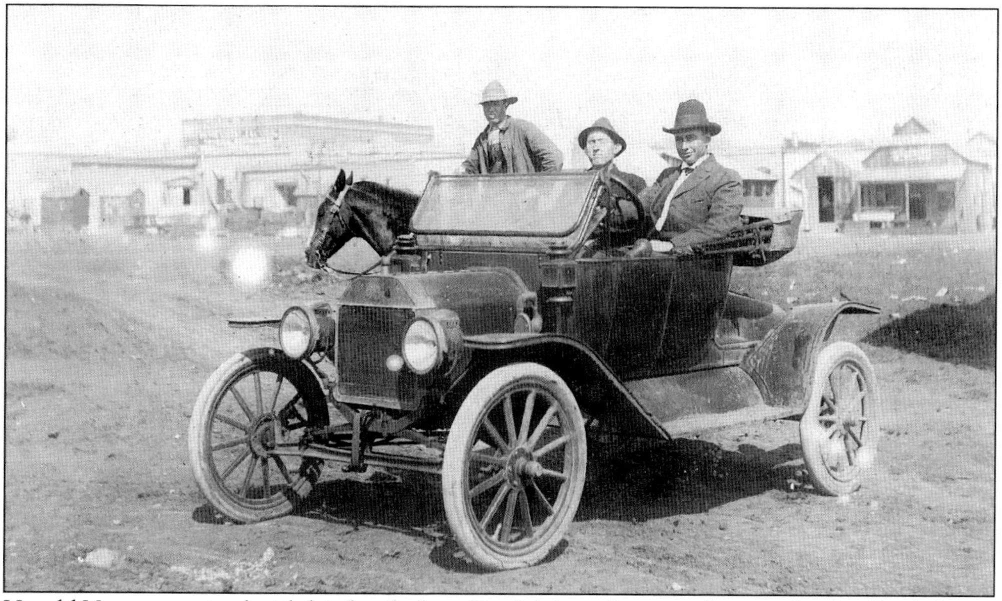

Harold Vertrees arrived with his family from Des Moines, Iowa, at the age of eight. His father, a Des Moines city councilman for many years, was 70. The Vertrees family bought riverfront land from Thomas J. Hooks and built a home near the Champion General Store. Once each month the family went to Brownsville for supplies. After the devastating flood of 1909, the Vertrees family moved to Donna. Harold Vertrees worked for Ed Ruthven in his general store. To earn $10 per week, Harold worked 15 hours a day, 7 days a week. Here Harold Vertrees is shown in 1912, driving a car in downtown Donna.

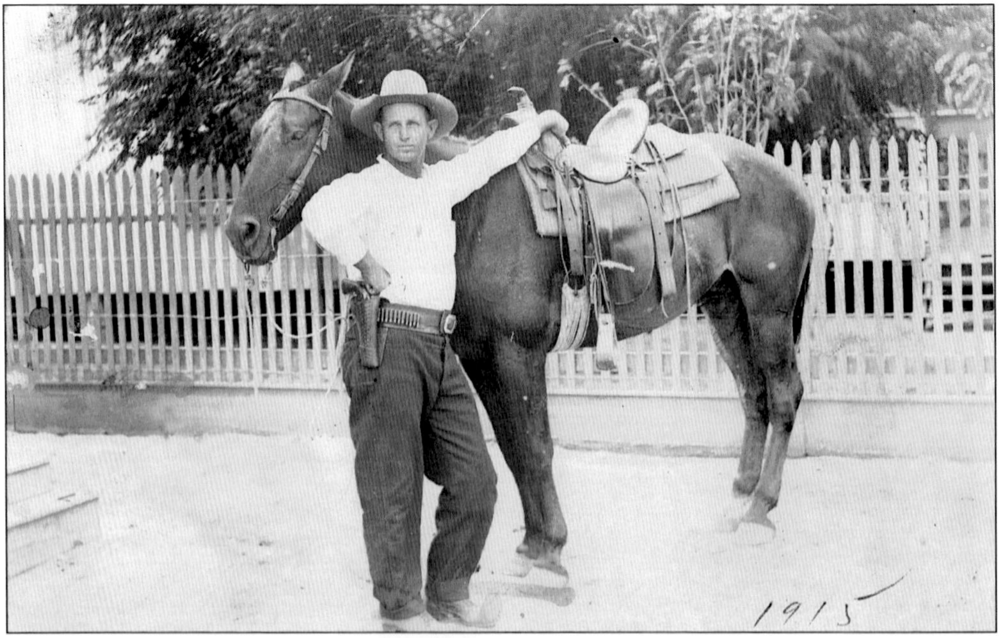

Sam Barnard became the first deputy sheriff for Donna. He is shown here in 1915 with his horse Diablo ("devil"). During the bandit raid period (1910–1920) when the U.S. military intervened, Deputy Barnard settled fights involving soldiers as well as civilians. The tin ceilings of Donna's famous Blue Goose Saloon were pockmarked with bullet holes. Deputy Barnard's calming presence was welcome at all of the local "watering holes."

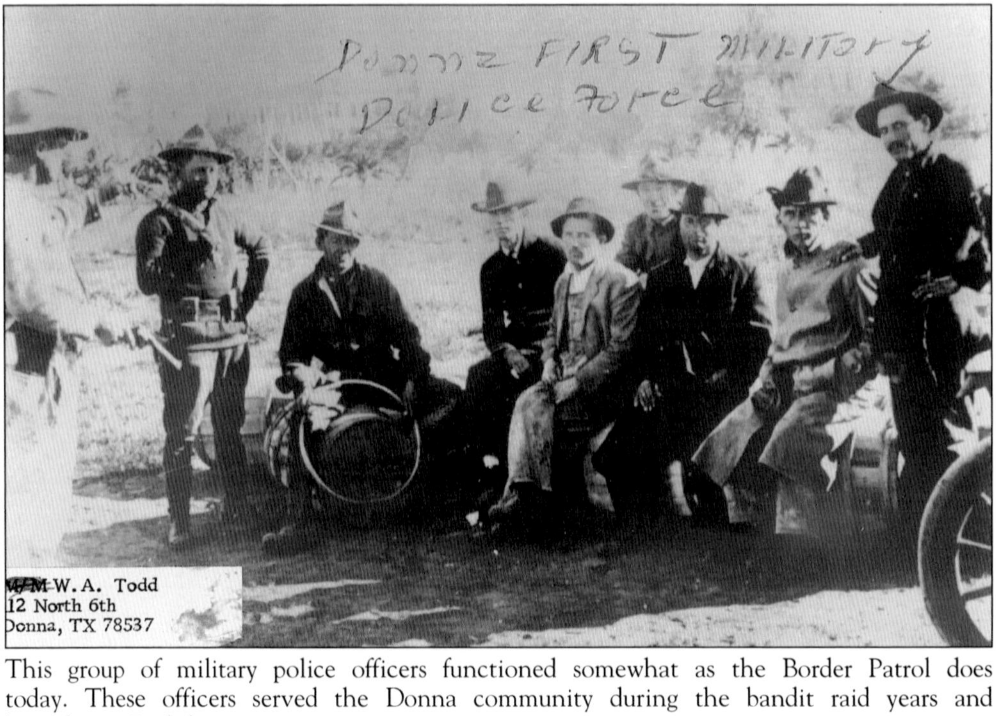

This group of military police officers functioned somewhat as the Border Patrol does today. These officers served the Donna community during the bandit raid years and later during Prohibition.

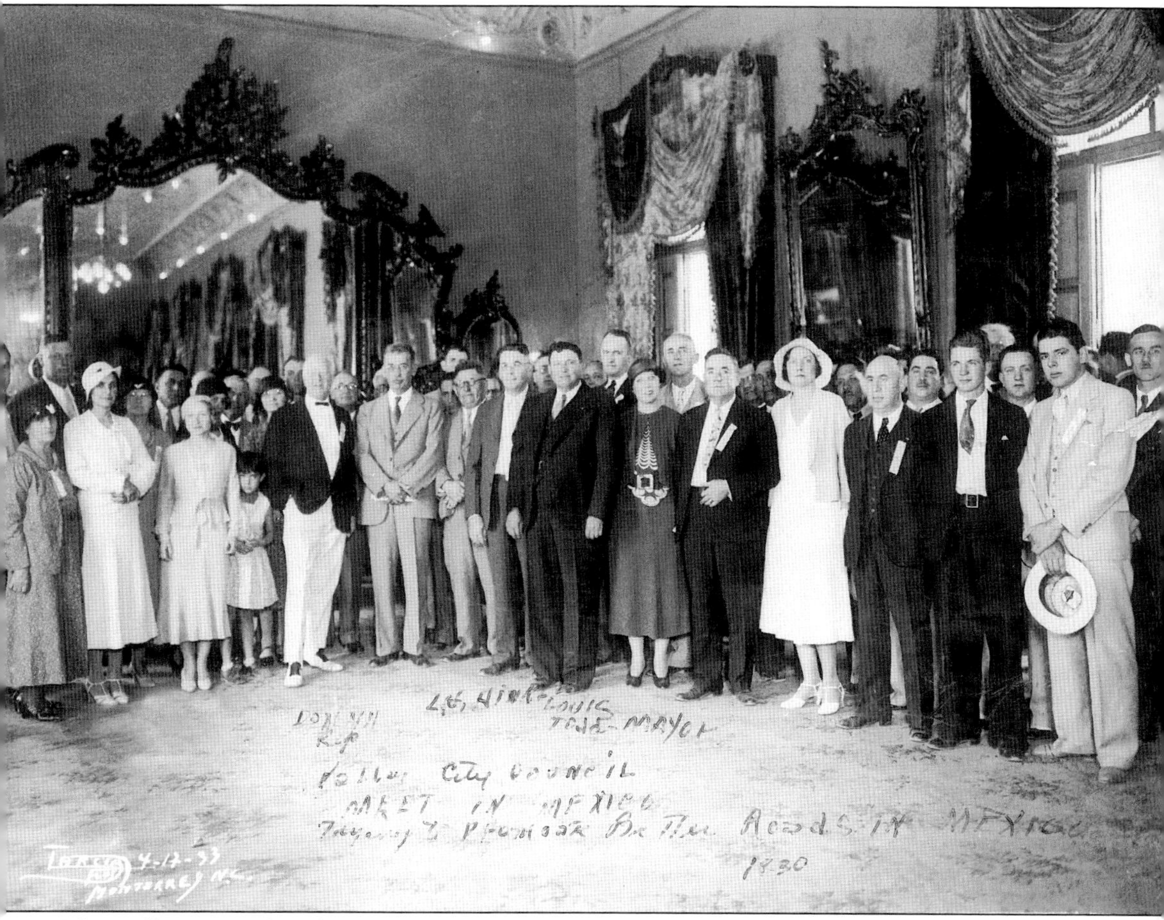

The Valley Council and Mexican officials met at this ornate hotel in Monterrey, Mexico, in 1930 to negotiate a plan for constructing better roads in Mexico. Donna mayor Louis Todd stands in the center.

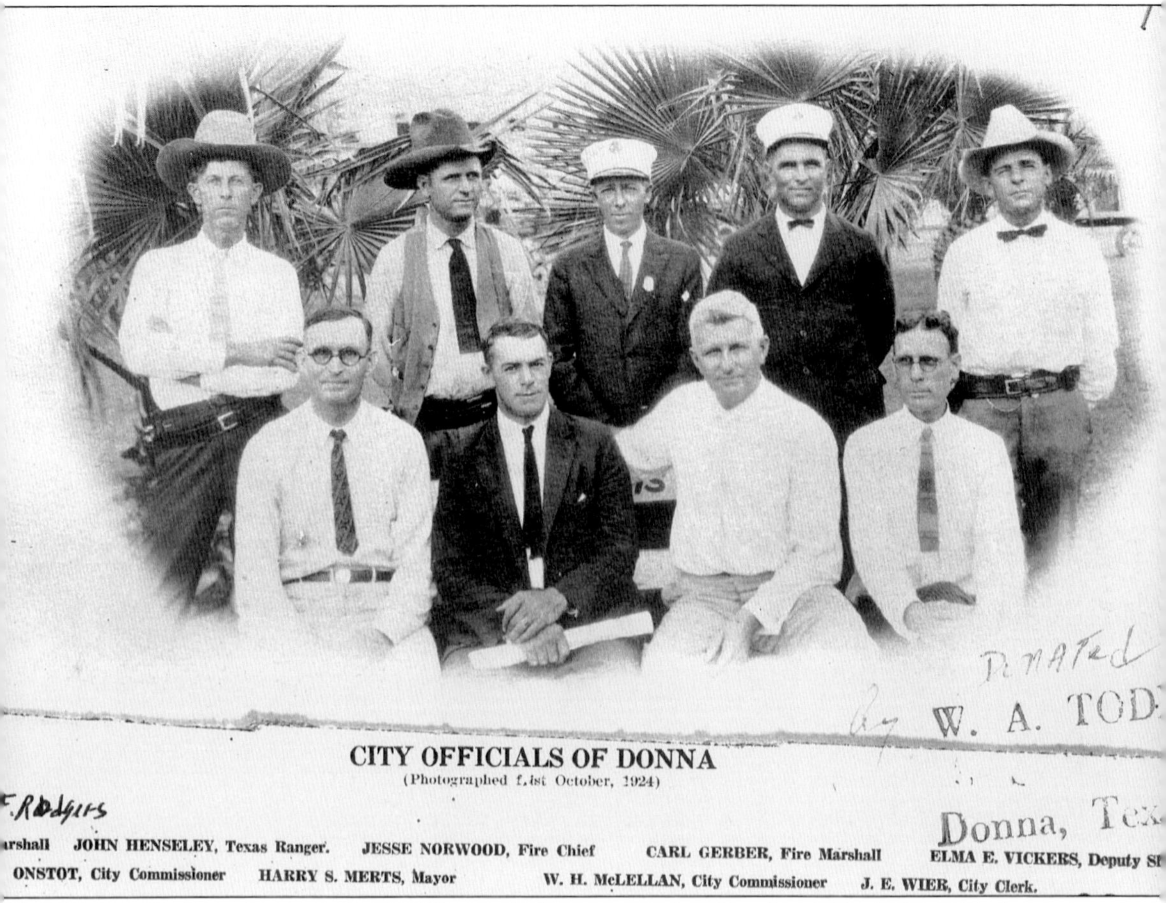

Pictured are the city officials of Donna as they appeared on October 1, 1924. Seated, left to right, are: H.H. Onstot, city commissioner; Harry S. Merts, mayor; W.H. McLellan, city commissioner; and J.E. Weir, city clerk. Standing, left to right, are: Ben F. Rodgers, city marshal; John Henseley, Texas Ranger; Jesse Norwood, fire chief; Carl Gerber, fire marshal; and Elmer E. Vickers, deputy sheriff. Minutes for the first meeting of the Donna City Commission are dated April 23, 1919. Present were mayor C.M. Paine, commissioner A.F. Hester Jr., city clerk A.J. Whiteside, and city attorney Walter Weaver Sr.

Five

DONNA: THIS IS MY LIFE

Donna Hooks Fletcher was the daughter of Thomas J. Hooks, one of the founders of the Donna town site. She was born on June 22, 1879, the third of 10 children born to Thomas and Virginia Hooks. At the time, the family was living in Pineville, in East Texas. Donna Hooks married Clyde W. Fletcher, one of her father's business partners in1895, but the marriage failed and by 1908 she was on her own. She became a successful pioneer farmer, rancher, and businessperson.

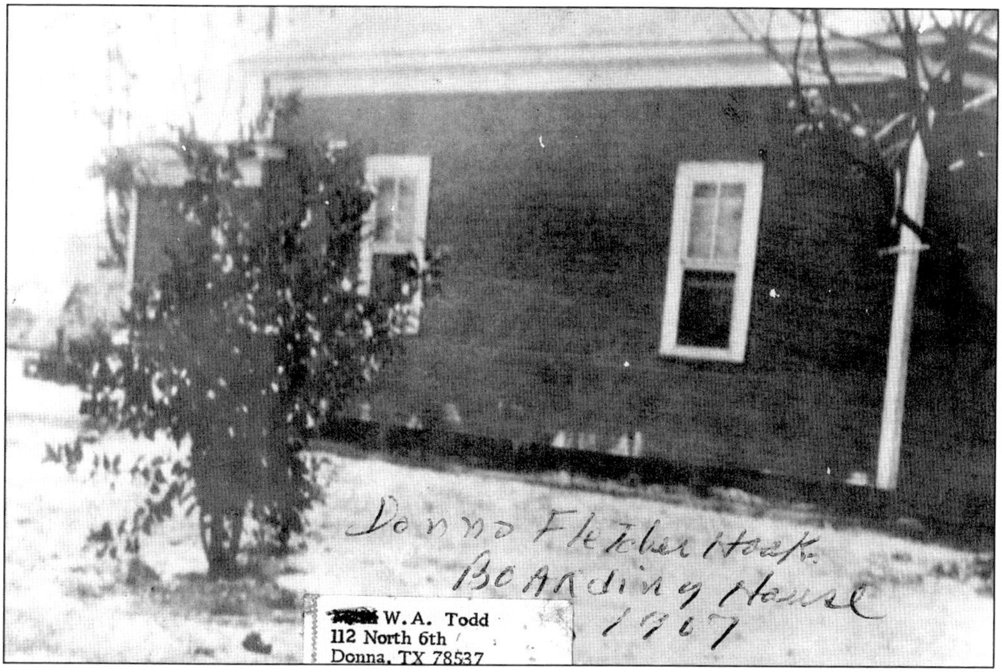

This is a side view of the Donna Hooks Fletcher boarding house soon after it opened in 1907. Donna held many "first" occupation titles. Not only did she own the boarding house, but she also owned an office building (1908), a hotel (1909), a movie theater, and was the first postmaster of Donna. During the 1920s, she established and operated a department store, which built a reputation as the finest in the Valley. Her Alameda Ranch, with the first herd of registered Jersey cattle in the area, produced the "Melrose" brand of butter, distributed throughout the Valley. She grew crops of corn, cotton, and alfalfa on her model farm.

SEASON OF 1908 PRICE $25

Annual Membership Card

TARPON BEACH CLUB

Issued to Mrs. D. H. Fletcher

Transferable only on the books of the Company.

PADRE ISLAND DEVELOPMENT CO.

No. 440 .... Treas.

This 1908 membership card, costing $25, entitled Donna to the following privileges: transportation between Point Isabel (now Port Isabel) and Tarpon Beach (now South Padre Island), plus the use of bathhouses, suits, and towels at "club rates." In addition, the membership provided privileges of the clubhouse, landing at the club's wharfs or other property, and the use of boardwalks and beaches.

Membership in the Tarpon Beach Club entitles the holder to the following privileges:

1.—Transportation between Point Isabel and Tarpon Beach on launches and boats operated or licensed by the Company at club rates.

2.—Use of bath houses suits, towels, etc. at club rates.

3.—Privilege of club hous

4—Privilege of landing at Company's wharfs, or any part of Company's property, and use of Board Walks and Beaches.

Rates for Non-Members After May 1, 1908, Visitor's Tickets to Tarpon Beach, good for one day only, will be sold at $1 the round trip from Point Isabel. Bath house tickets, 25 cents each.

Visitors will not be allowed the use of Club House unless introduced by a Club member.

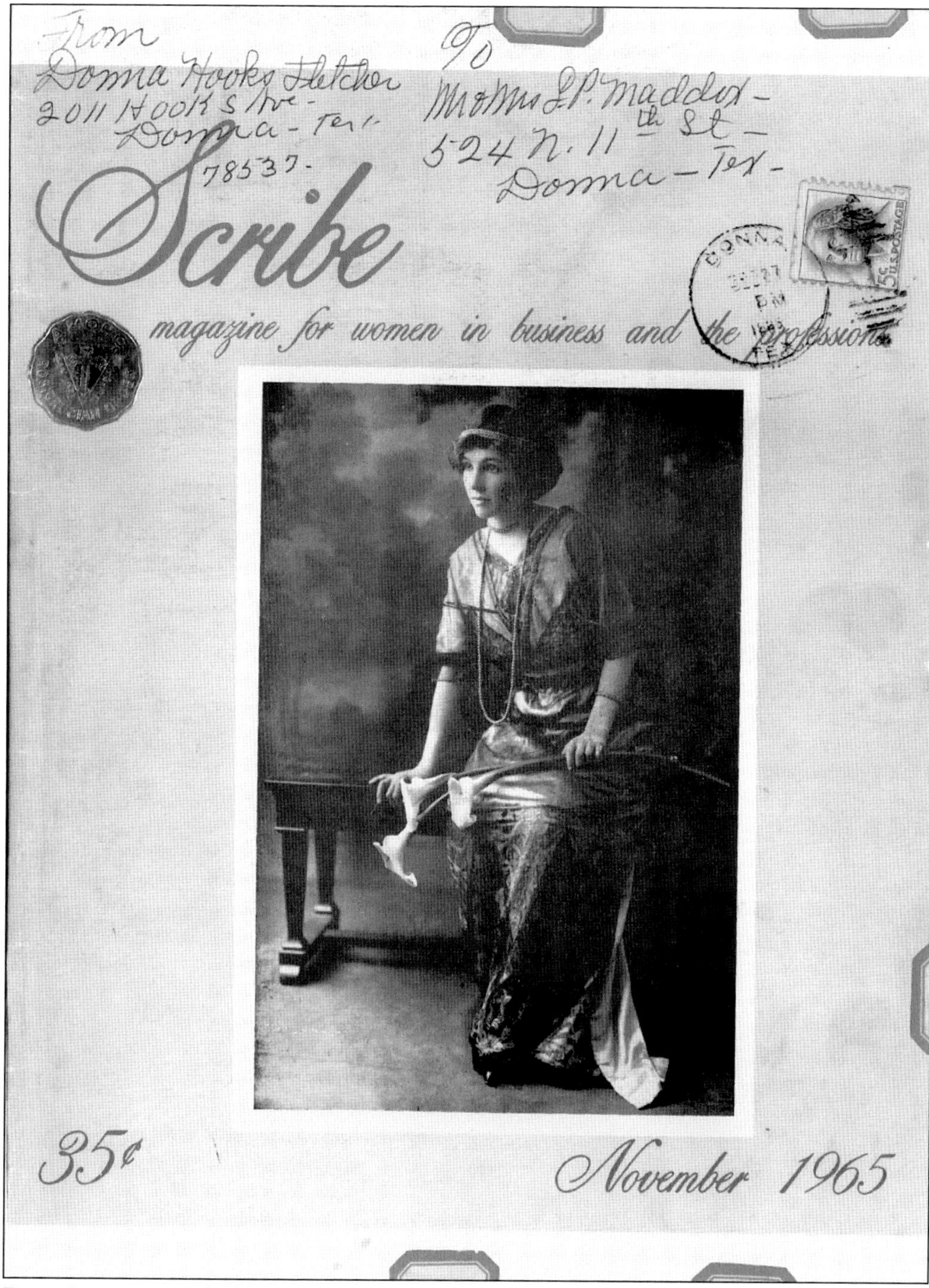

Donna's portrait made the front cover of the November 1965 issue of *Scribe* magazine published in Dallas, Texas. The cover story highlighted Donna as a "Pioneer Woman of Yesterday." According to the article, "this woman helped open the Valley of Texas with a Bible in one hand and a gun in the other. She erected a chapel as a meeting place for study and worship. This building, which is located on the eastern outskirts of Donna, almost hidden in shrubbery, is now her home."

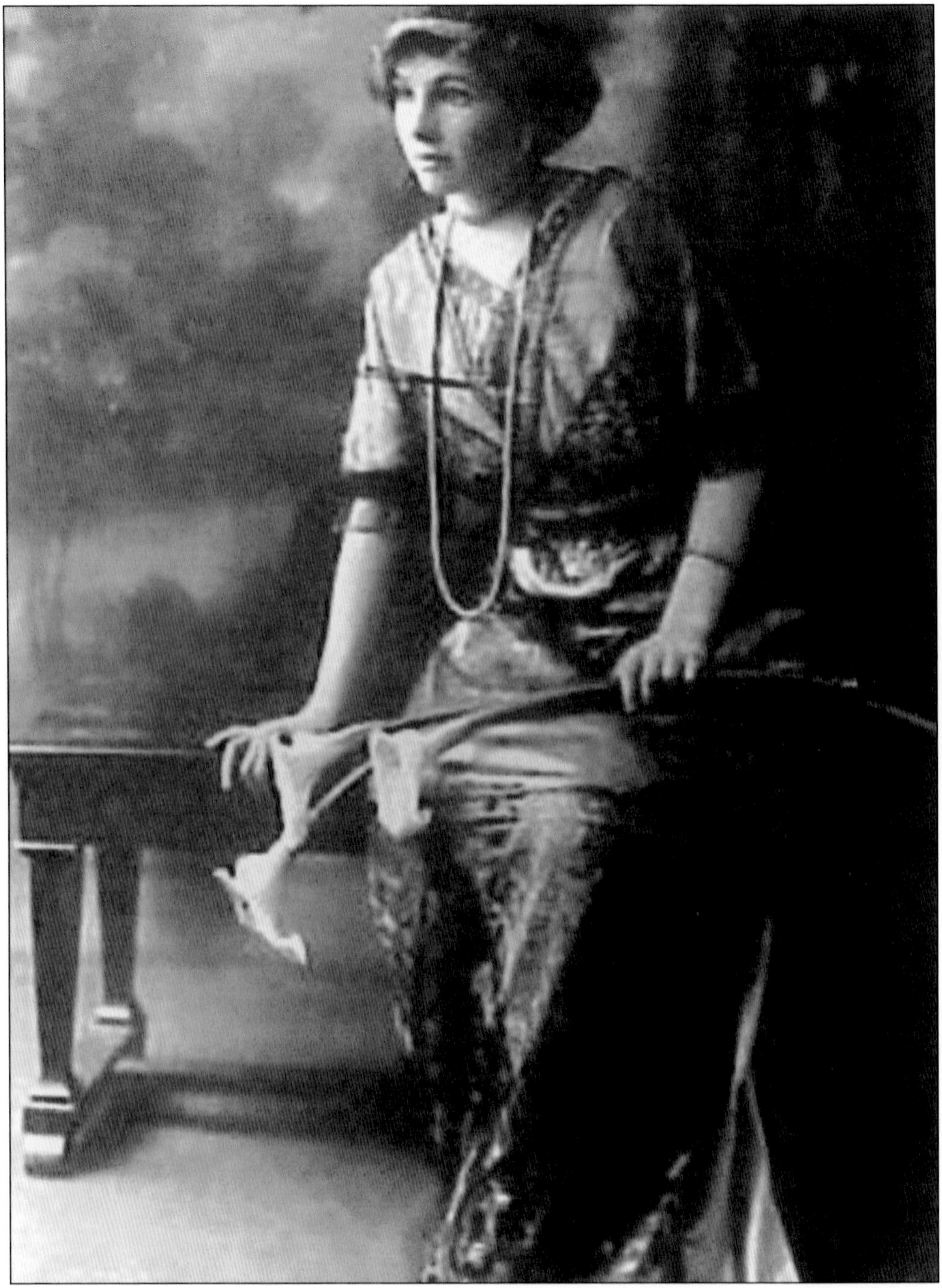

This famous portrait shows Donna Hooks Fletcher at the turn of the century, possibly at the age of 21. The photo was probably taken at a studio in Brownsville, 45 miles east of Donna. Being more cosmopolitan than other Valley towns, Brownsville offered the luxury of photo studios. The flowers she is holding, of Mexican origin, are known as "the Alcatraz," a type of calla lily.

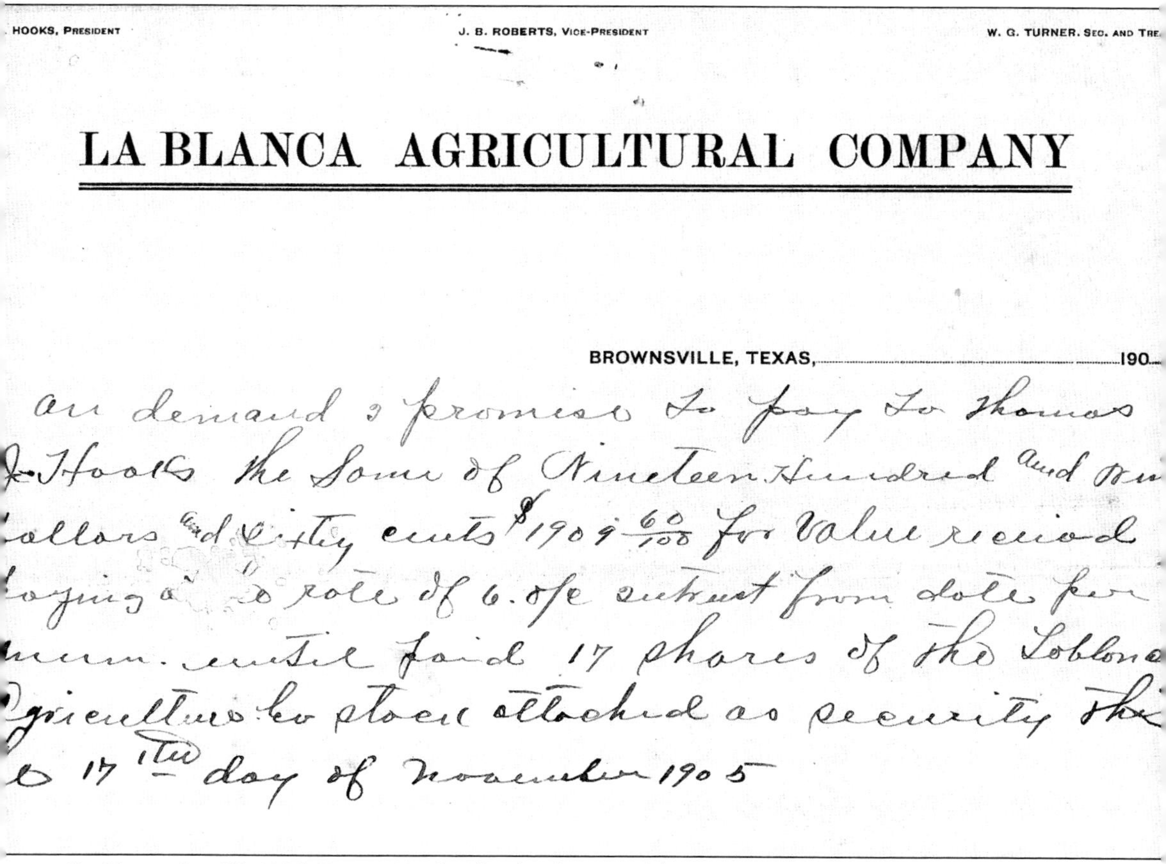

HOOKS, PRESIDENT J. B. ROBERTS, VICE-PRESIDENT W. G. TURNER, SEC. AND TRE

LA BLANCA AGRICULTURAL COMPANY

BROWNSVILLE, TEXAS, ... 190..

On demand I promise to pay to Thomas J. Hooks the Sum of Nineteen Hundred and Nine Dollars and Sixty cents $1909 60/100 for Value received paying at the rate of 6. % interest from date per annum until paid 17 shares of the La Blanca Agriculture Co stock attached as security the 17th day of November 1905

On November 17, 1905, Donna Hooks Fletcher borrowed $1,909.60 at 6 percent interest from the La Blanca Agricultural Company, using 17 shares of La Blanca stock as security for the note. The interest rate was lowered to 4 percent in 1909, when Donna paid the interest due on the note. Her father, Thomas J. Hooks, wrote that he received another payment on October 6, 1910.

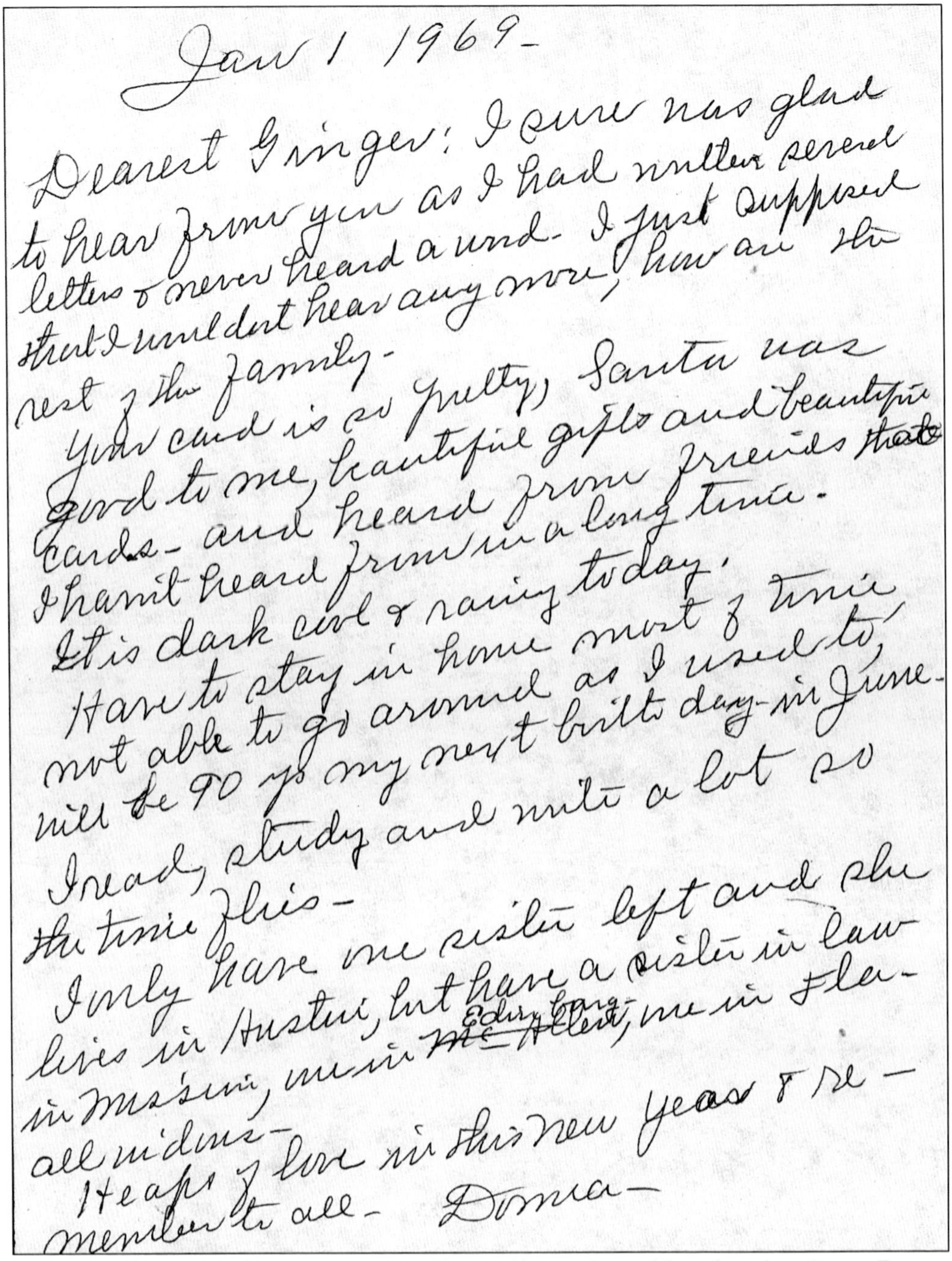

Jan 1 1969 -

Dearest Ginger: I sure was glad to hear from you as I had written several letters & never heard a word - I just supposed that I would not hear any more, how are the rest of the family -

Your card is so pretty, Santa was good to me, beautiful gifts and beautiful cards - and heard from friends that I haven't heard from in a long time -

It is dark cool & raining today,

Have to stay in home most of time not able to go around as I used to, will be 90 yrs my next birth day - in June -

I read, study and write a lot so the time flies -

I only have one sister left and she lives in Austin, but have a sister in law in ~~McAllen~~ Edinburg, one in Fla - in Missouri, [illegible] all widows -

Heaps of love in this new year & remember to all - Donna -

At the age of 89, Donna began to correspond less and less with good friends such as Ginger Fegette of Fresno, California. In the letter, dated January 1, 1969, she described the Christmas holiday and the weather being cool and rainy for the time of year. In addition to "staying in the house most of the time not able to go around as I used to, will be 90 years my next birthday in June." Donna passed away soon after reaching that birthday in June of 1969.

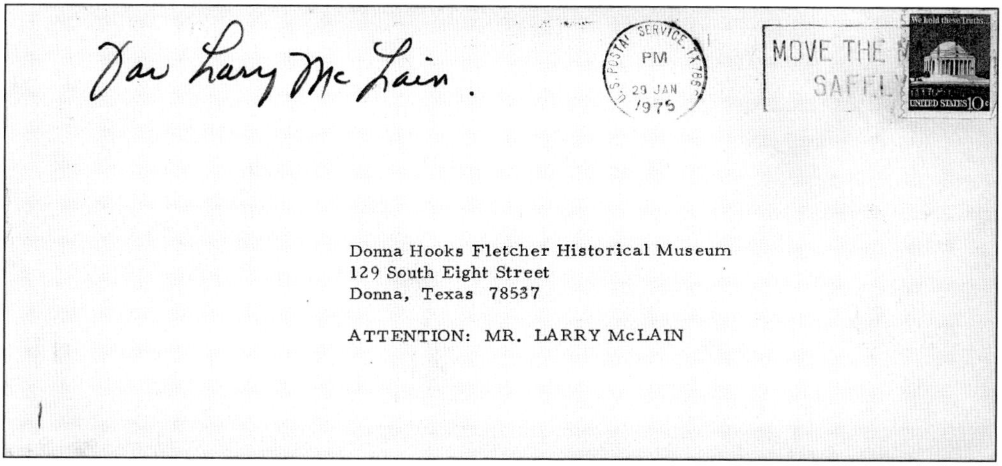

Donna Hooks Fletcher Historical Museum
129 South Eight Street
Donna, Texas 78537

ATTENTION: MR. LARRY McLAIN

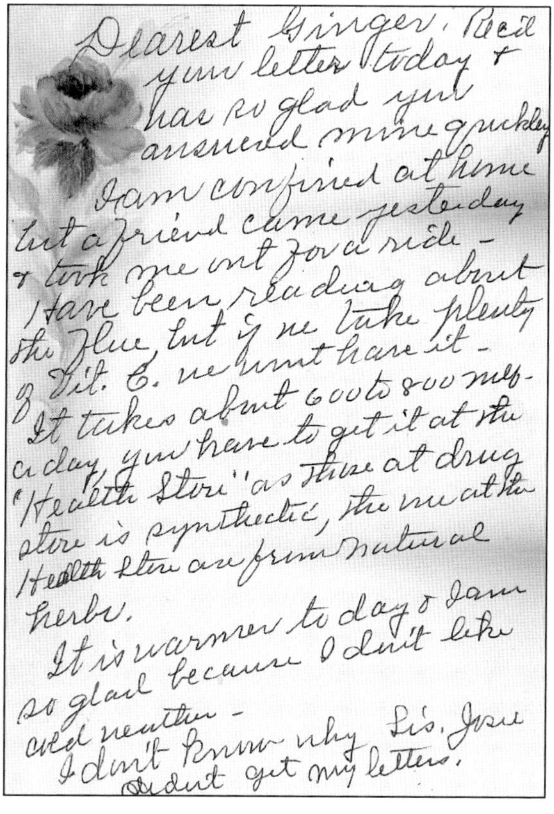

Dearest Ginger. Rec'd your letter today & was so glad you answered mine quickley. I am confined at home but a friend came yesterday & took me out for a ride - Have been reading about the Flue, but if we take plenty of Vit. C. we won't have it - It takes about 600 to 800 mg. a day, you have to get it at the "Health Store" as those at drug store is synthetic, the ones at the Health Store are from natural herbs.

It is warmer today & I am so glad because I don't like cold weather - I don't know why Sis. Josie didn't get my letters.

The letter, addressed to the attention of Mr. Larry McLain, coordinator of the Donna Hooks Fletcher Historical Museum, is postmarked 1979. Accessioned into the archives of the Donna Museum is a handwritten letter by Donna to her good friend Ginger Fegette. The Donna Museum has many handwritten letters from Donna, who enjoyed corresponding with friends and relatives.

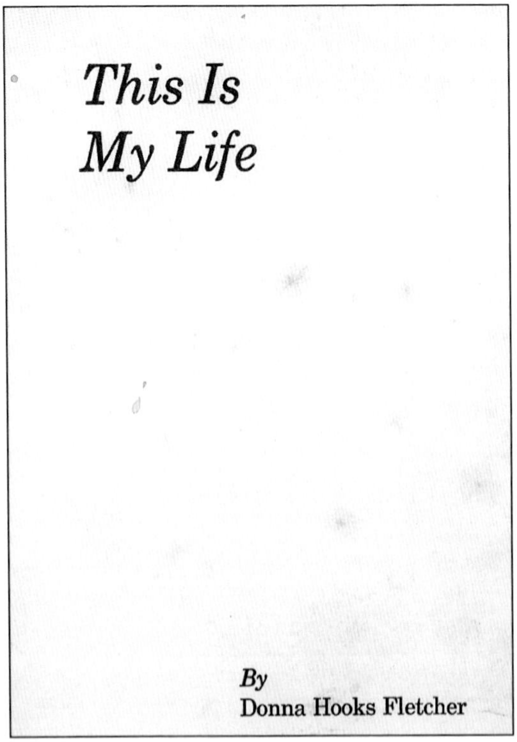

Donna's autobiography was printed in June of 1959, which was also her 80th birthday. Entitled *This Is My Life*, the book includes chapters such as "Move to Texas (1849)," "School Days," "Lured to the Valley," "LaBlanca Agriculture Company," "First to Ride Train Out of Valley," "Birth of the City of Donna," "Early Days of Donna," "Became a Pioneer Developer," and "My Pet Wildcat."

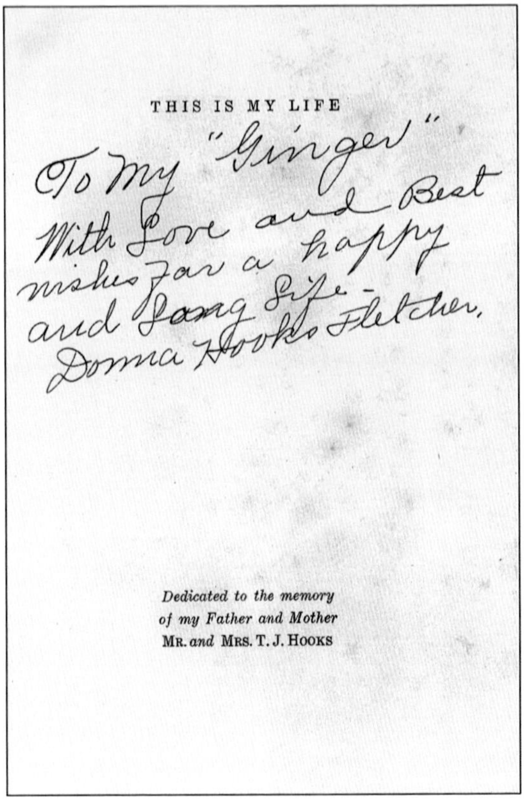

Published as a limited edition, Donna's autobiography was dedicated to her mother and father. She added a handwritten note to the recipient of each of the few distributed copies. In addition to *This Is My Life*, Donna authored several religious handbooks.

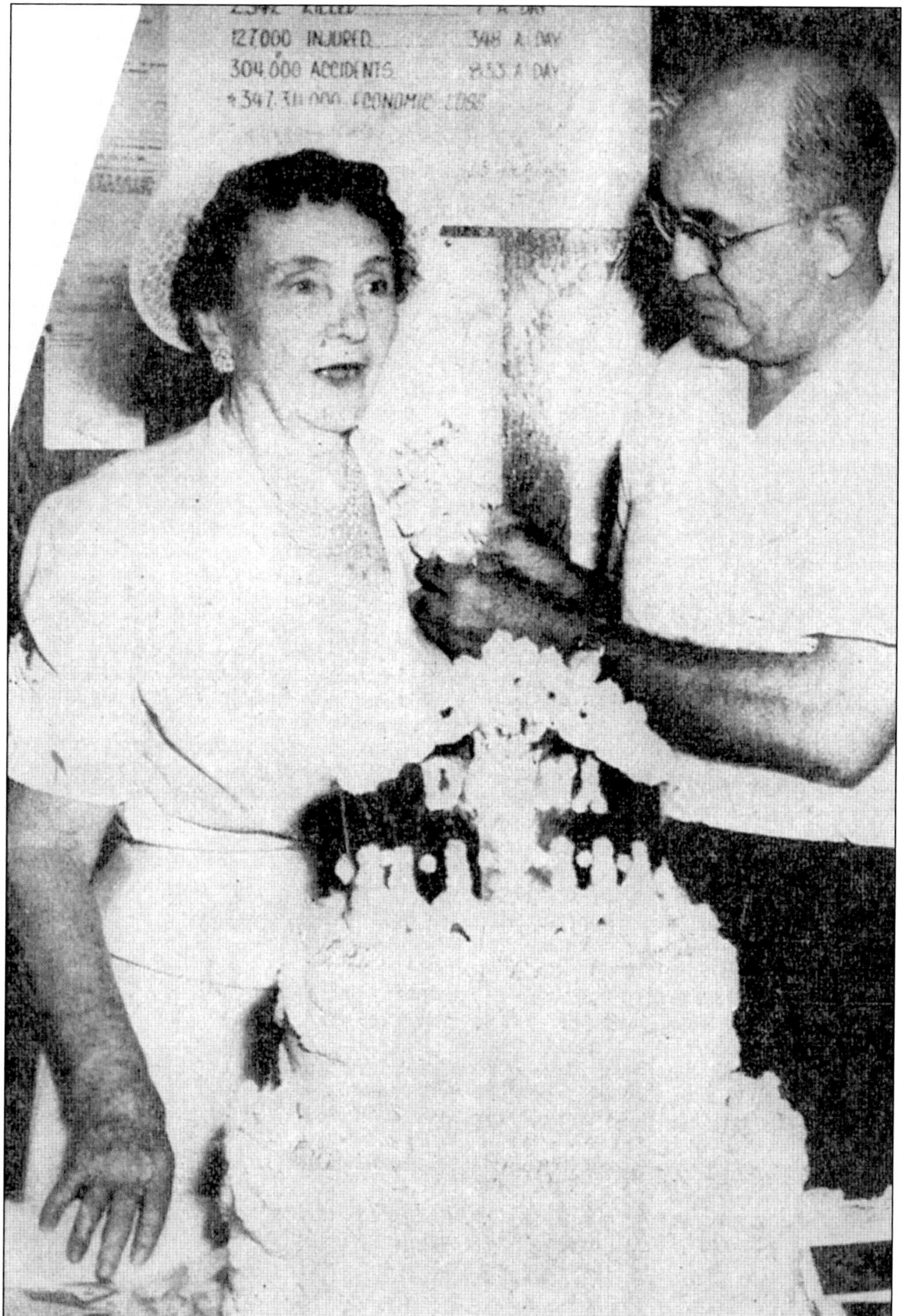

This June 1959 image from *The Donna News* shows mayor Gordon B. Wood pinning a corsage on the legendary Mrs. Donna Hooks Fletcher in honor of her 80th birthday.

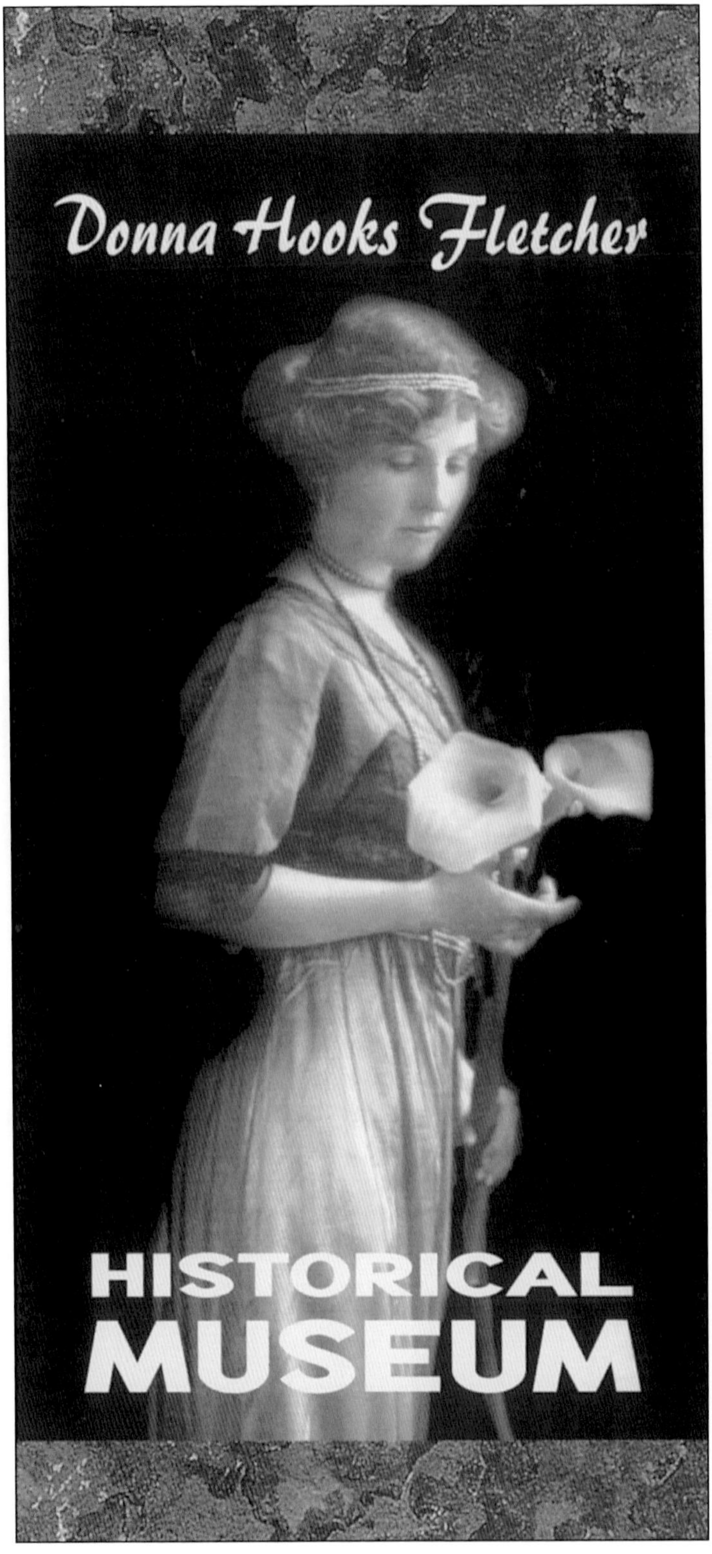

The Donna Hooks Fletcher Historical Museum brochure debuted in the fall of 2000. The Museum, now in its 28th year, received the Mitchell A. Wilder Award for excellence in publication and media design from the Texas Association of Museums in Austin. The portrait is popularly identified with the Donna Museum, which receives many compliments and commentary on the everlasting beauty of Donna Hooks Fletcher.

Six

Border Safeguard

The 35-year-old regime of Porfirio Diaz, president of the Republic of Mexico, collapsed under the weight of a revolution that began in October 1910. Diaz was forced to resign on May 25, 1911. Francisco I. Madero was sworn into office as president of Mexico on November 6, but he was killed in February 1913. General Victoriano Huerta became the next president. Hated as much as he was feared, Huerta was unable to restore order to the country, which saw the rise of such leaders as Pancho Villa and Emiliano Zapata. The Texas-Mexico border became fertile ground for bandits, with or without political goals, who raided Valley farms and ranches for livestock, burned railroad bridges and a pump station, and robbed and killed U.S. citizens. Deployment of U.S. soldiers, Texas state militia, and National Guardsmen to the border stopped the raids and restored peace. By 1920, under new leadership, Mexico also found peace.

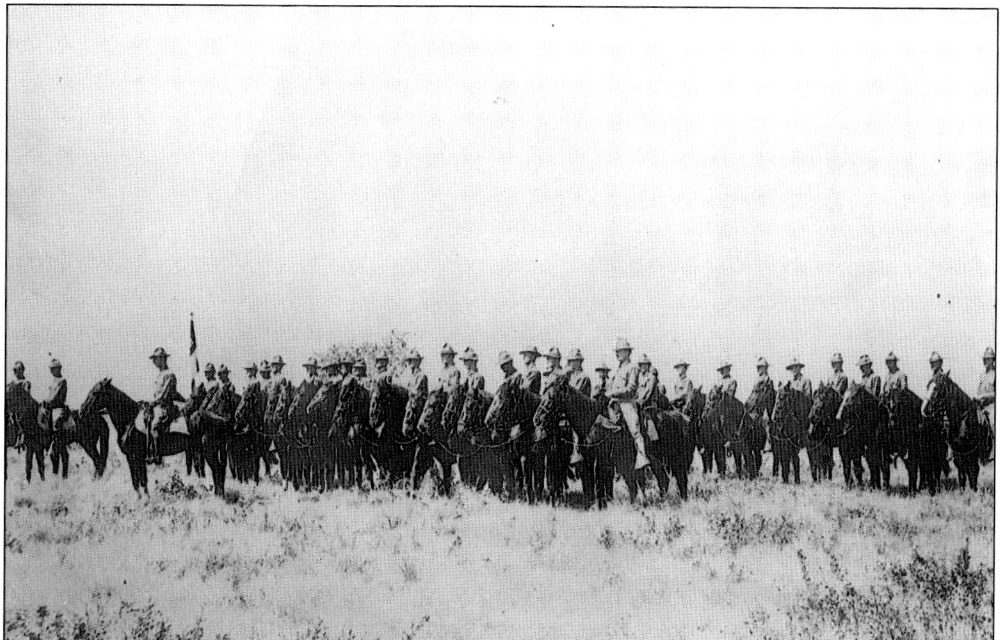

The 12th U.S. Cavalry arrived in May 1914 and remained for about one year. Here, troops prepare for military exercises at Donna.

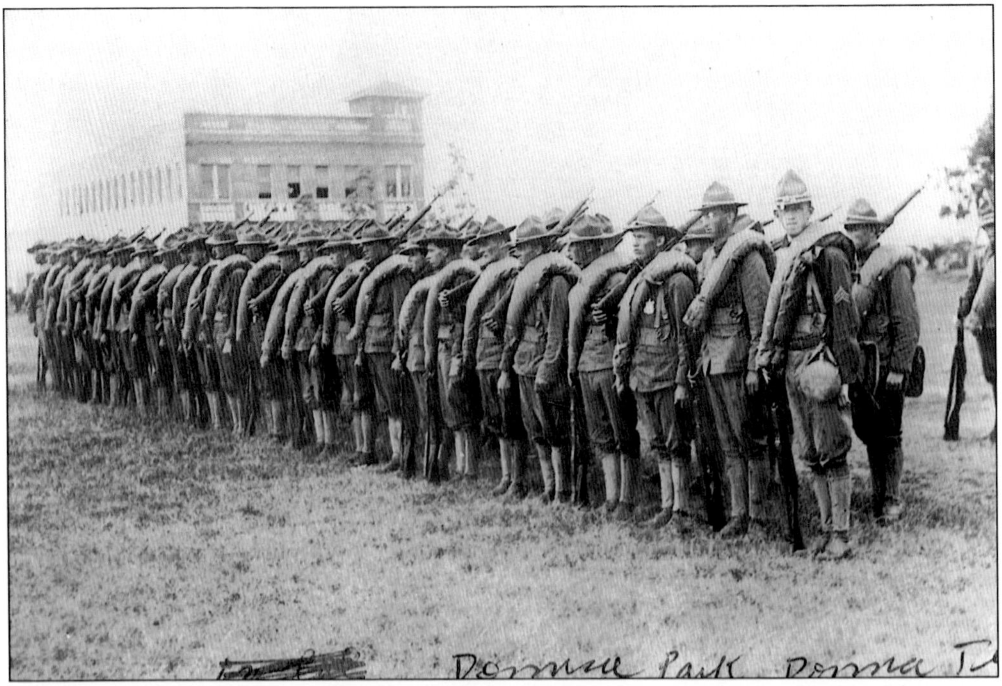

Carrying bedrolls, canteens, and rifles, soldiers line up at the city park in Donna. The troops took part in daily four-hour training exercises, two hours of instruction, as well as inspections and parades. Hester Mercantile stands in the background.

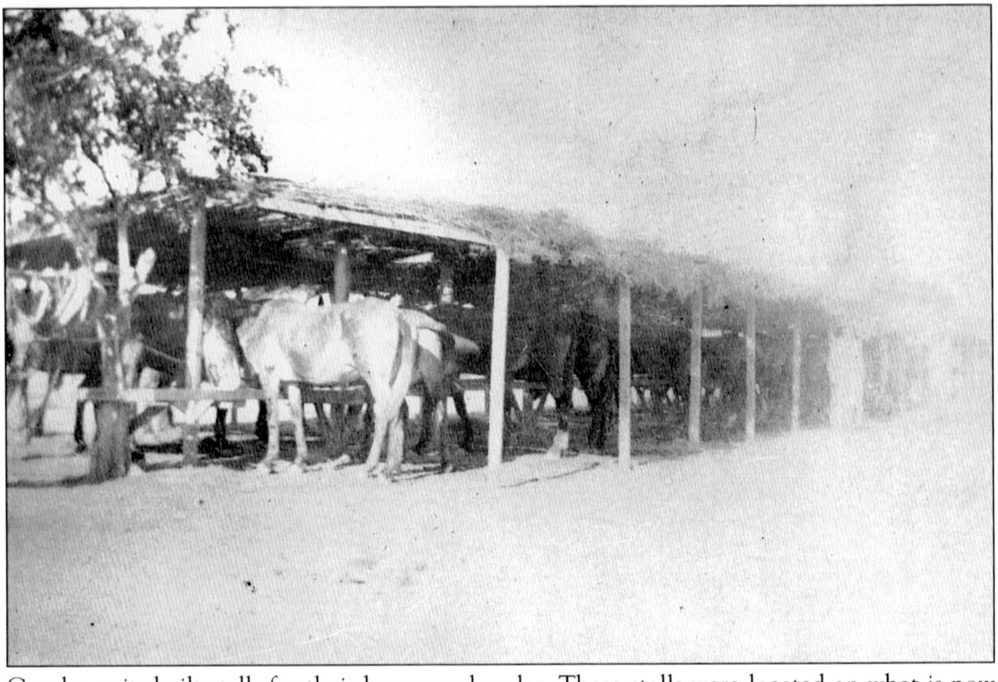

Cavalry units built stalls for their horses and mules. These stalls were located on what is now North 4th Street in Donna.

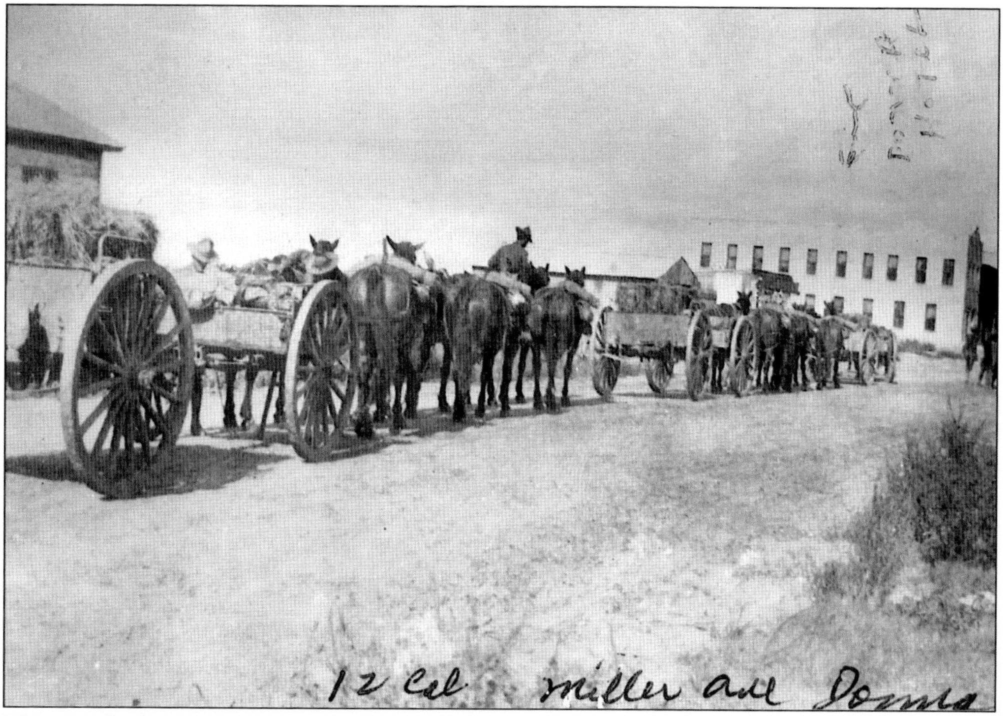

These mule-drawn wagons, belonging to the 12th U.S. Cavalry, are carrying tack, clothing, and field equipment down Miller Avenue. The Donna Hotel appears on the far right.

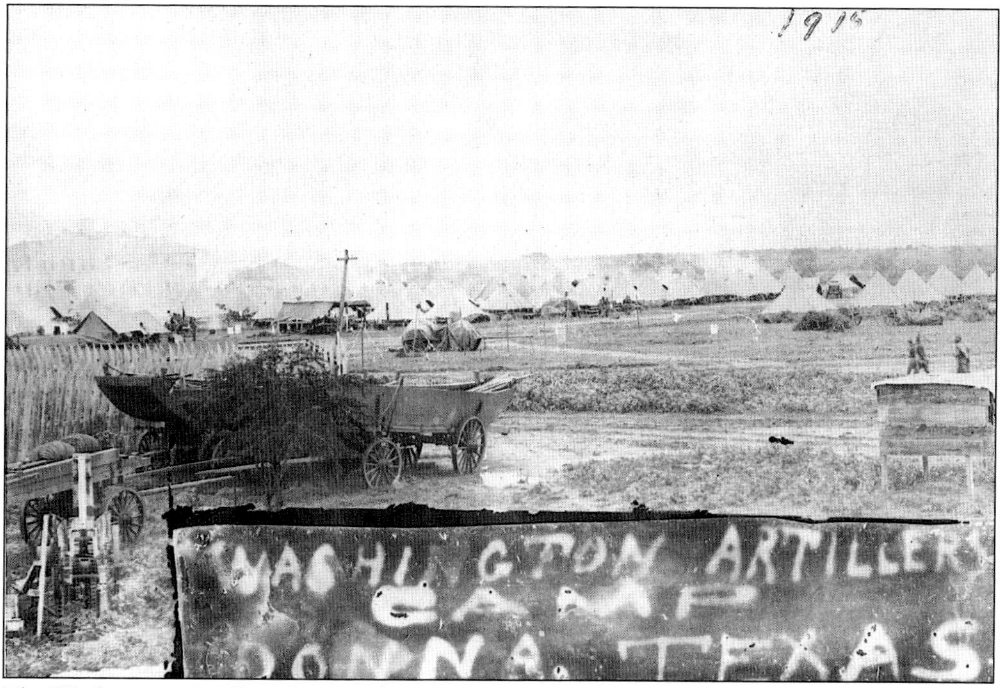

The Washington Artillery Camp is shown in 1915. The first Donna Junior High School appears in the left background.

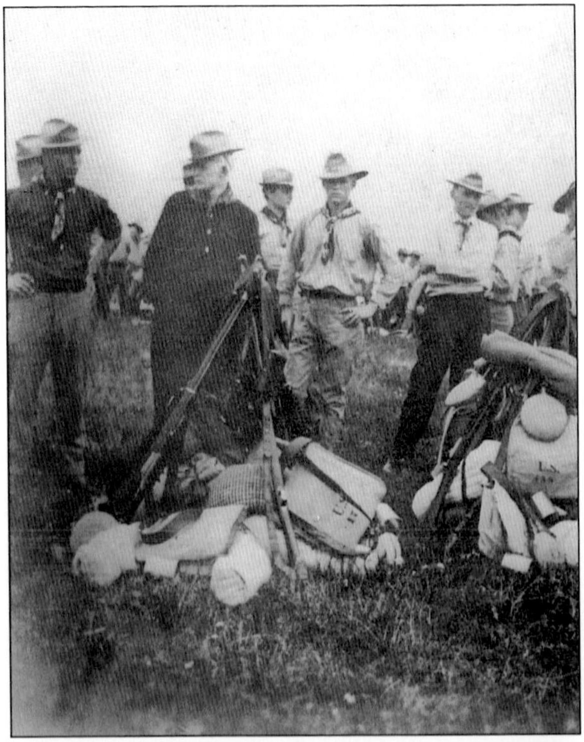

Training for the soldiers lasted about five months. Once their camps were set up, the troops cleared brush, dredged channels for drainage, and built and repaired roads. They also patrolled the river, engaged in small arms and artillery practice, and took part in large-scale maneuvers.

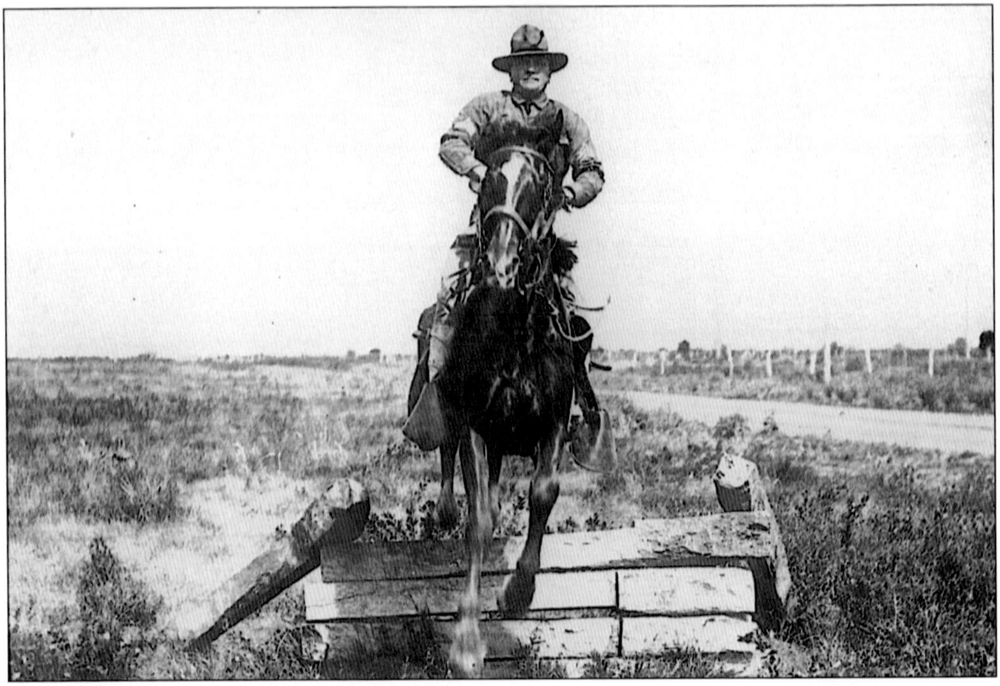

An early newspaper caption stated that Sergeant Borges, "a skilled rider, jumped his mount in a demonstration put on for the troops." Performances such as this, boxing and wrestling contests, parades, and field days broke the monotony for the heat- and brush-weary soldiers.

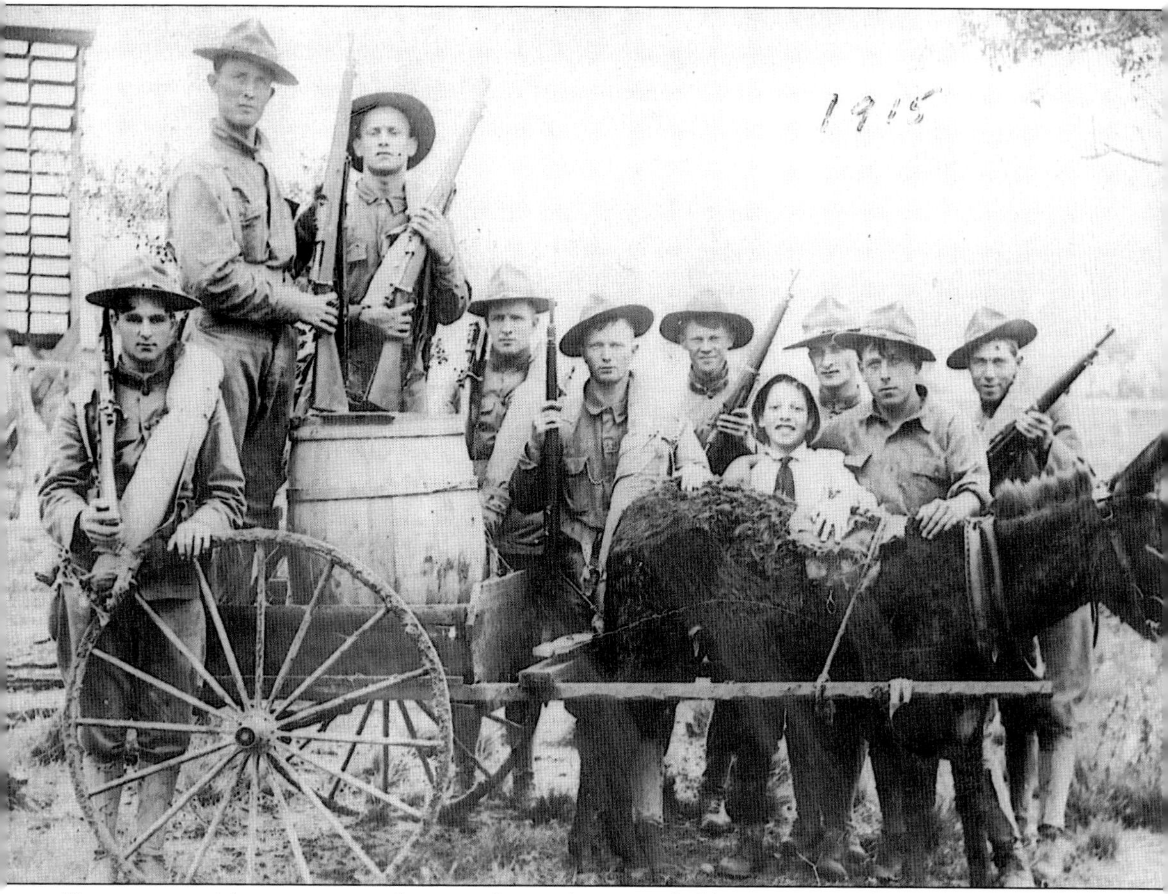

Troops pose with a youngster who is washing a burro, probably using water from the barrel on the cart. This 1915 image reveals the humor in everyday events, but the young men appear to be very serious about their role in safeguarding the Valley.

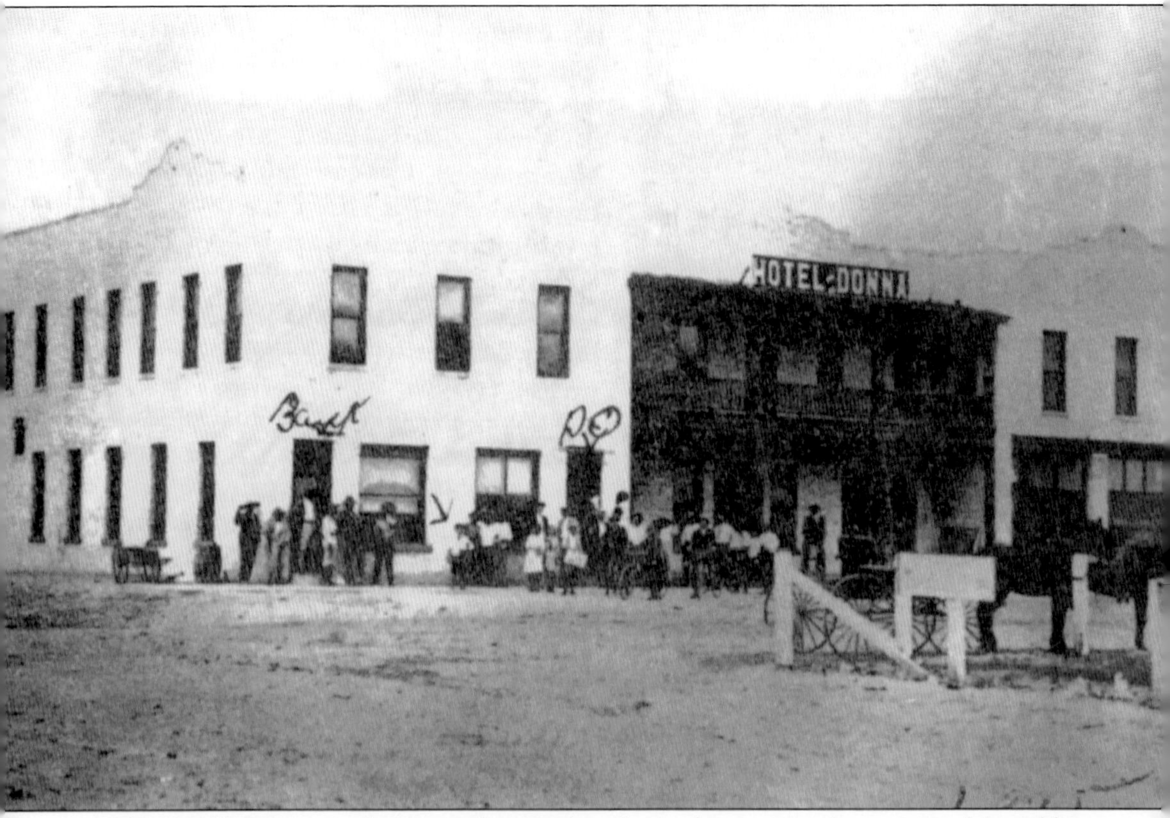

The Hotel Donna was a favorite gathering place for residents to watch activities of the soldiers, who often conducted exercises on the grounds of the city park across the street. This 1915 image identifies the locations of a bank and the post office.

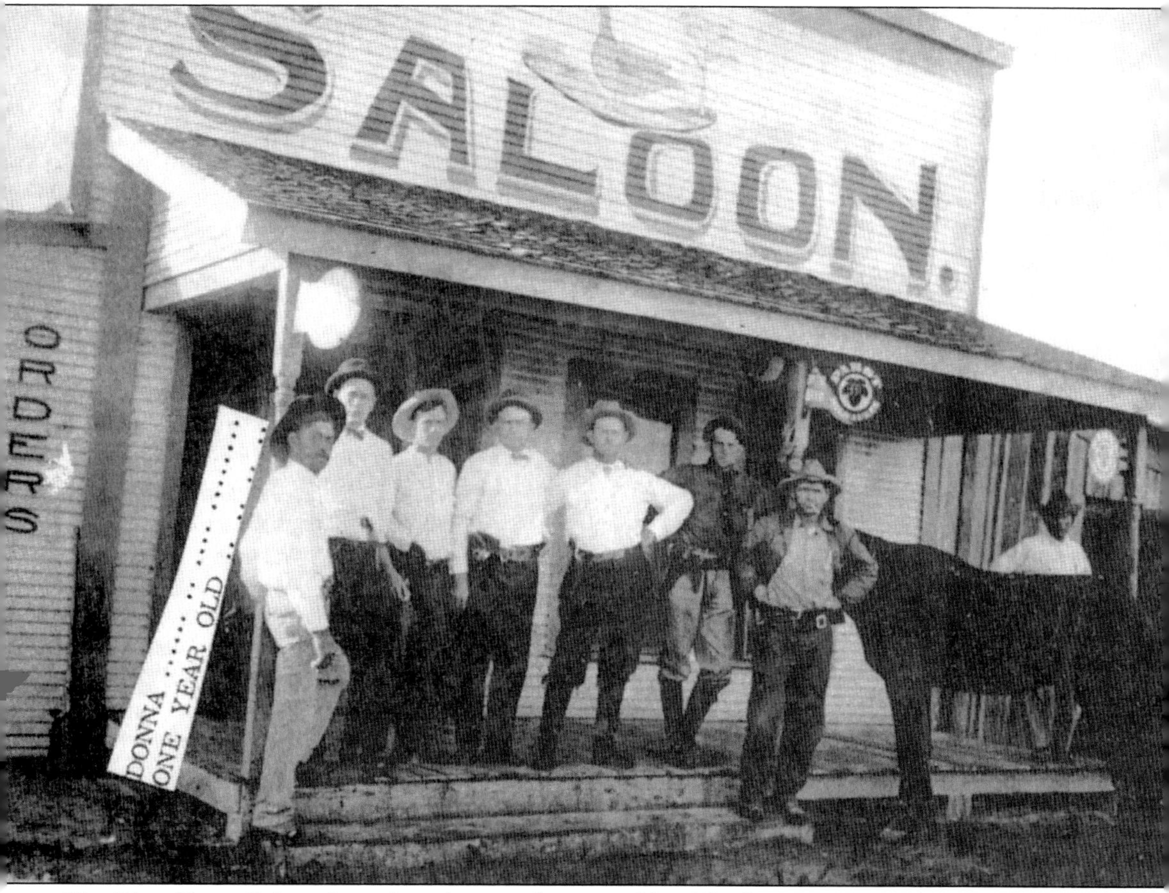

The Blue Goose Saloon hosted civilians and troops alike. The lawmen, shown here in 1912, are identified, from left to right, as "Ice" Brown, Cliff Bowen, Sam Barnard, Homer Bryson, Les. L. Barnard, Rube Stamford, and John Pilkey. When vaudeville shows and silent movies were not enough entertainment for the soldiers, they congregated at the Blue Goose Saloon and provided their own.

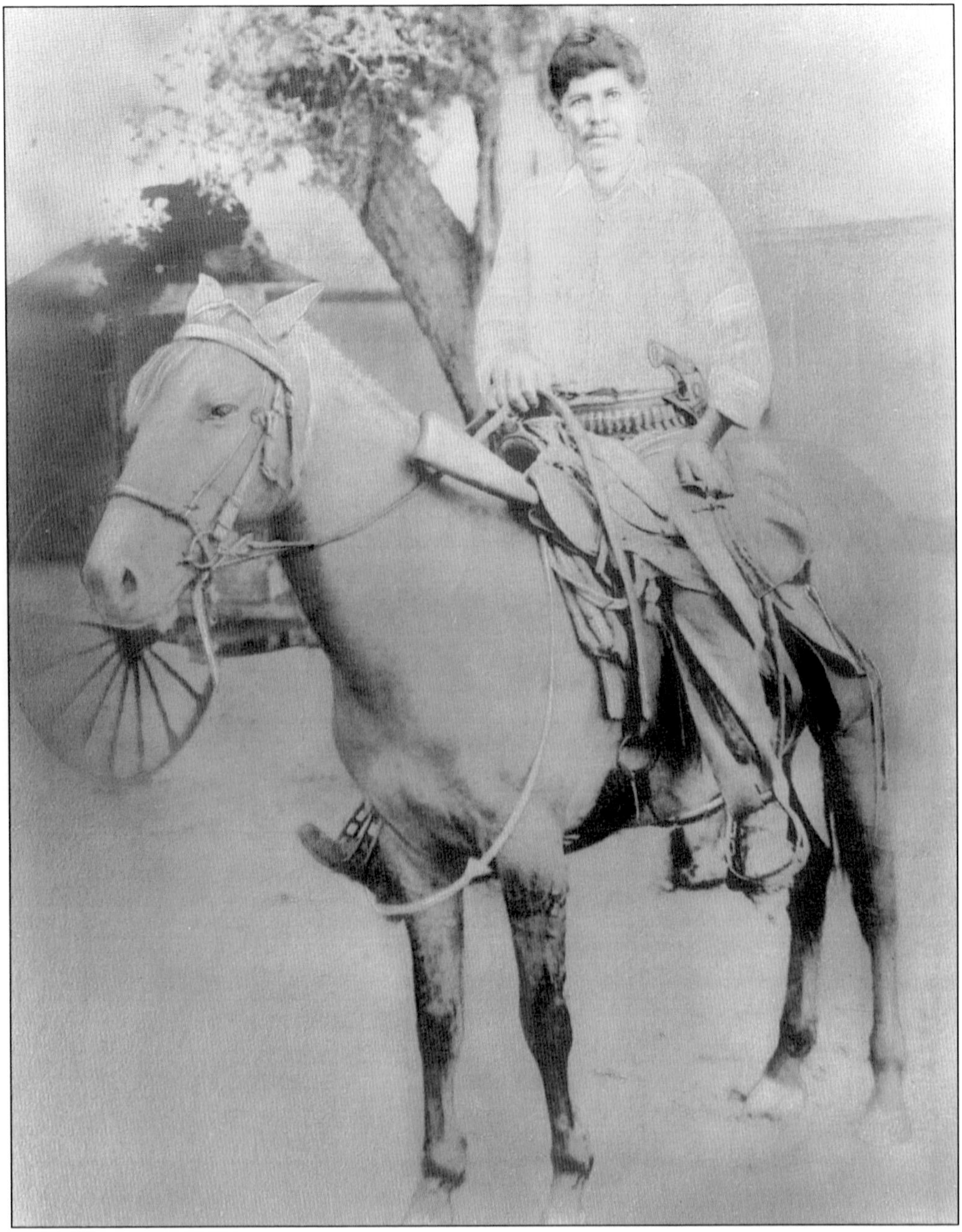

Gregorio Ybarra (1876–1964), a U.S. Cavalry scout, is shown on his horse "Old Mexico." Bandit raids into Texas led to the arrival of the 12th Cavalry Regiment in 1914. The troops were deployed throughout the Donna area. The regimental commander needed a scout familiar with the people and terrain of the brush country, a man who was also trustworthy. Andrew Champion Sr. recommended his ranch foreman, Gregorio Ybarra. The 6-foot-6-inch Ybarra received a commission as a Federal scout for the 12th Cavalry, which included the right to bear arms. Lean and tough, Ybarra was reputed to have the fastest reflexes and the quickest draw in the Valley. Ybarra served as a scout until 1915, when the 12th Cavalry completed its tour of duty in the Lower Rio Grande Valley.

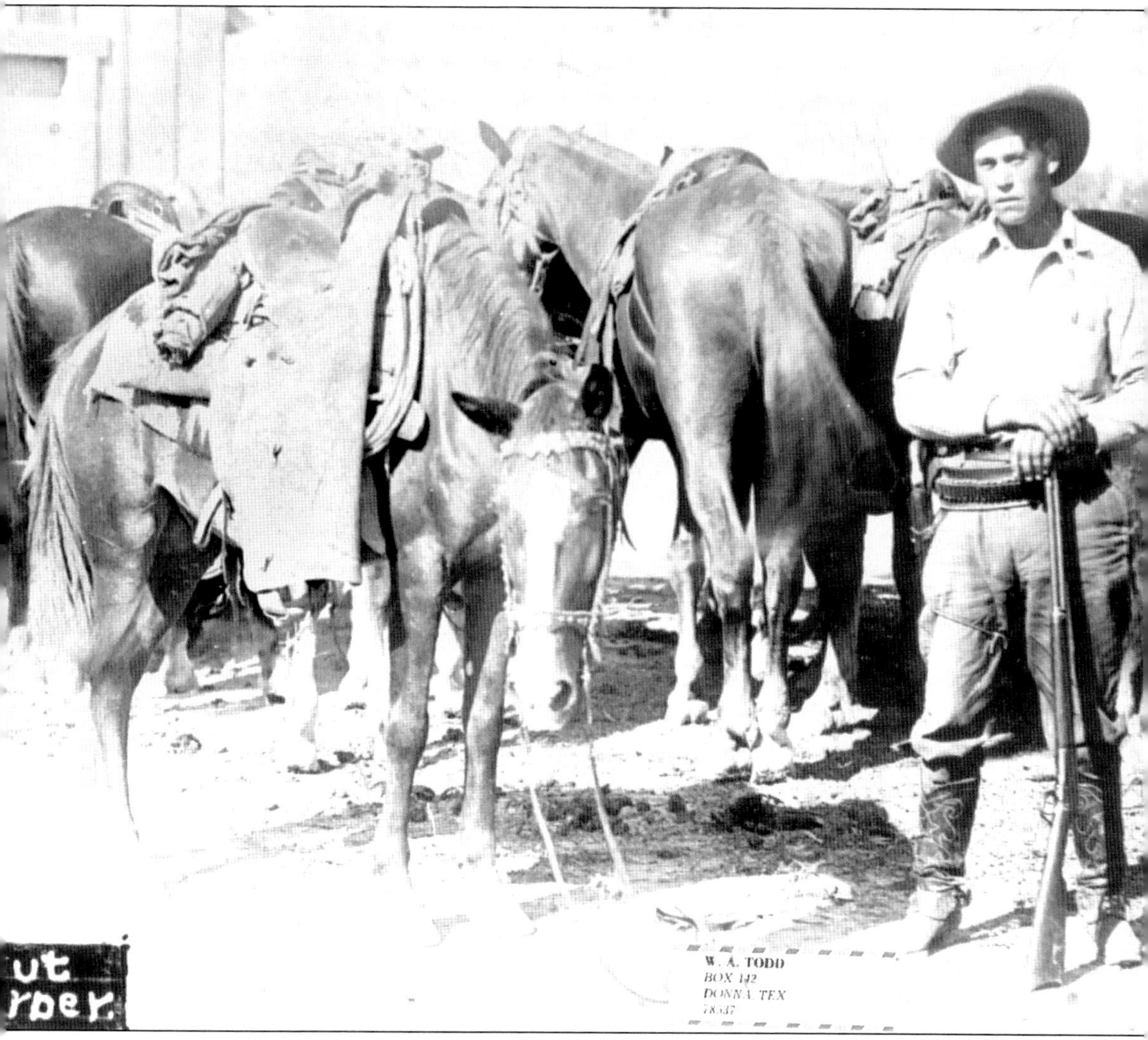

This heavily armed border scout, probably commissioned by the military, would have known the trails and back roads, farms and ranches, area residents and their cattle brands, as he searched the brush country for signs of bandits. The horse carries his bedroll and rain gear, chaps to protect his legs from thorns, and rope.

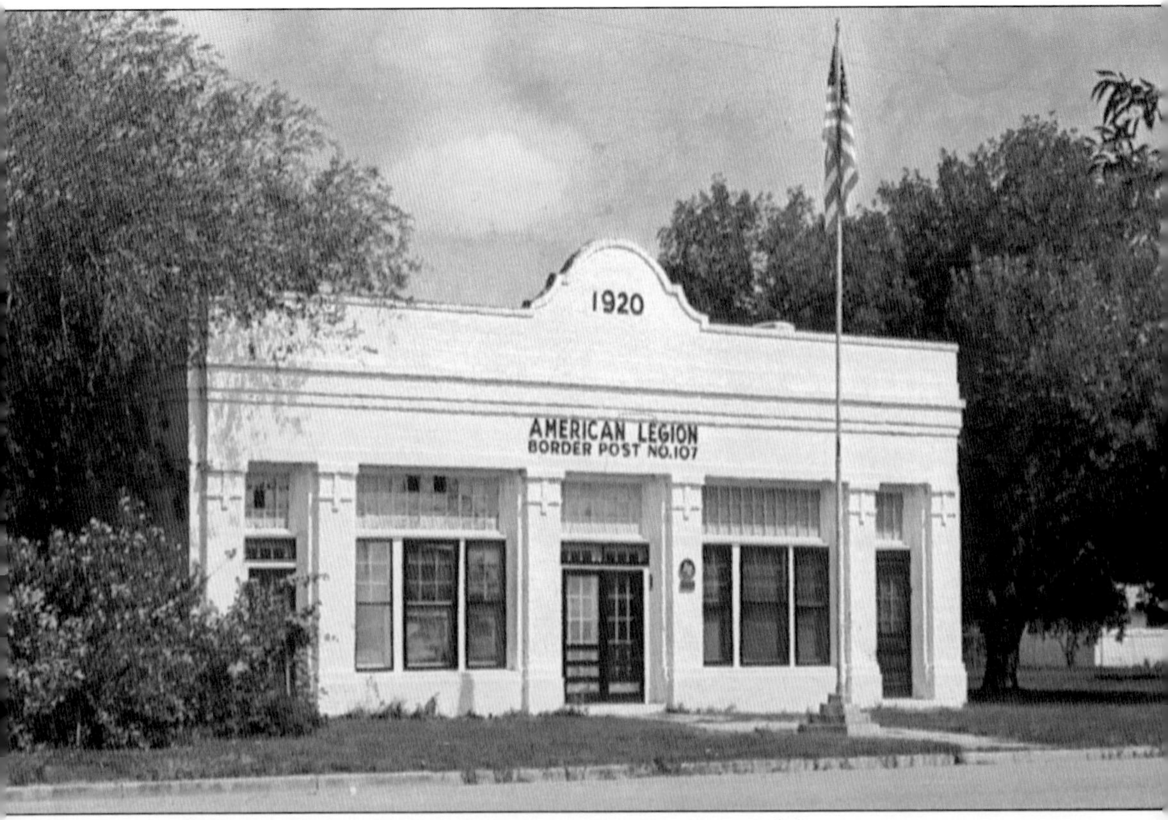

On April 6, 1917, the U.S. declared war on Germany. Many of the troops were sent overseas, where their months of border service, including artillery practice, made them highly desired by their superior officers and greatly feared by the enemy. After the war, returning soldiers established American Legion Border Post 107. They raised funds to build the American Legion Hall in Donna, the first hall to be constructed by any American Legion post in the world.

Seven

Breaking Ground

Donna's long history is one of continually "breaking ground." From the coming of the railroad and construction of the pumphouse and irrigation system, to the laying out of farms and groves, and finally to the building of a town, Donna residents saw the potential of their chosen land. Brush country gave way to orchards, river delta soil produced enormous crops of vegetables and citrus fruits, and the muddy streets of the new town were paved. In a few short years, Donna became a modern 20th-century city with an unlimited future. Almost 100 years later, it still is.

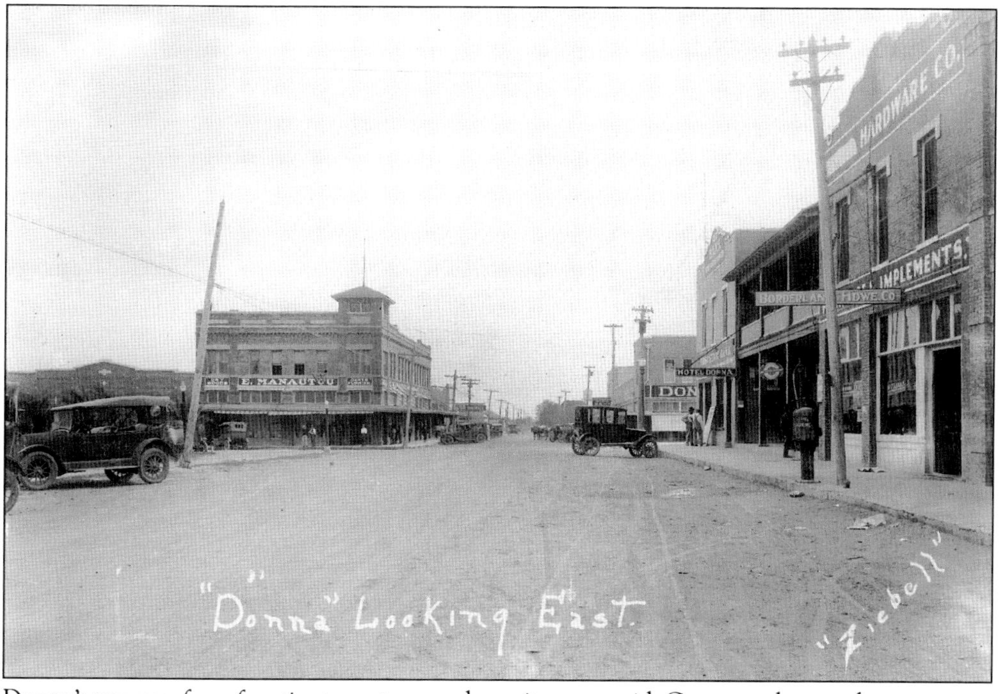

Donna's progress from frontier town to a modern city was rapid. Gone are the wooden structures from the early days. In their places stand imposing brick buildings graced with sidewalks. Poles for electric lines extend the entire length of the east-facing street. The street is not yet paved, but it has been graded smooth for easy passage of automobiles.

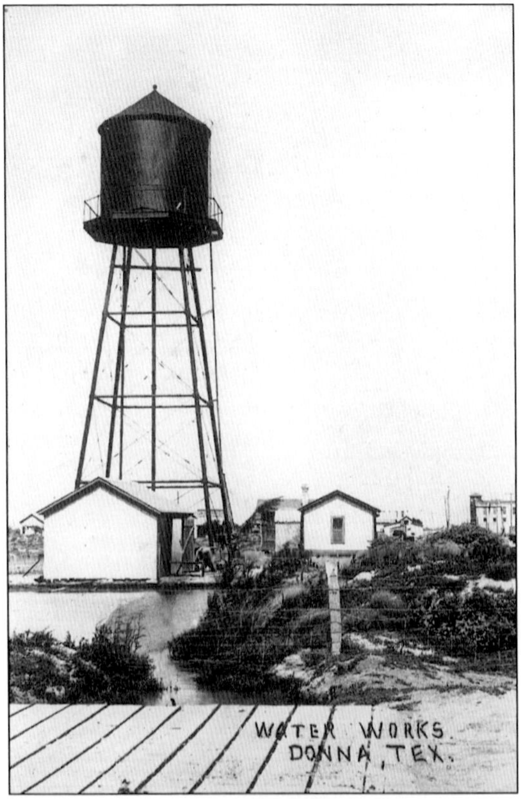

The Donna water works and tower, constructed in 1908, provided a dependable supply of water, and led to a surge in the city's growth.

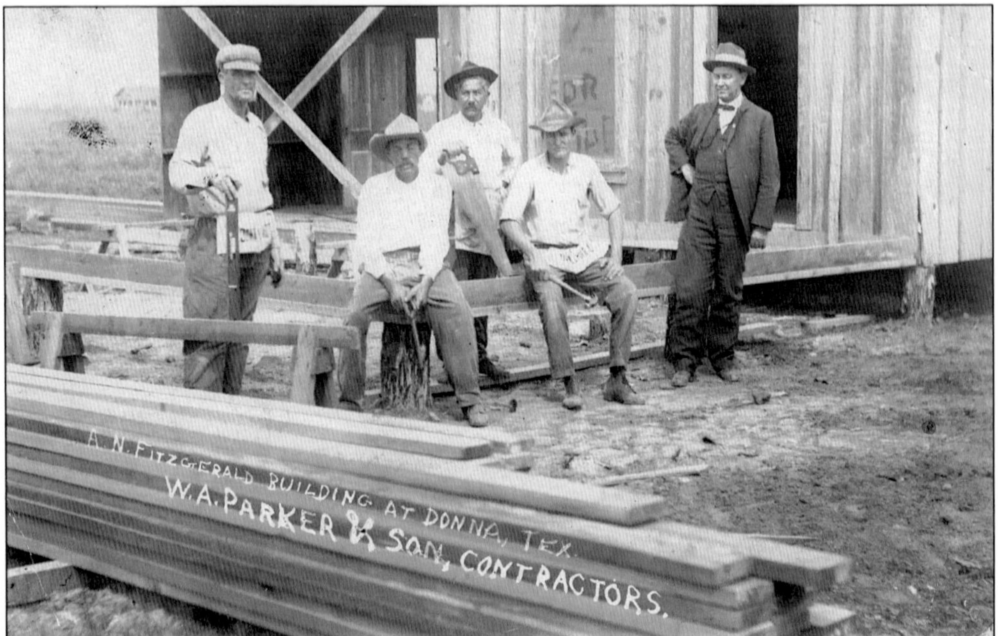

New homes and businesses needed builders and construction supplies. Contractor W.A. Parker is pictured with carpenters and supplies for the Fitzgerald Building.

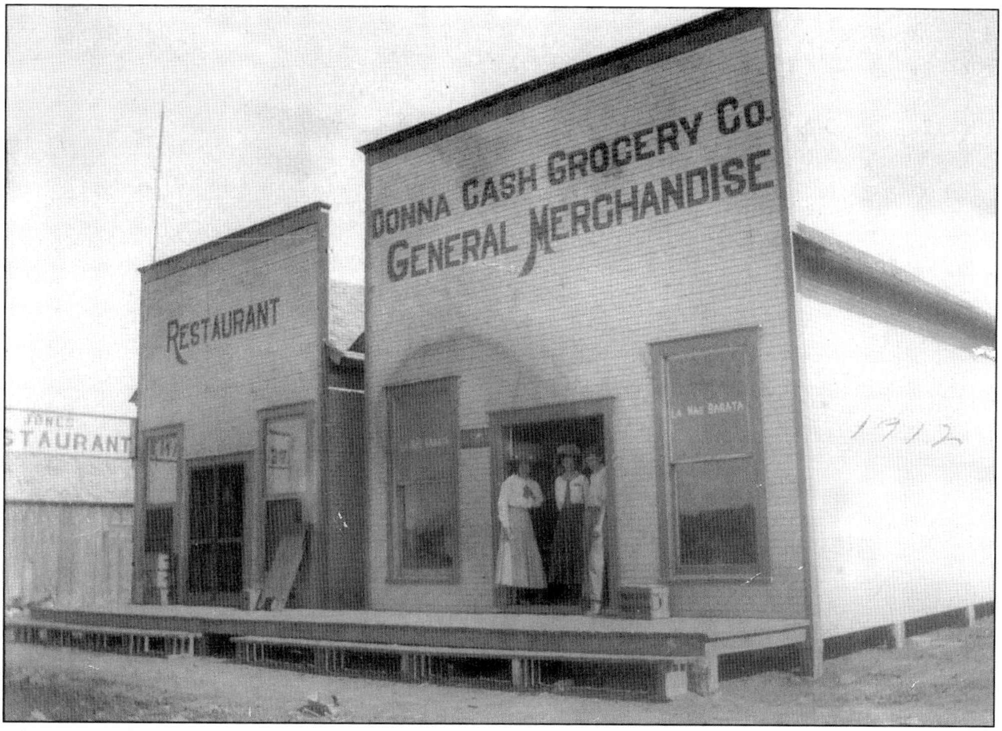

This 1912 photograph shows the adjacent buildings of the Bill Dobby Restaurant and the Donna Cash Grocery Co. general store. A sign on the store window reads "*La mas barata*," Spanish for "the cheapest in town."

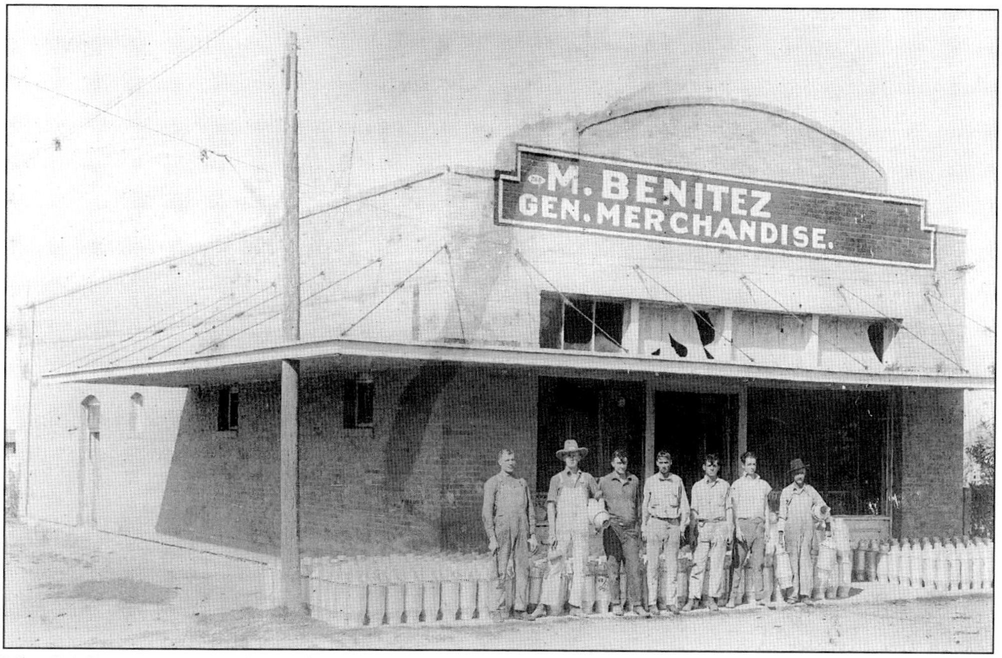

The M. Benitez general merchandise store was owned and operated by the Benitez family, who sold everything from rope to milk cans, shown here in the mid-1930s.

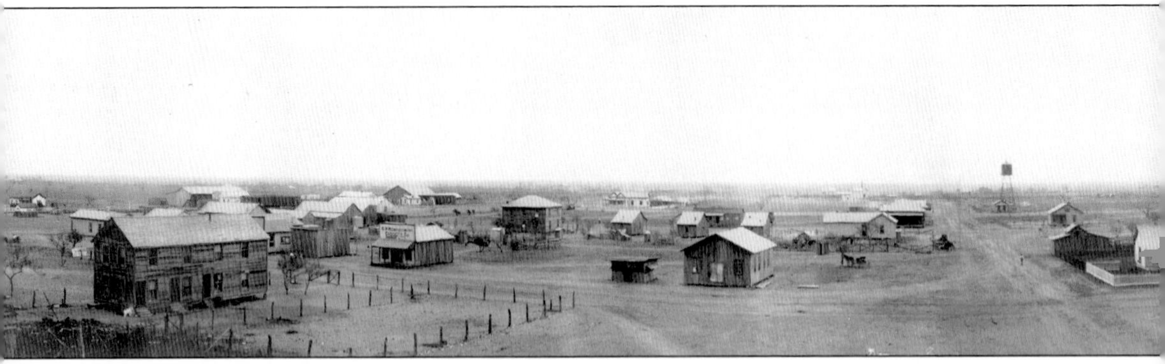

This panorama view of the Donna town site on February 14, 1911, depicts the many wooden homes, businesses, churches, and farmhouses built in the seven years since Donna was founded.

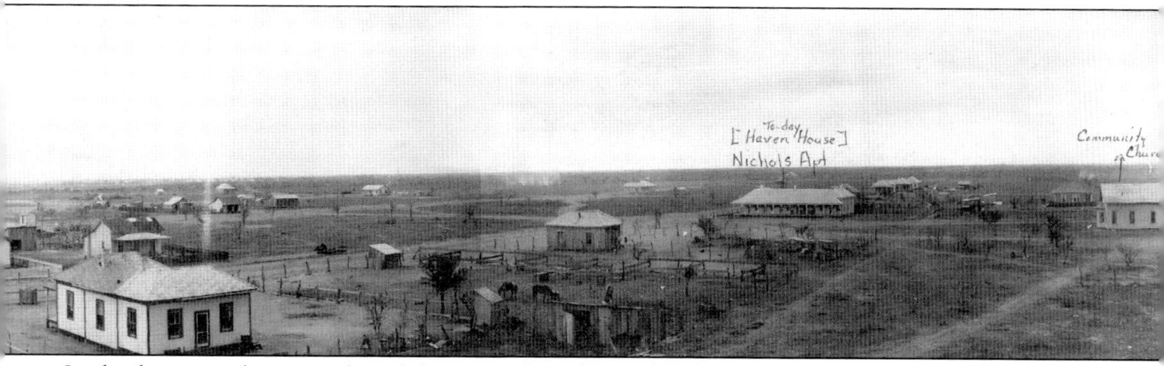

In the foreground are corrals with horses and small woodsheds. The image shows open land and dirt roads, broken only by a few trees and sparse foliage.

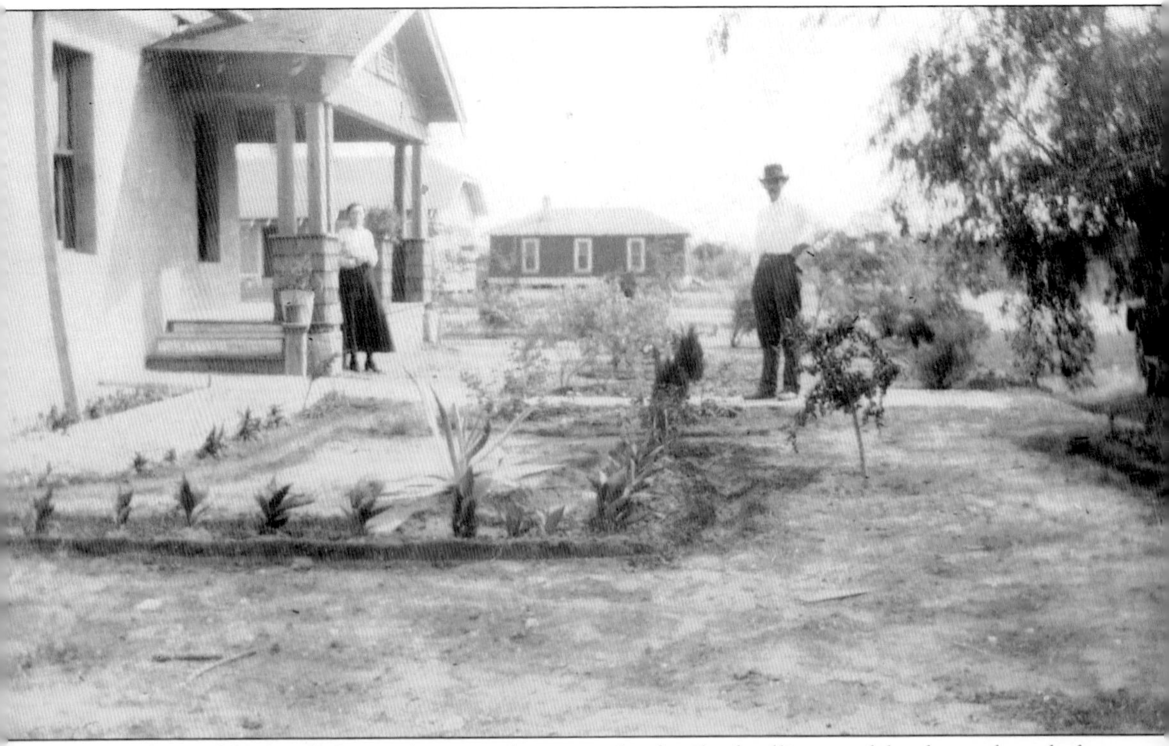

Early neighborhoods boasted new architecture for family dwellings and landscaped yards for visiting with new neighbors. Harold Vertrees is standing in the yard of the Loch home.

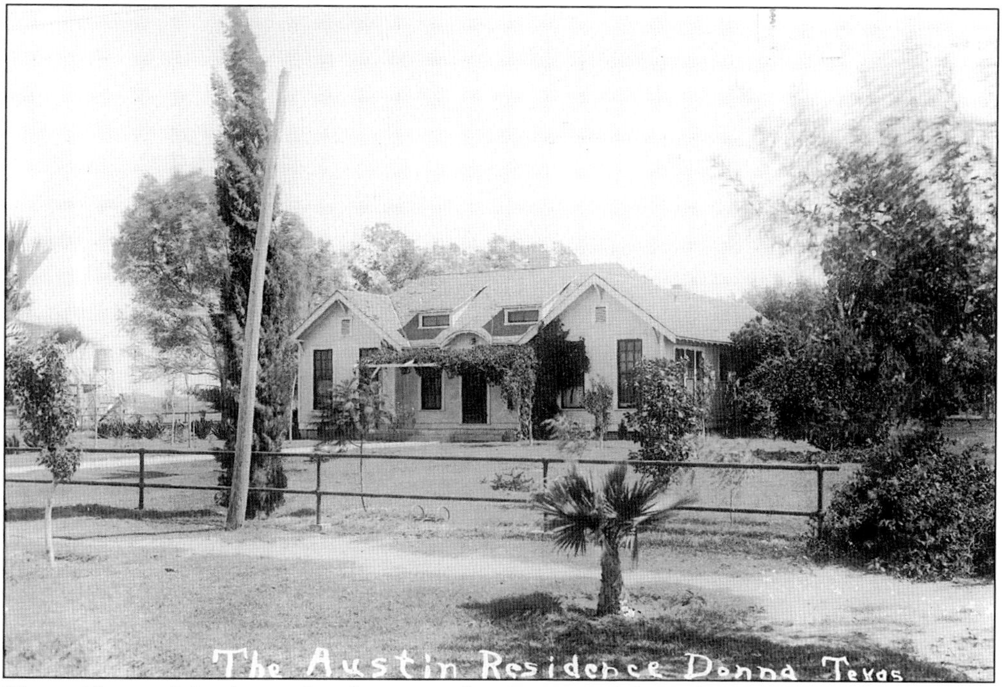

The residence of the Austin family was another large wood frame home.

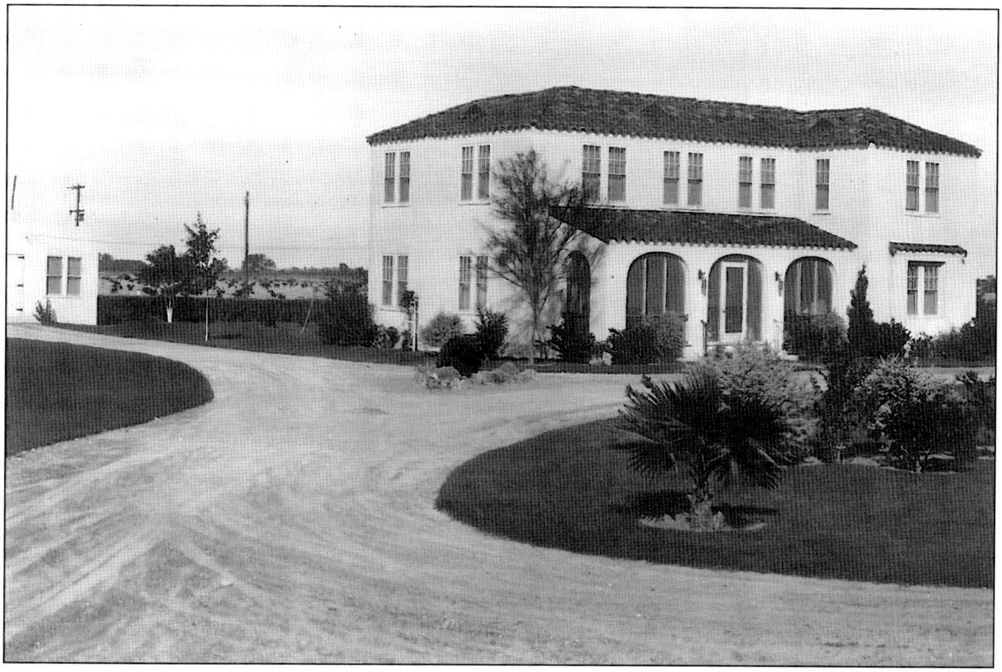
This handsome structure was a clubhouse for guests and potential land buyers of the Valley Orchards Develop-ment Company, Inc. Citrus trees surrounded the clubhouse. It is now a private residence.

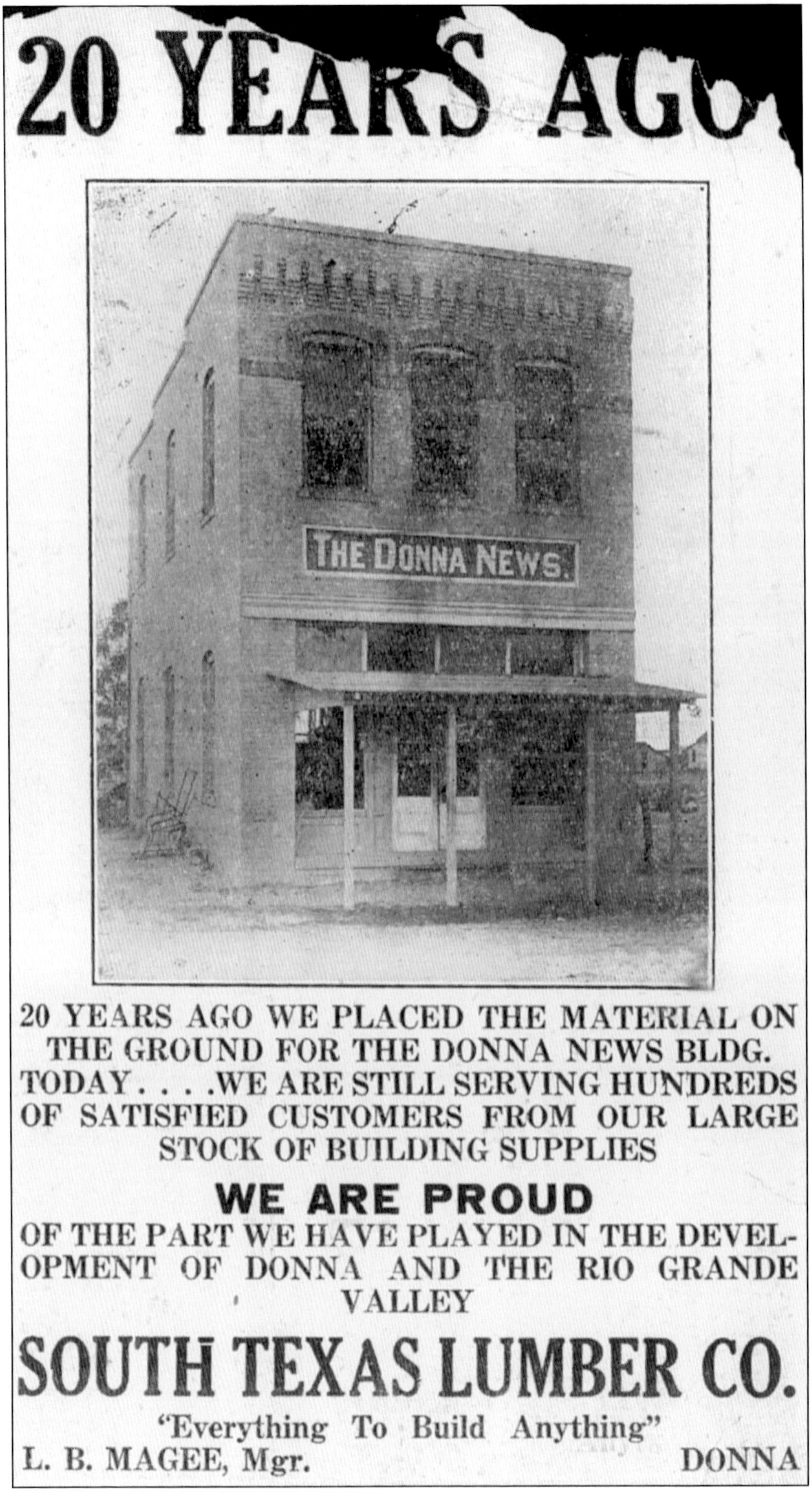

This newspaper advertisement for the South Texas Lumber Company shows the *Donna News* building on the square; the building was constructed in 1920.

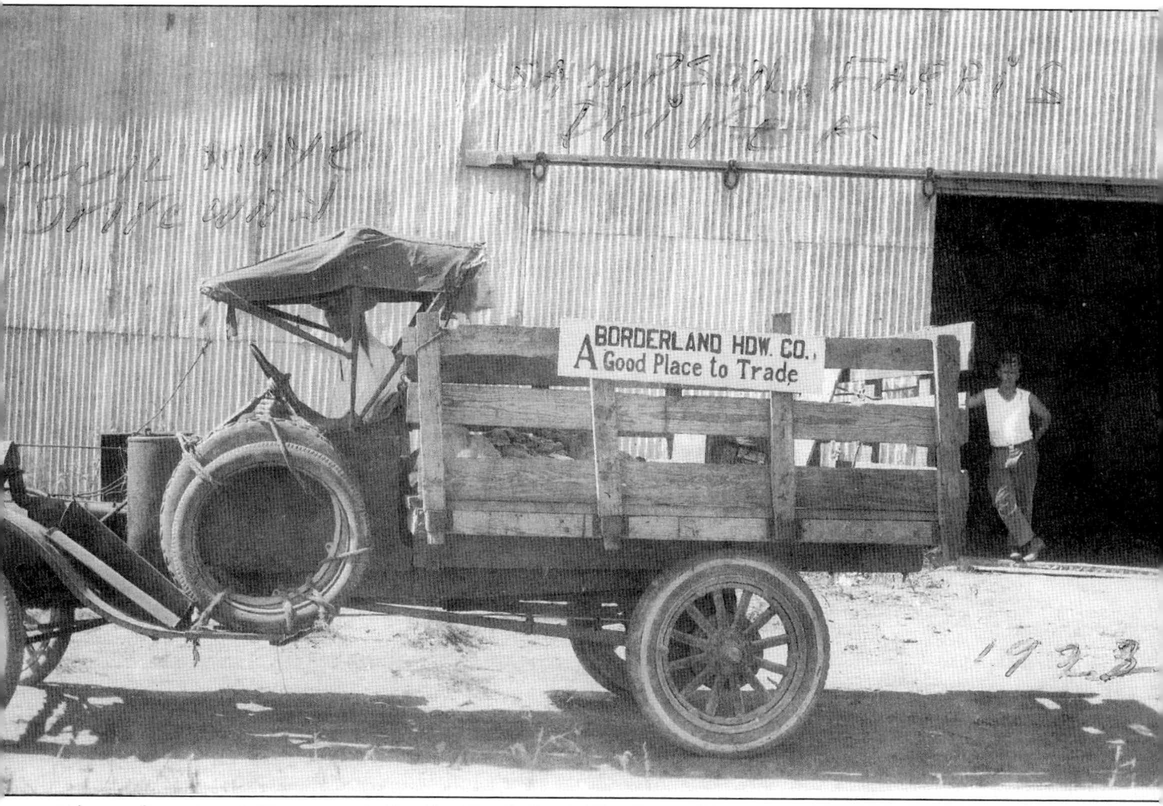

Shown here is a delivery truck for the Borderland Hardware Company in 1922.

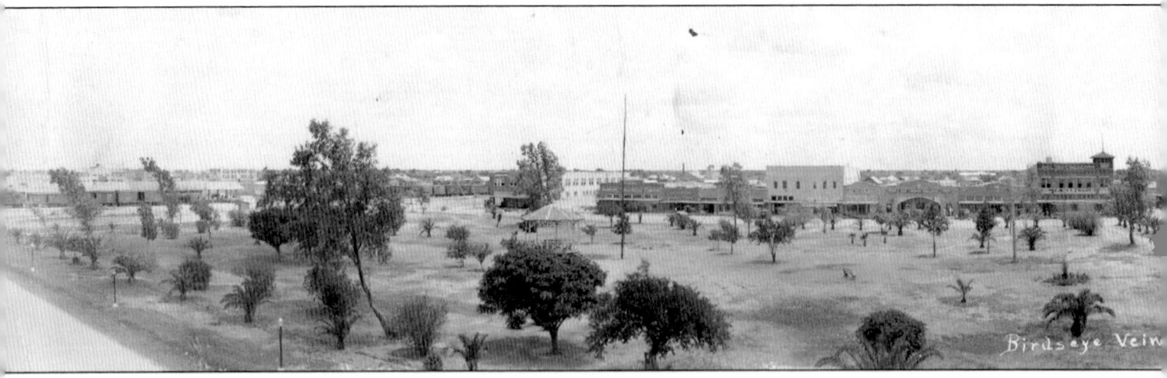

This "birds eye view" of Donna, taken on August 18, 1920, shows the progress of the past nine years. On the far left is a line of railroad cars. Brick buildings line Main Street and hug the southeast side of the square. Added to the central area are more commercial buildings,

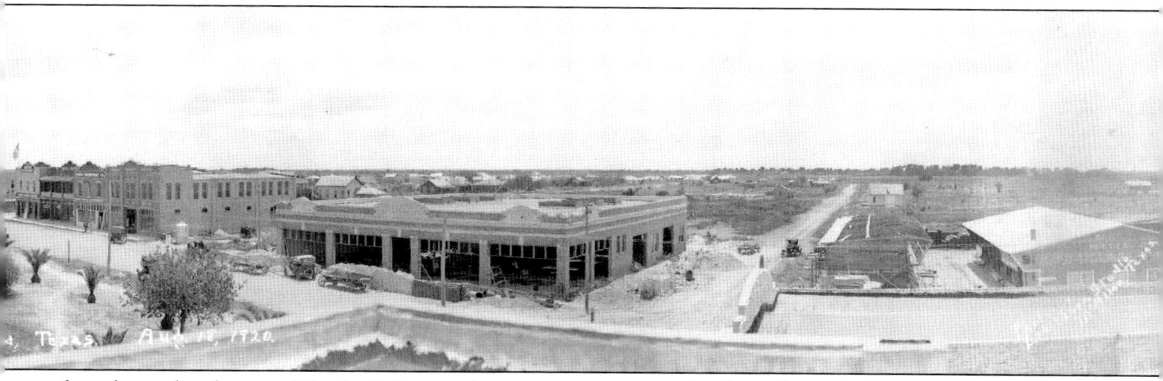

hotels, and a theater. The building under construction on the far right is the Knapp Chevrolet auto dealership. Knapp Chevrolet, first located in Donna, remains in business with dealerships throughout the Valley.

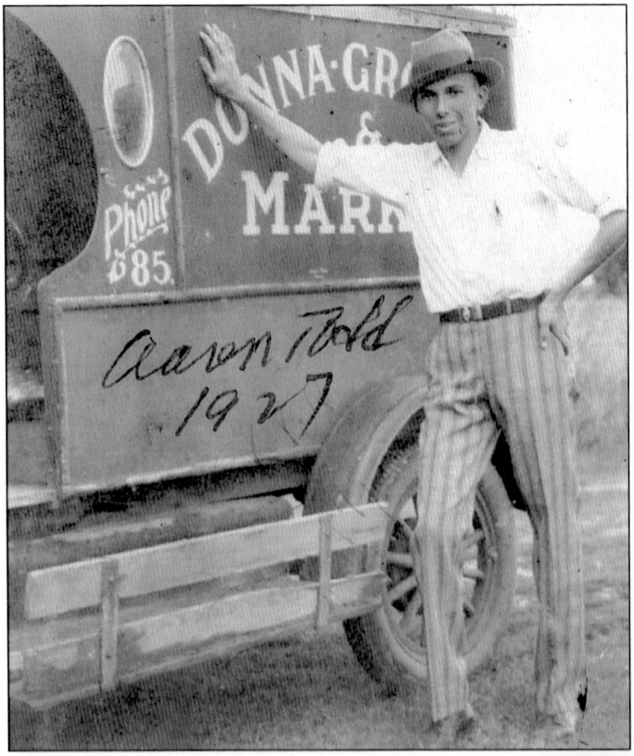

W.A. (Aaron) Todd first visited the Valley in 1918. He returned to his home in Mississippi, but moved to Donna in 1925. His father operated Donna's first ice plant. W.A. Todd served on the school board, as a deacon of the Baptist church, and as a member of the Rotary Club. This photo, dated 1927, shows Todd standing beside a delivery truck. Todd gathered many early photographs of Donna, and his collection is preserved at the Donna Hooks Fletcher Museum.

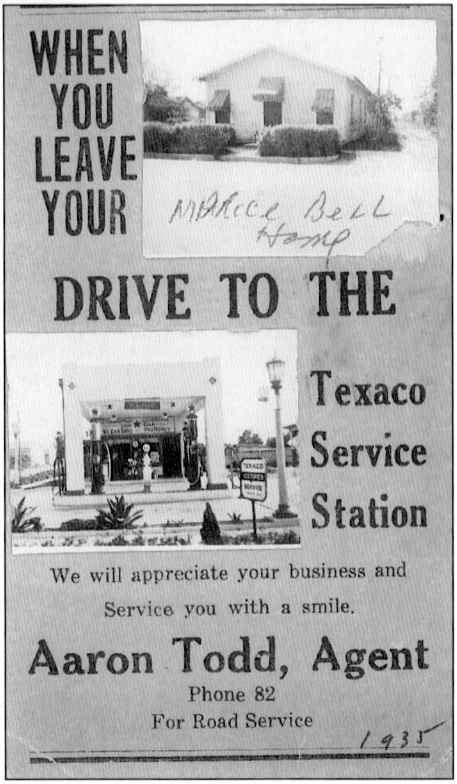

An advertisement for the Texaco station owned and operated by Aaron Todd used photos to complete the catchy slogan. The ad lists a two-digit telephone number, which seems primitive compared to phone numbers of the 21st century. The Donna Museum is indebted to Mr. Todd for donating his entire collection to the Museum.

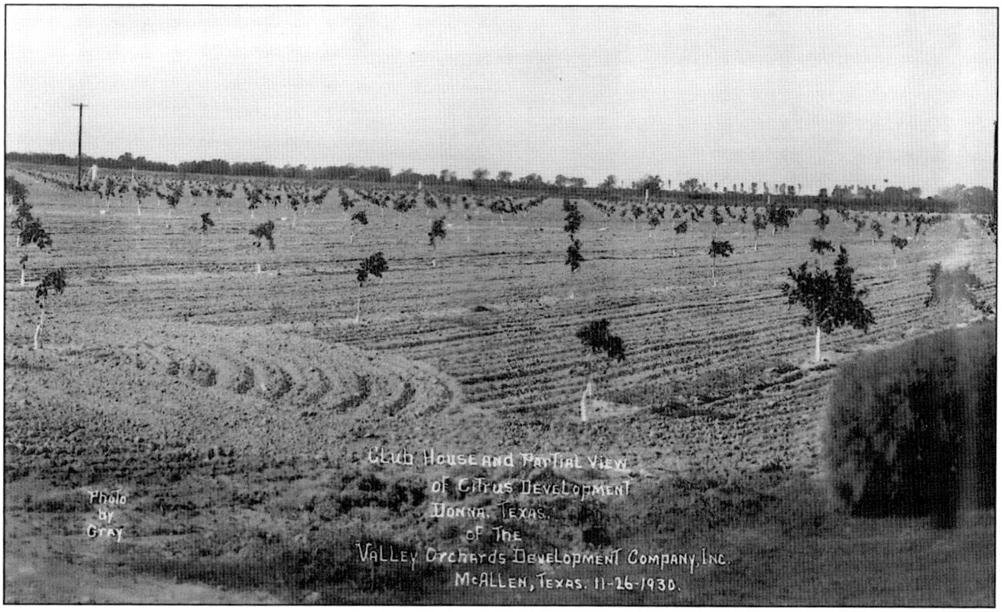

In addition to its clubhouse, the Valley Orchards Development Company of McAllen, Texas, established groves of citrus trees to promote the richness of its land. This grove is shown on November 26, 1930.

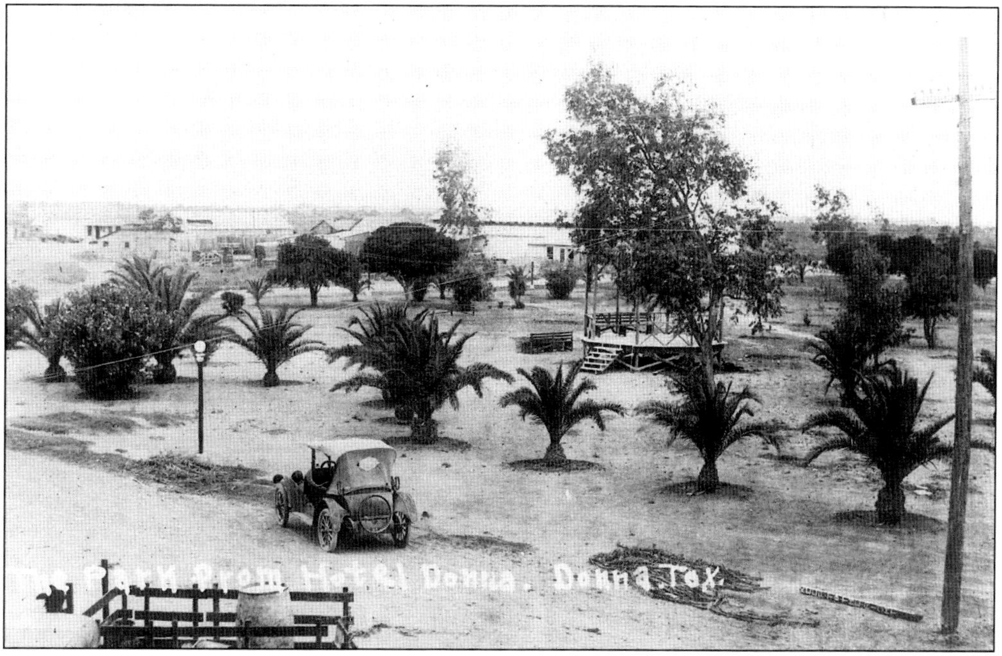

This 1915 view of the Donna City Park shows a variety of young trees surrounding a gazebo. The Donna Women's Club, organized on November 11, 1911, established a public library, improved the new cemetery, and beautified the city park by planting grass, shrubs, and trees. The Donna Women's Club raised funds to build a clubhouse and library for the use of women's organizations, the first of its kind in the Valley. The Donna Women's Club later joined the Texas State Federation of Women's Clubs.

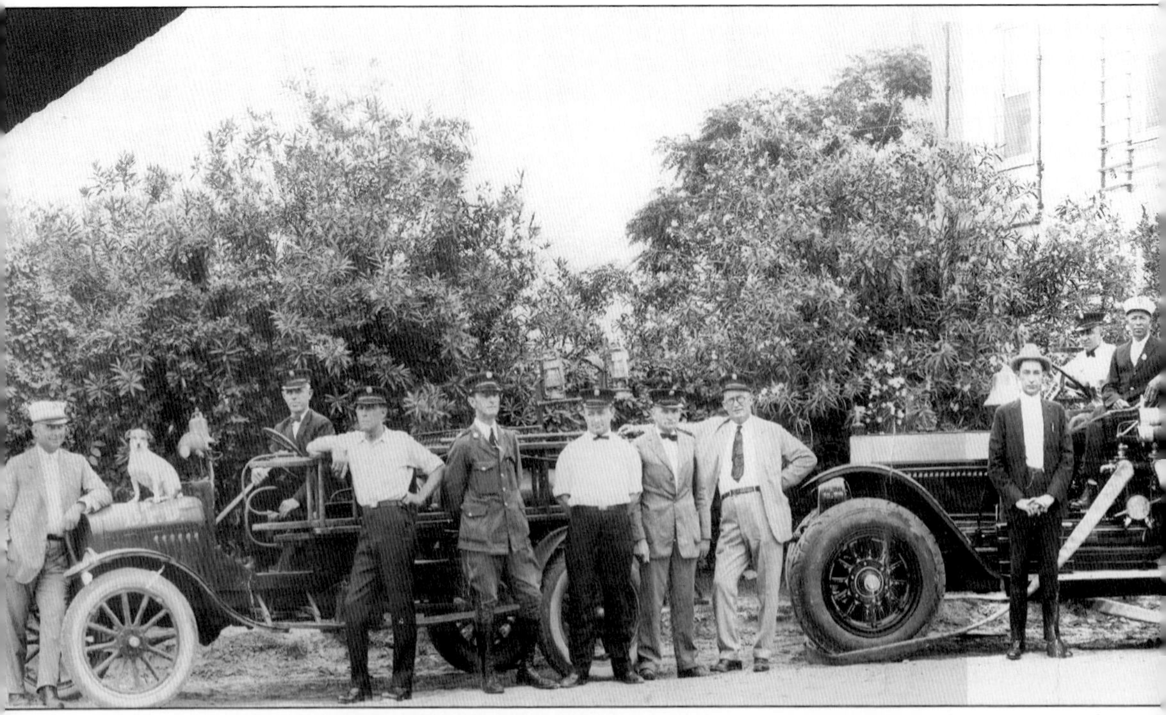

The Donna Volunteer Fire Department was photographed on May 8, 1926, in front of one of the first buildings on the west side of the town square, which housed the *Donna News*. The firefighters show pride in their new equipment and in their mascots, perched on the hoods of the vehicles (far left and far right). Constructed in 1920, the building provided a home for the

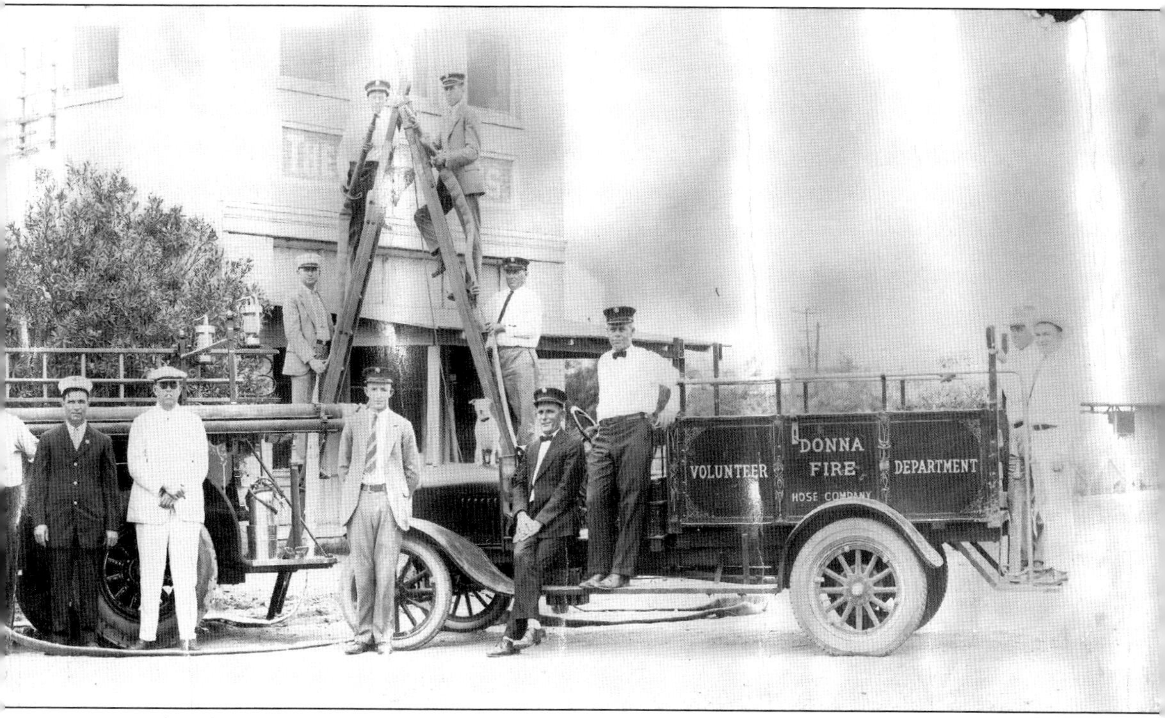

Donna Chamber of Commerce and the Donna Museum for many years. It caught fire in the late 1980s, and the Donna Museum moved to quarters in the American Legion Hall. The *Donna News* building will be refurbished to become the new home of the Donna Museum.

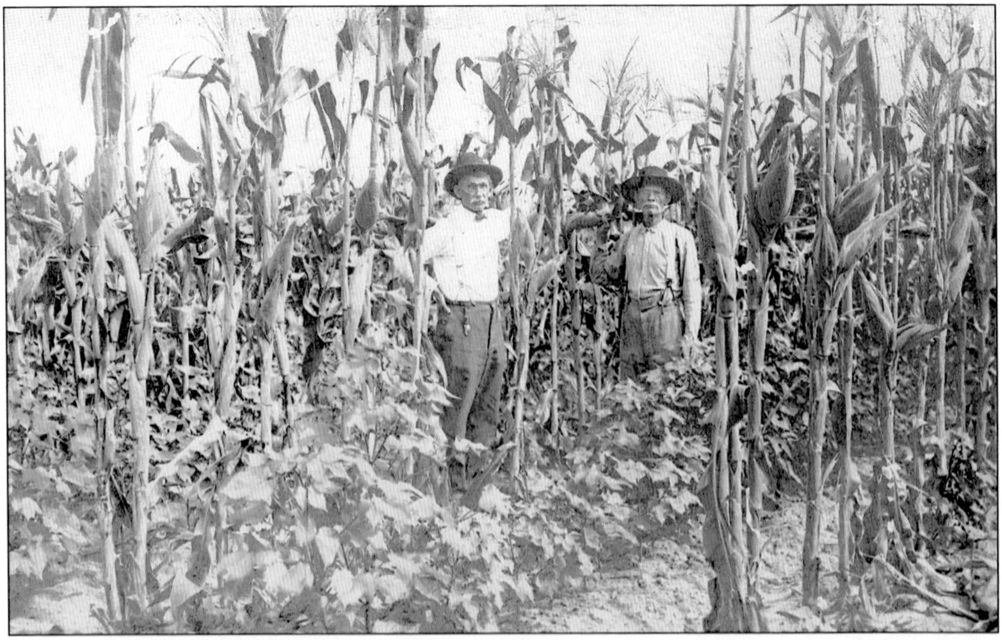

Undisturbed for thousands of years, the rich delta soil produced enormous crops in the early days. Standing in this cornfield are Mr. Thomas J. Hooks (left) and his foreman (right). Note the height of the corn stalks.

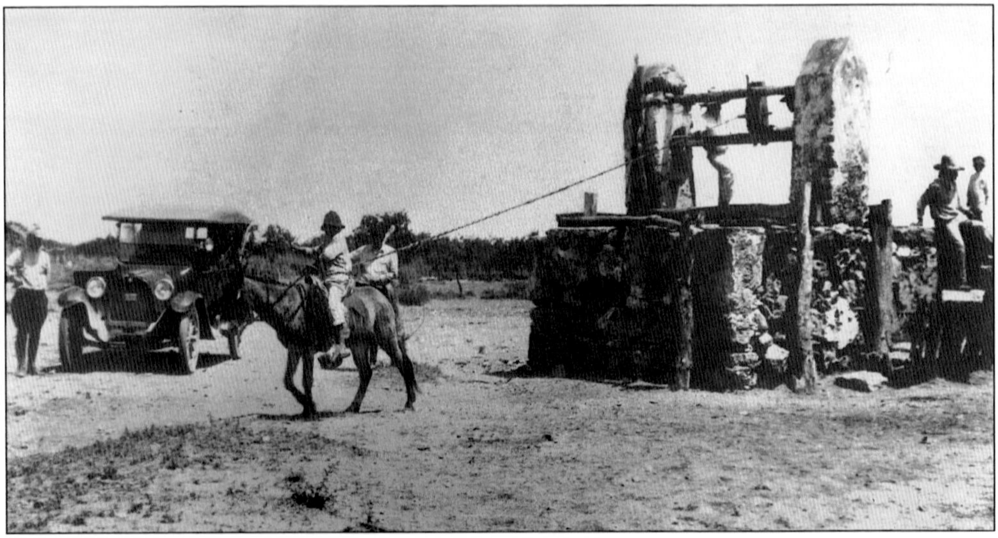

In the early days of settlement, the South Texas Frontier lacked sufficient water for growing crops. Installing a water well in the desolate landscape required strength, toughness, and ingenuity. Modern machinery reduces the physical effort that was needed in the past, but the shortage of water remains.

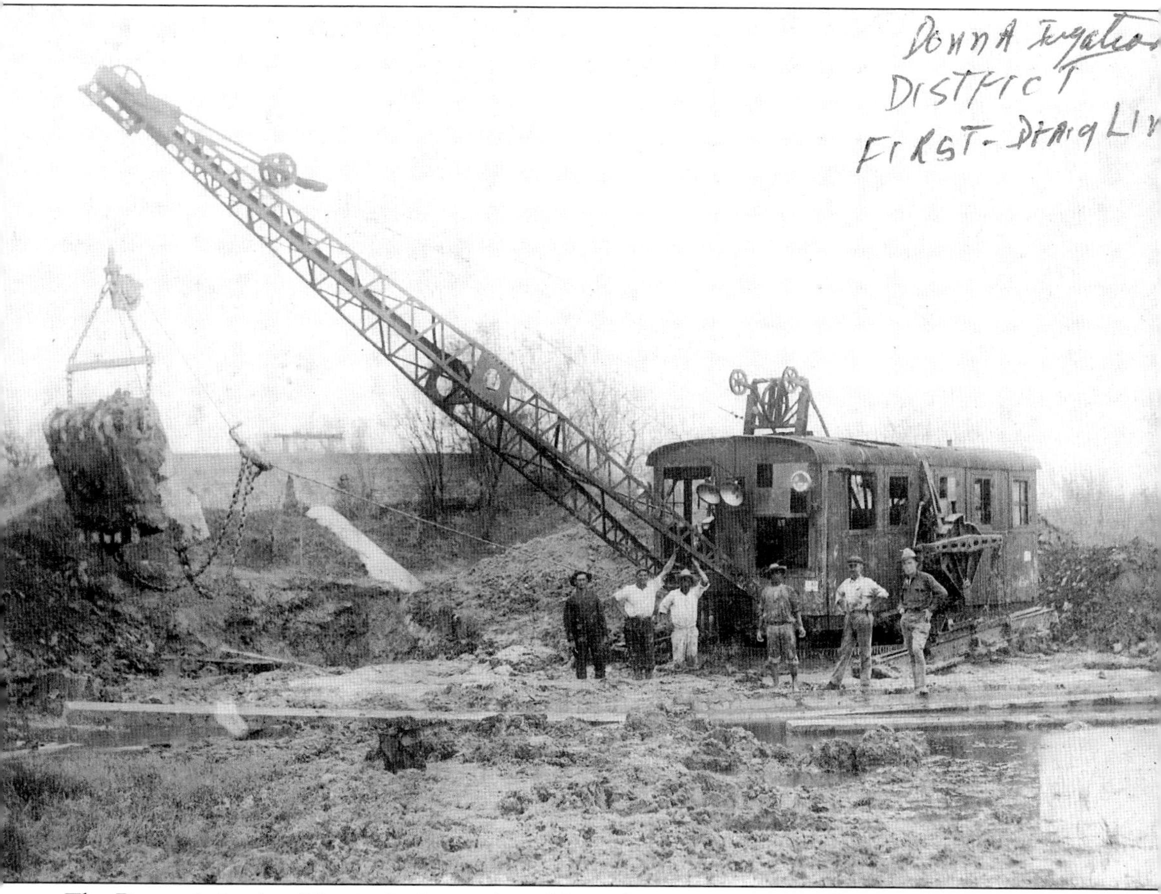

The Donna Irrigation District built canals and laterals to carry water to farms and groves near the City of Donna. Shown here is a drag line removing soil prior to the construction of a section of canal.

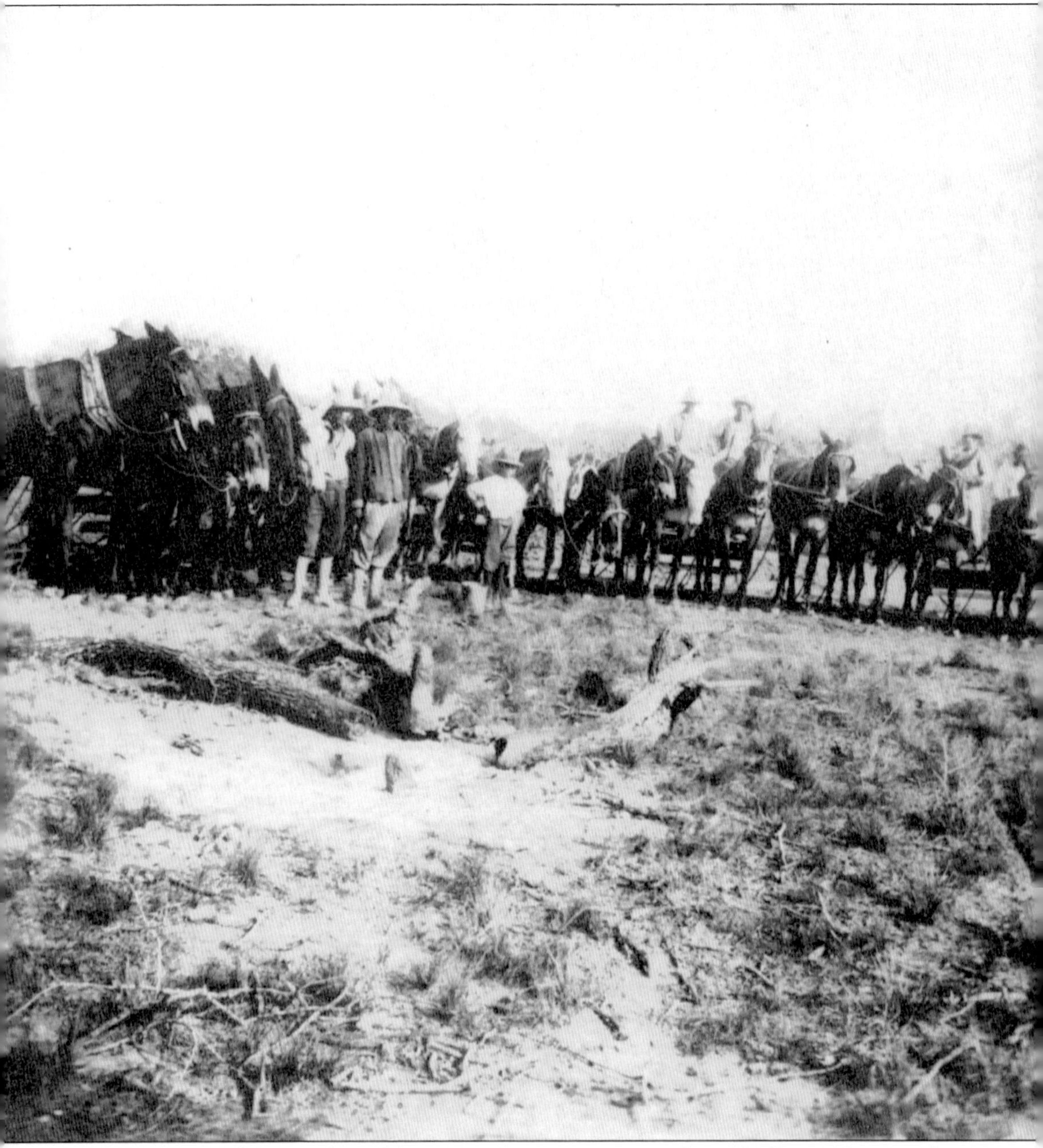

Construction of the canals was labor intensive, requiring great physical effort on the part of men and animals. The canal beds were scooped out with huge scrapers called "fresnos," which were pulled by mule teams. The banks on either side were of tightly packed earth. The canals and banks were later lined with concrete to prevent erosion.

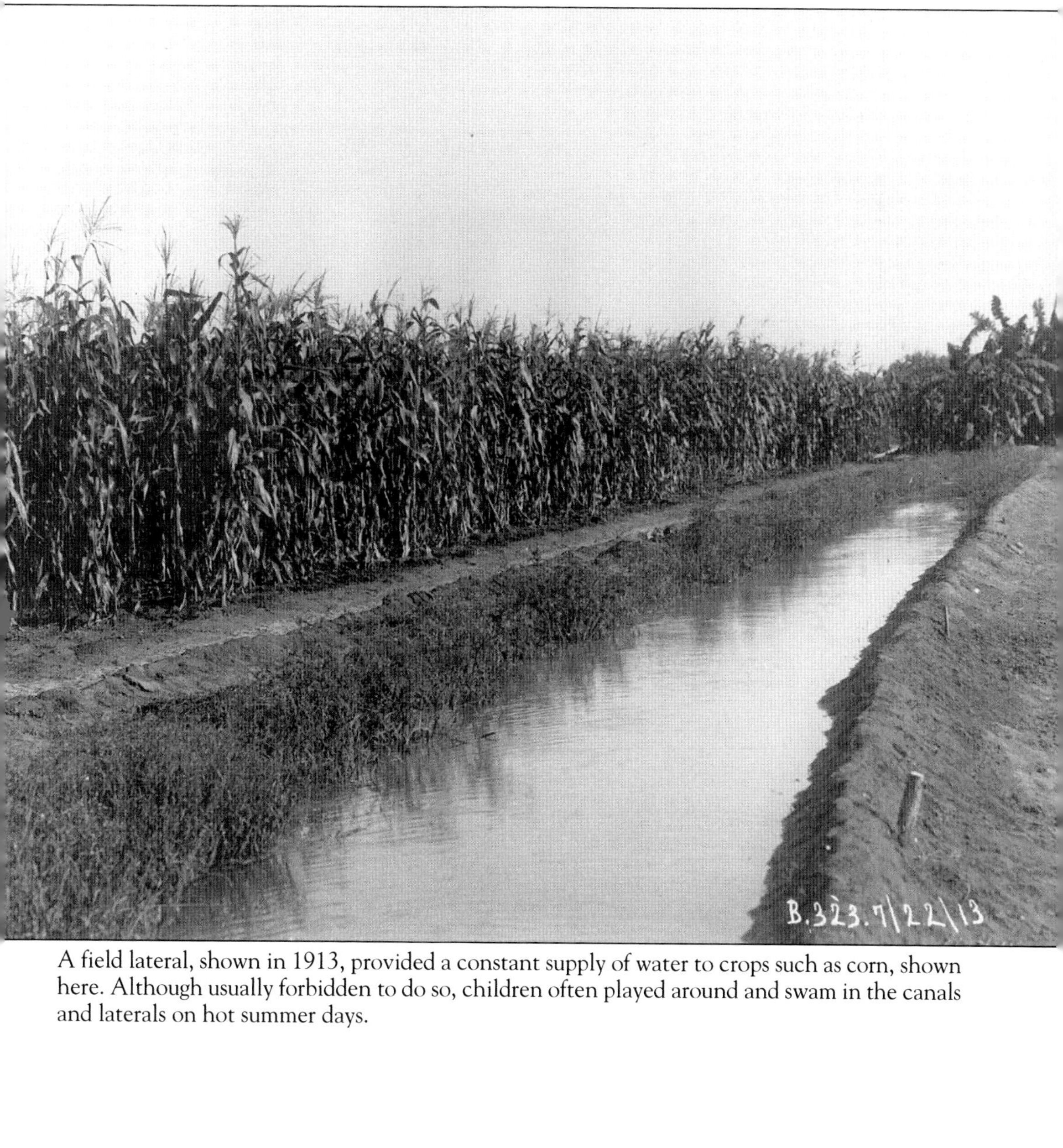

A field lateral, shown in 1913, provided a constant supply of water to crops such as corn, shown here. Although usually forbidden to do so, children often played around and swam in the canals and laterals on hot summer days.

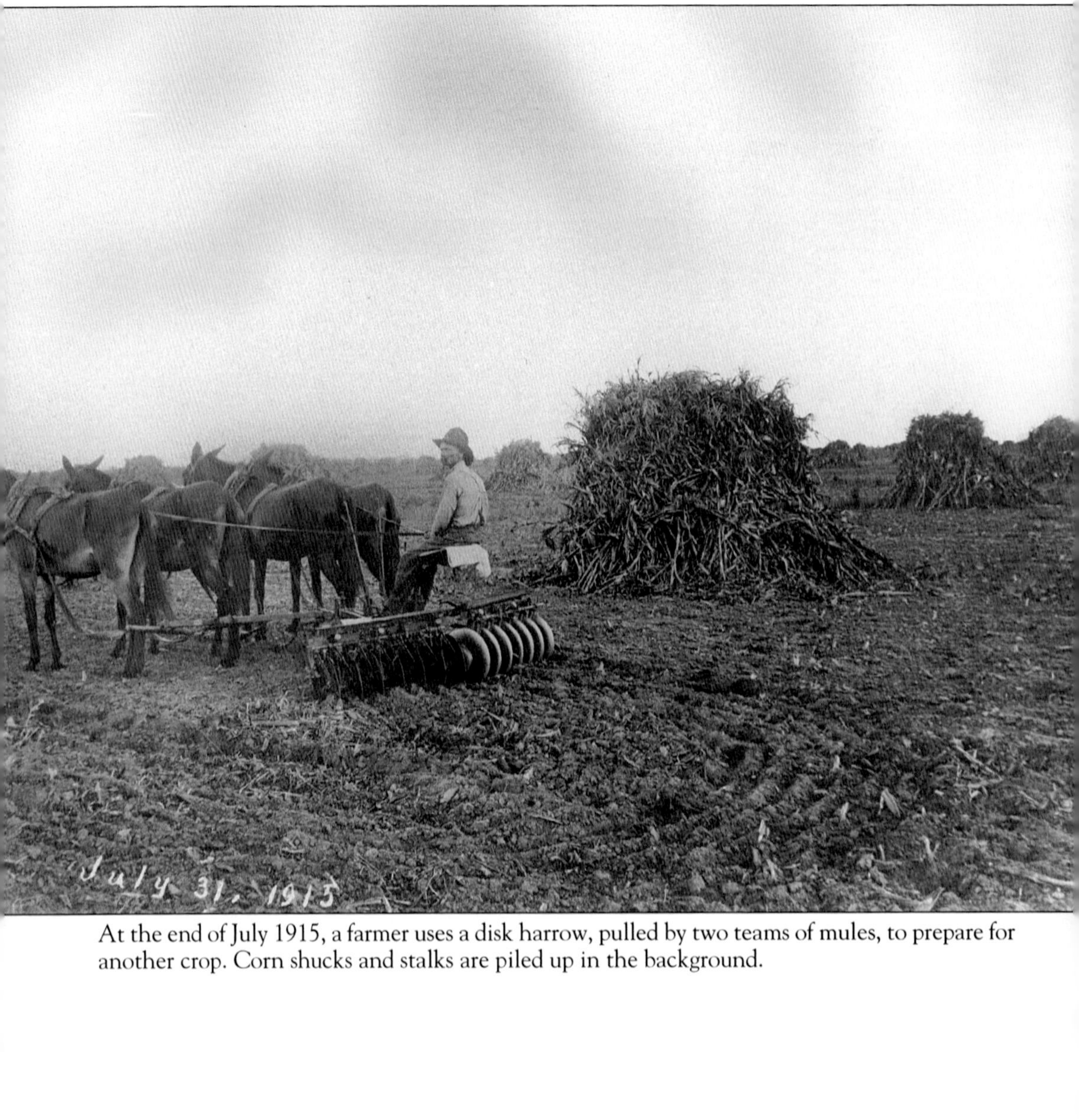

At the end of July 1915, a farmer uses a disk harrow, pulled by two teams of mules, to prepare for another crop. Corn shucks and stalks are piled up in the background.

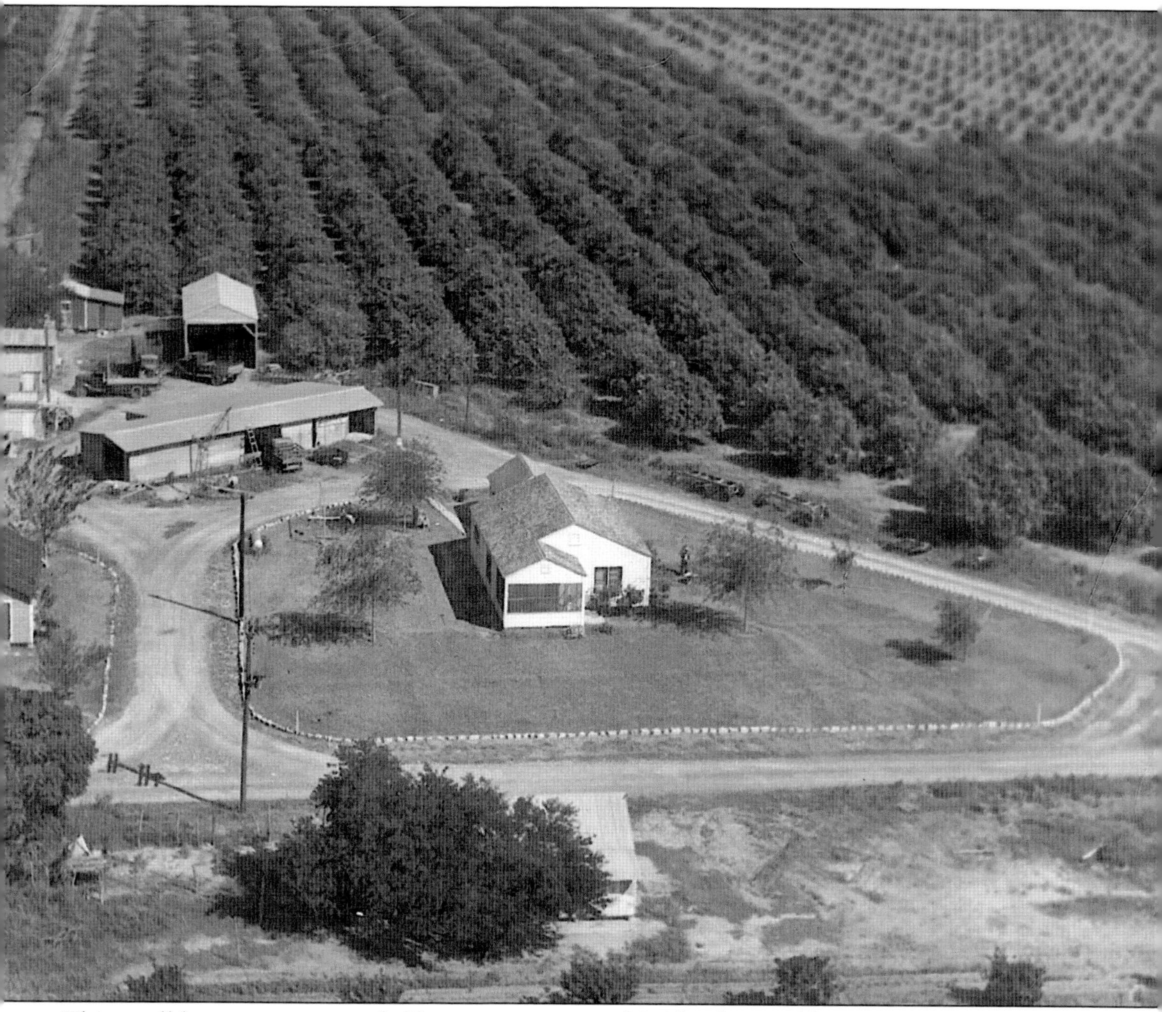

This small house was surrounded by citrus groves and fields of vegetables. Farm managers and their families lived in these houses.

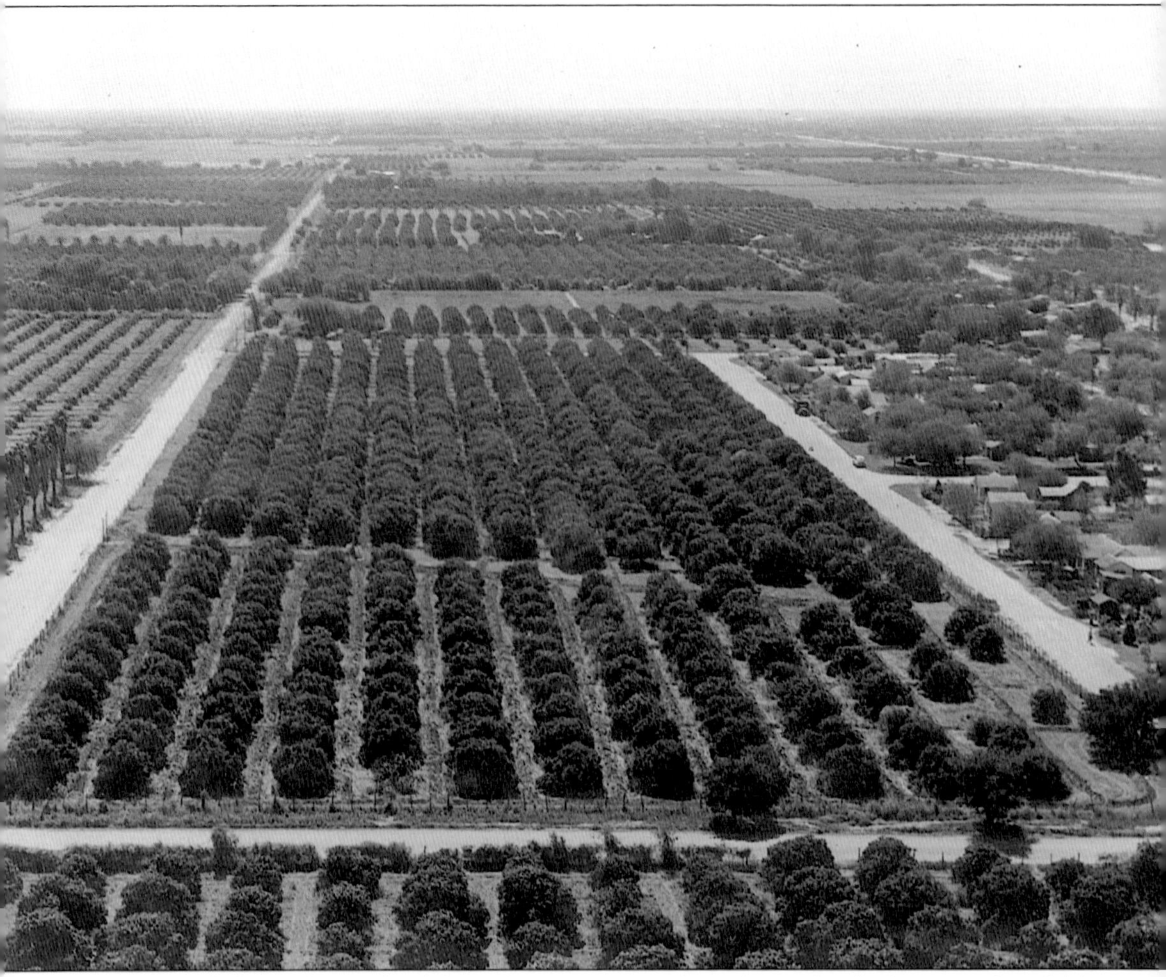

This aerial photo of an orchard shows how trees were planted to make the best use of available land and their placement relative to canals.

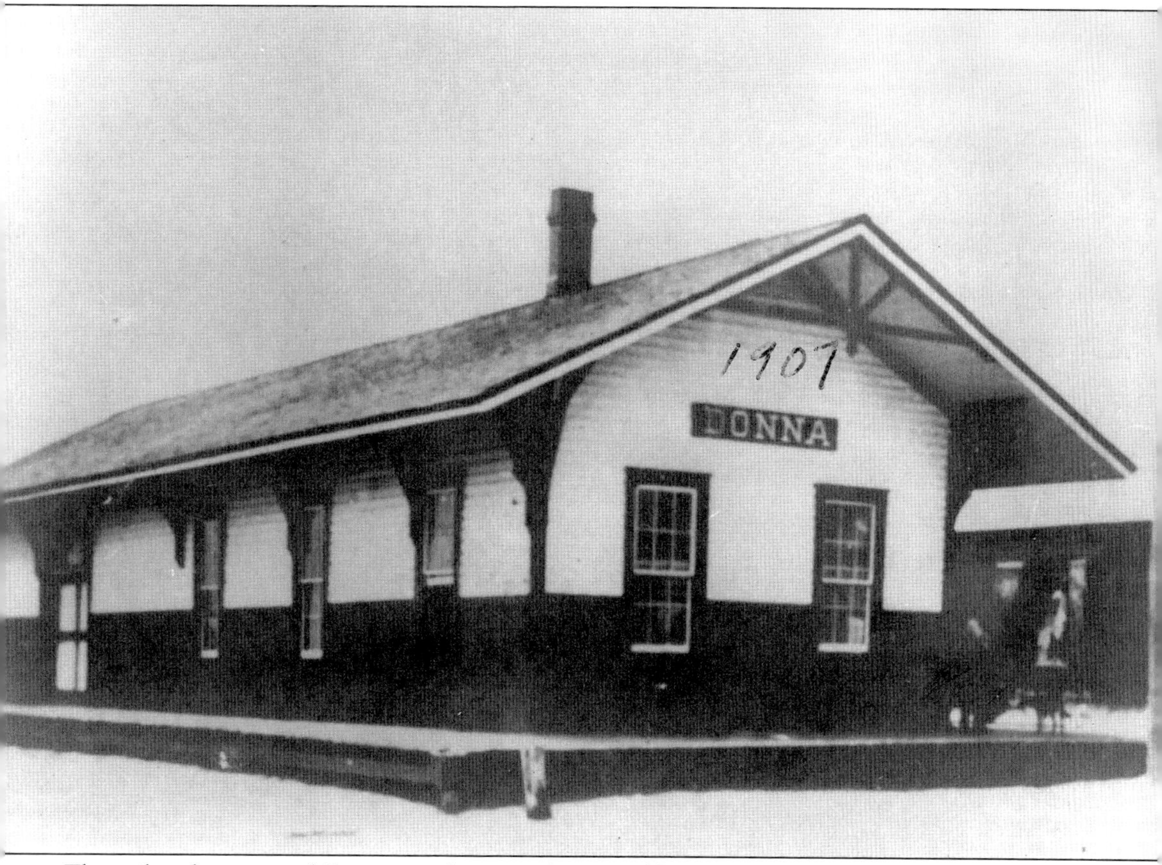

The railroad connected Donna residents to their neighbors in other towns and to the larger world beyond the Valley. This 1907 photograph shows the Donna passenger station for the Sam Fordyce extension of the St. Louis, Brownsville, and Mexico Railroad.

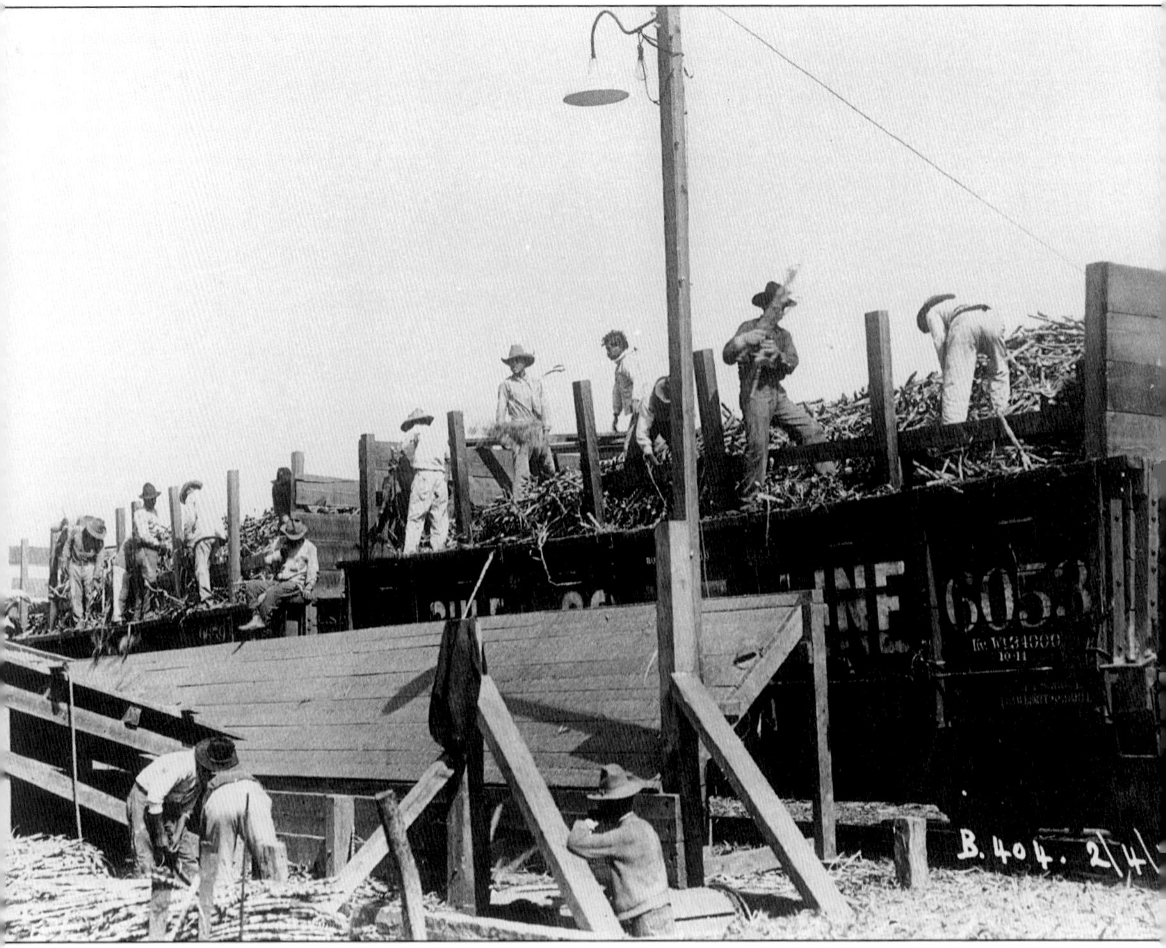

Workers unload tons of sugarcane from rail cars at the Donna sugar mill in this 1915 image

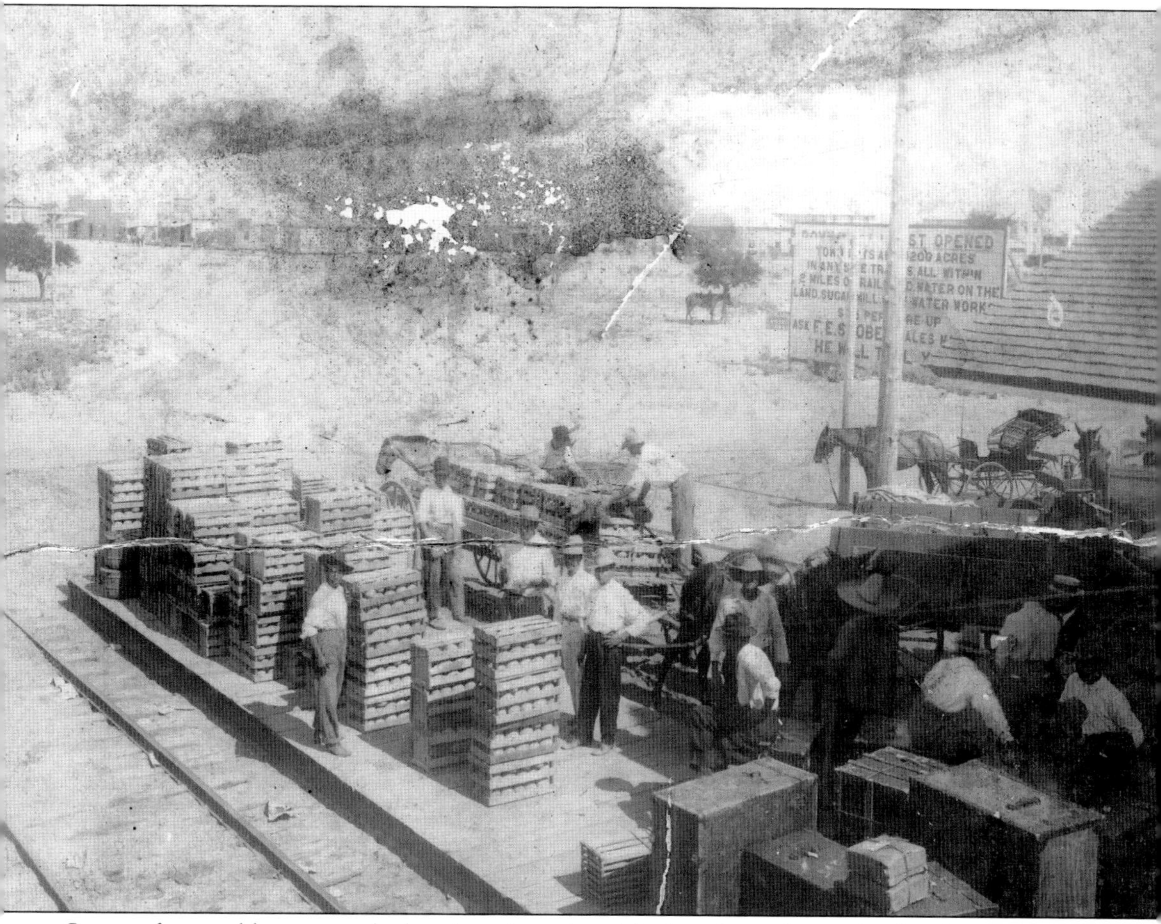

Crates of vegetables are stacked and ready to be picked up by rail cars. In the days before refrigeration, perishables were packed in sawdust and ice for shipment.

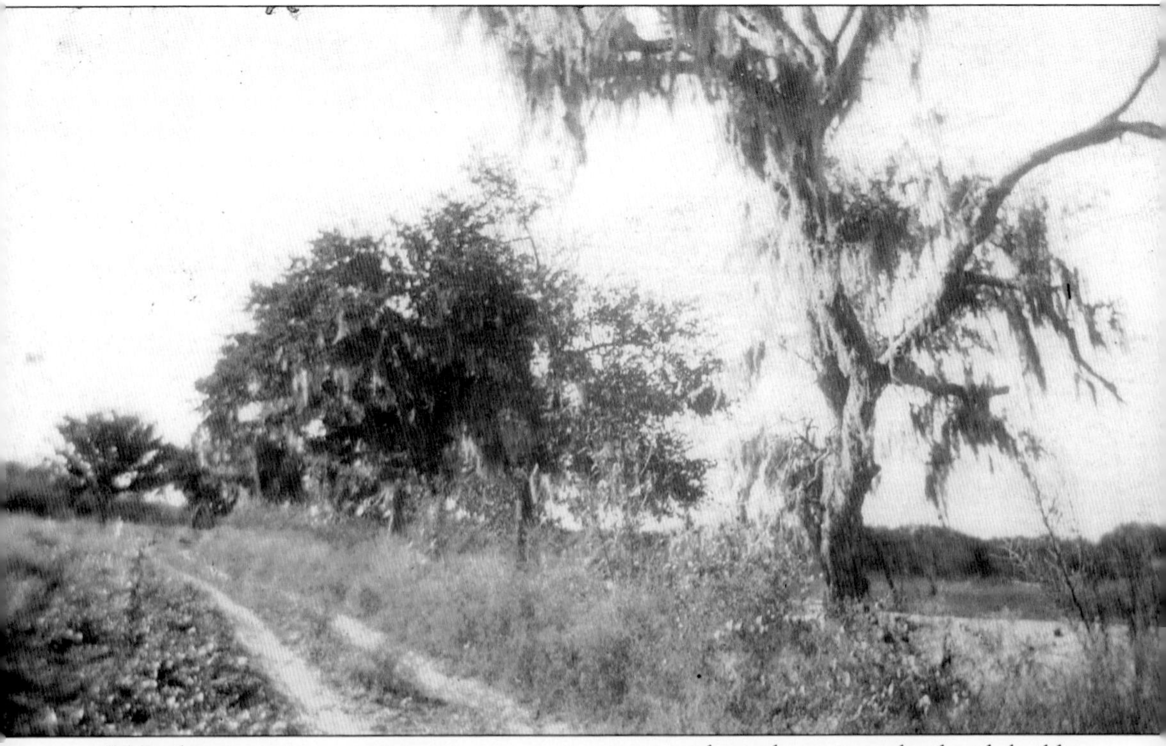

Ed Ruthven, engineer, postmaster, cotton gin owner, and merchant, is credited with building the first sugar mill, a small enterprise for brown sugar *piloncillos*. In 1908, the Donna Plantation Company received a charter to build a sugar mill 2.5 miles south of Donna. This image shows the well-worn road to the sugar mill in 1915. Sugar Mill Road became the first roadway in Donna, and extended south from Donna to the sugar mill, through Run, and ended at the pumping plant on the river.

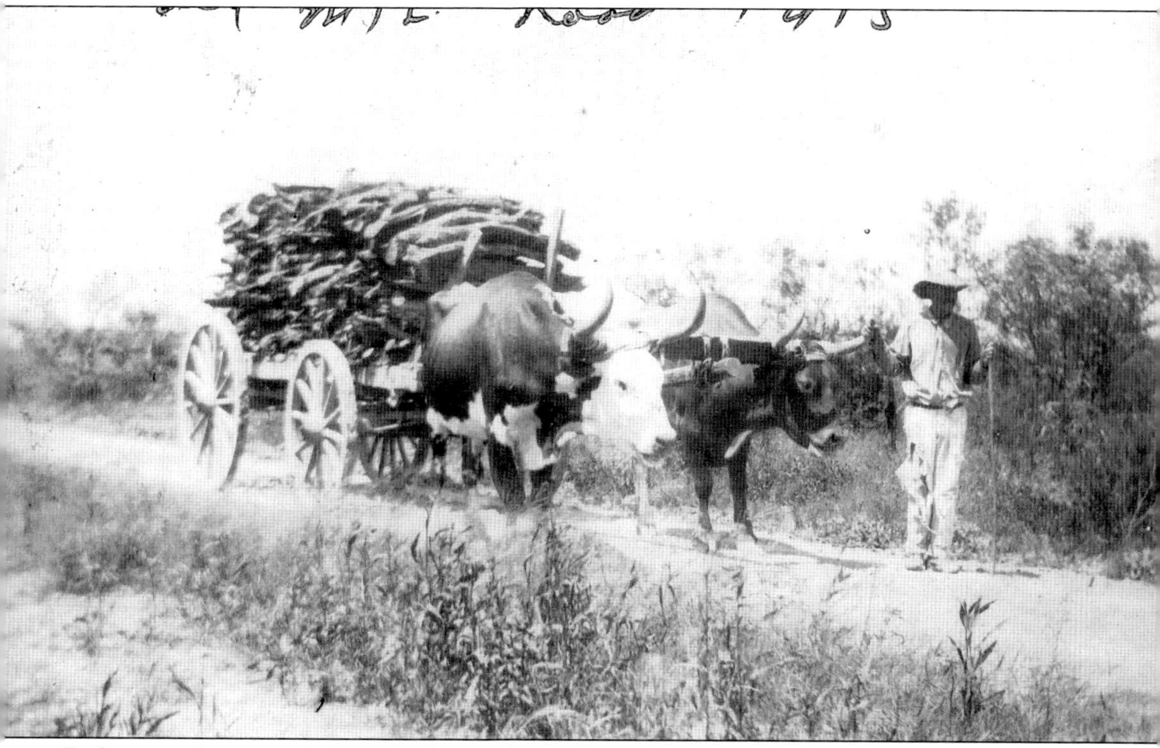

Early crops of sugarcane grew as high as 17 feet and produced between 30 and 40 tons of cane per acre. Its high sucrose content made it superior to sugarcane grown in East Texas and Louisiana. In 1922 the American Sugar Trust Company bought the Donna Plantation Company and the sugar mill, which it subsequently destroyed. This 1915 photograph shows an ox-drawn cart loaded with sugarcane on the road to the sugar mill.

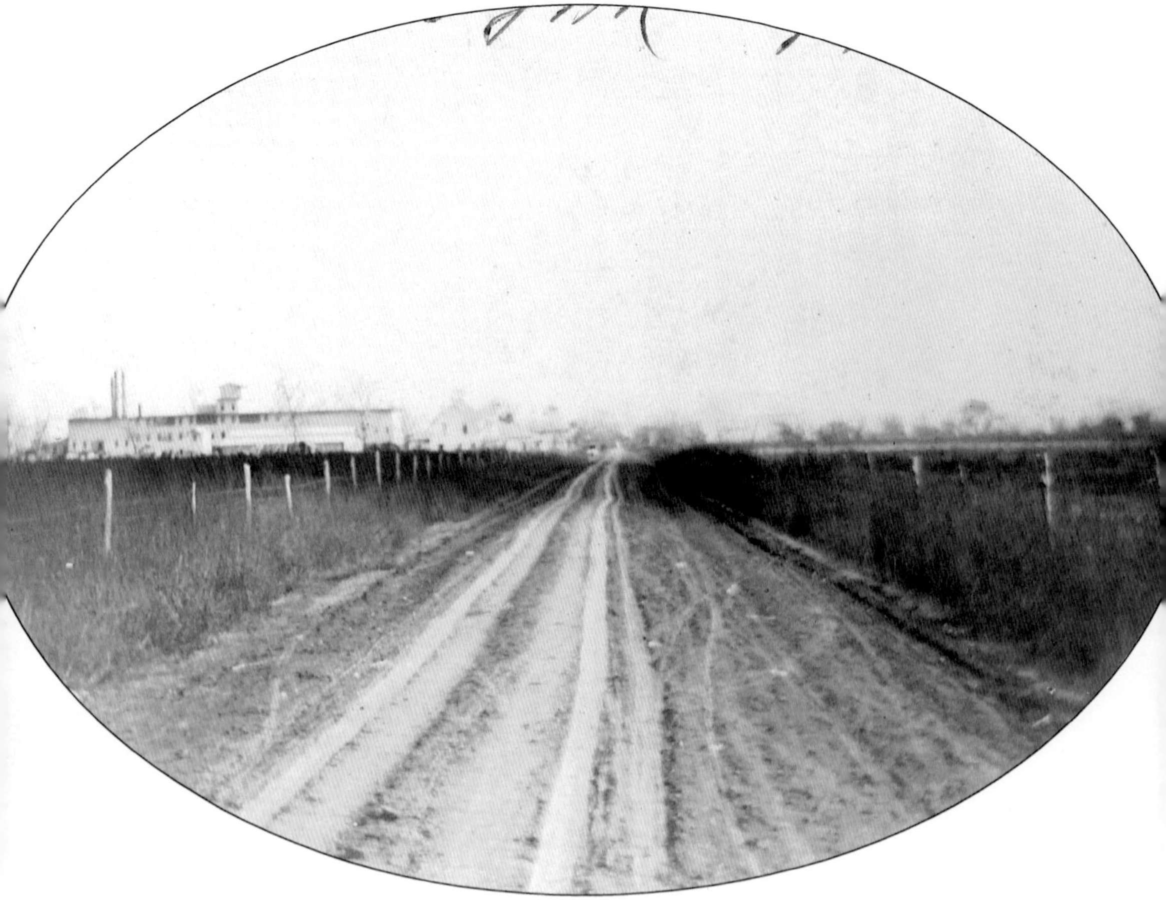

Sugar Mill Road was deeply rutted from the weight of heavily laden carts of sugarcane. The sugar mill is shown on the left.

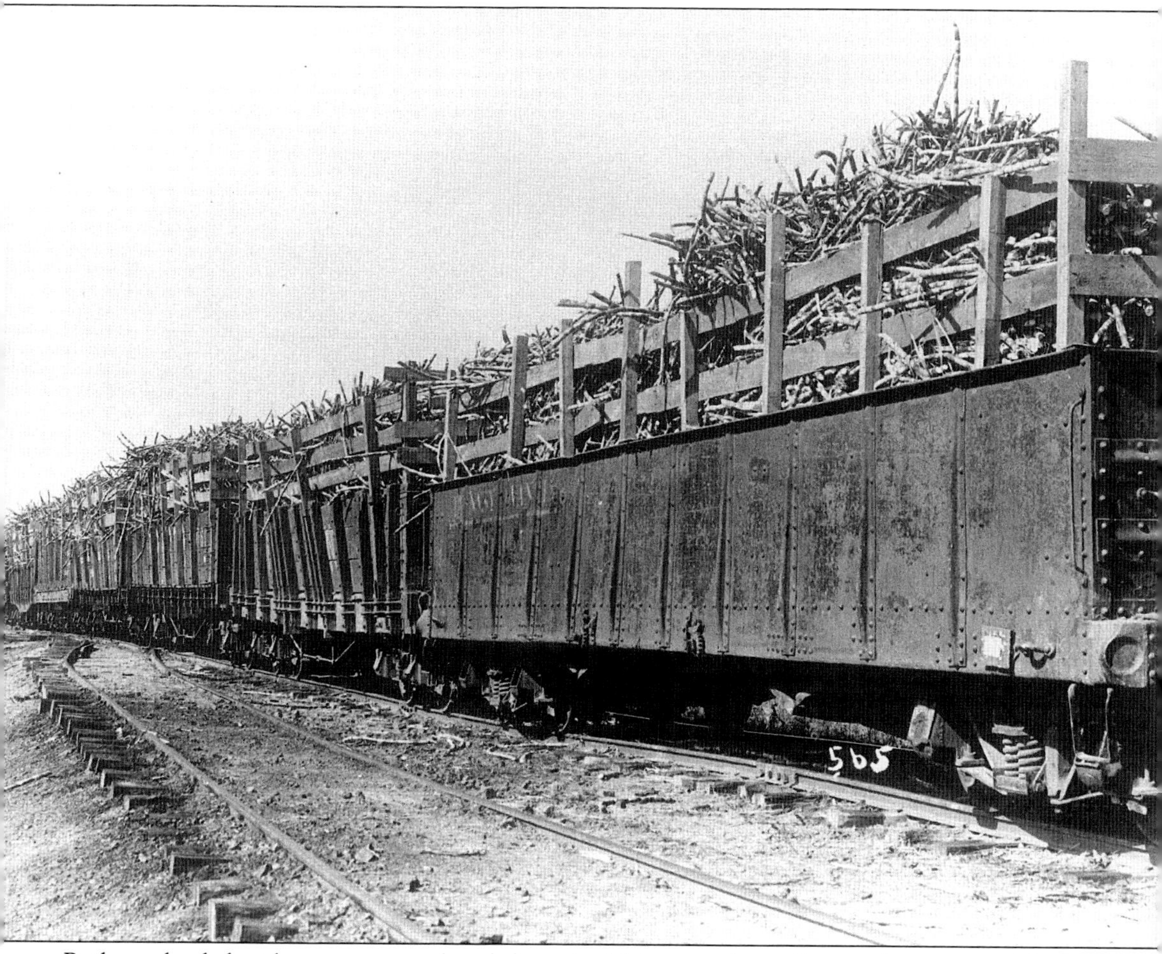

Rail cars loaded with sugarcane replaced the colorful, but much smaller, ox-drawn carts. The sugar mill at Donna processed 500 tons of sugar per day and had a weekly payroll of $3,000.

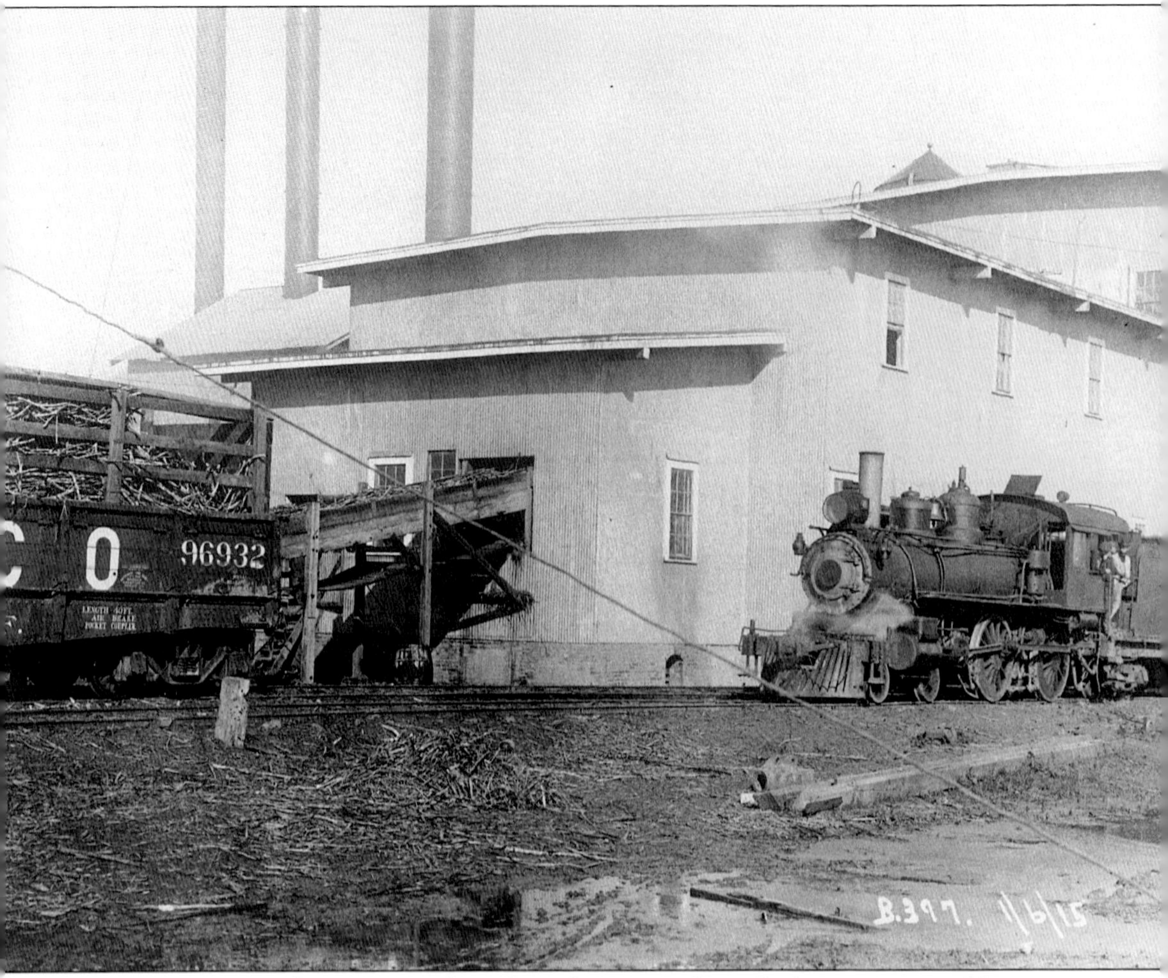

A conveyor transfers sugarcane from the rail cars into the mill. A steam-powered locomotive waits on a siding behind the mill.

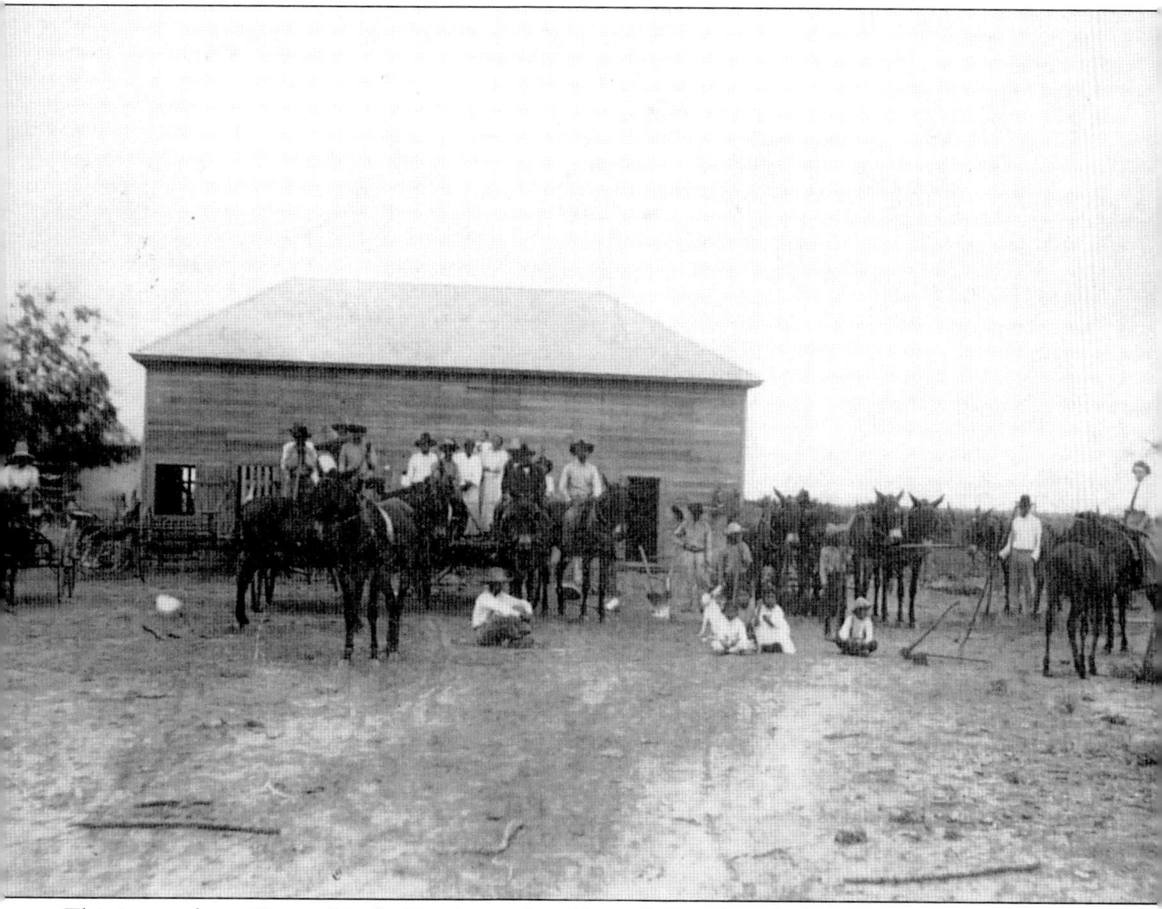

This image shows Donna Hooks Fletcher at her Alameda Ranch with the Mexican helpers who cleared the land and built her "a tiny, primitive shack hardly the size of a wood shed, bare of all modern conveniences" for her home. Eventually her ranch had 100 cleared and irrigated acres and became a model farm. In her autobiography, *This Is My Life*, she describes life on the Rio Grande as "colorful and dangerous," especially during the years 1914 and 1915. In one incident, unwanted trespassers on horseback surrounded her ranch house. Alerted by her dog, she stood at the doorway and frightened the intruders away at gunpoint.

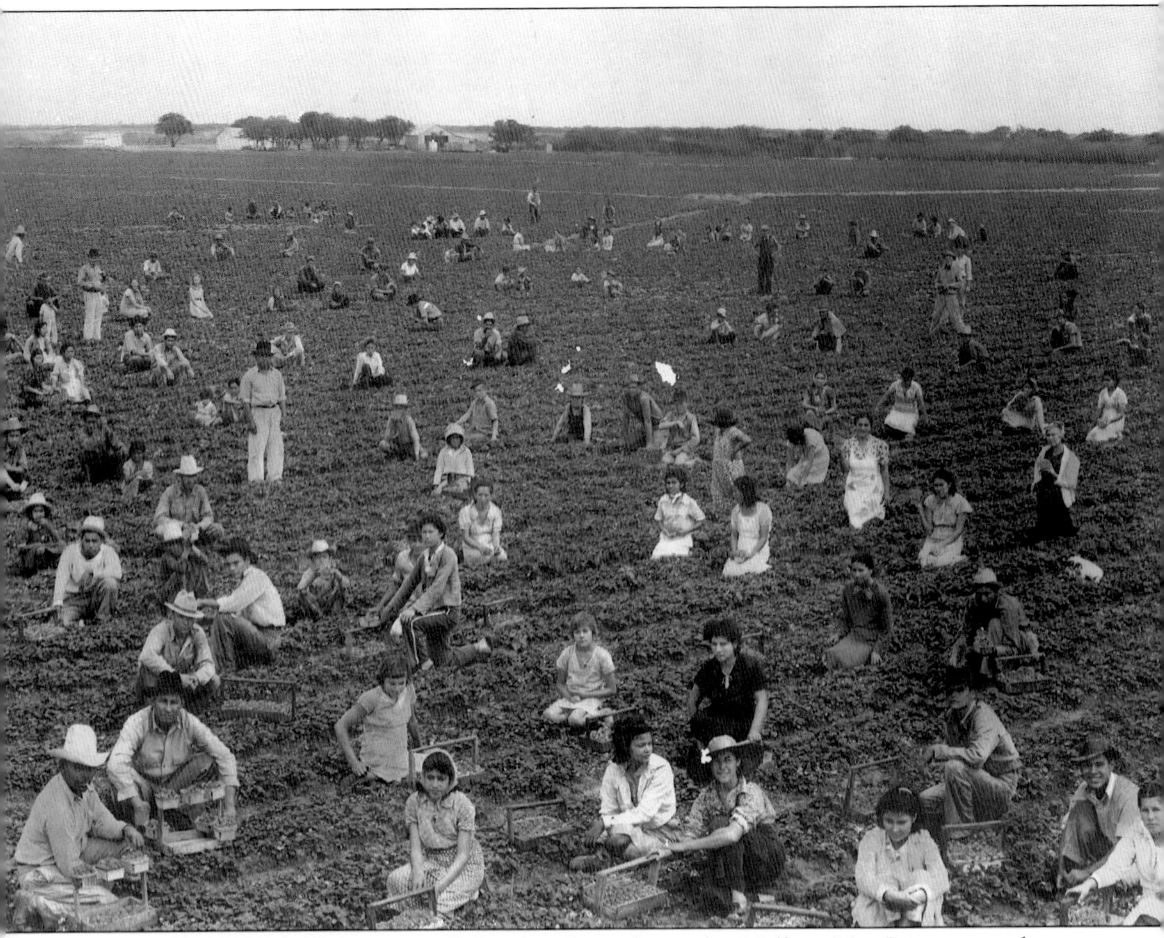

The Stites Berry Farm was well known throughout the Valley. Mr. Stites owned many acres and was recognized as the Strawberry King, since this was his primary crop. This mid-1940s photograph shows field workers posing with their pickings. Today young ladies who represent Donna in a Valley-wide citrus pageant are given the title "Duchess of Strawberry." Mr. Stites' business flourished to the mid-1960s, when more and more farmers turned to grain and sugarcane.

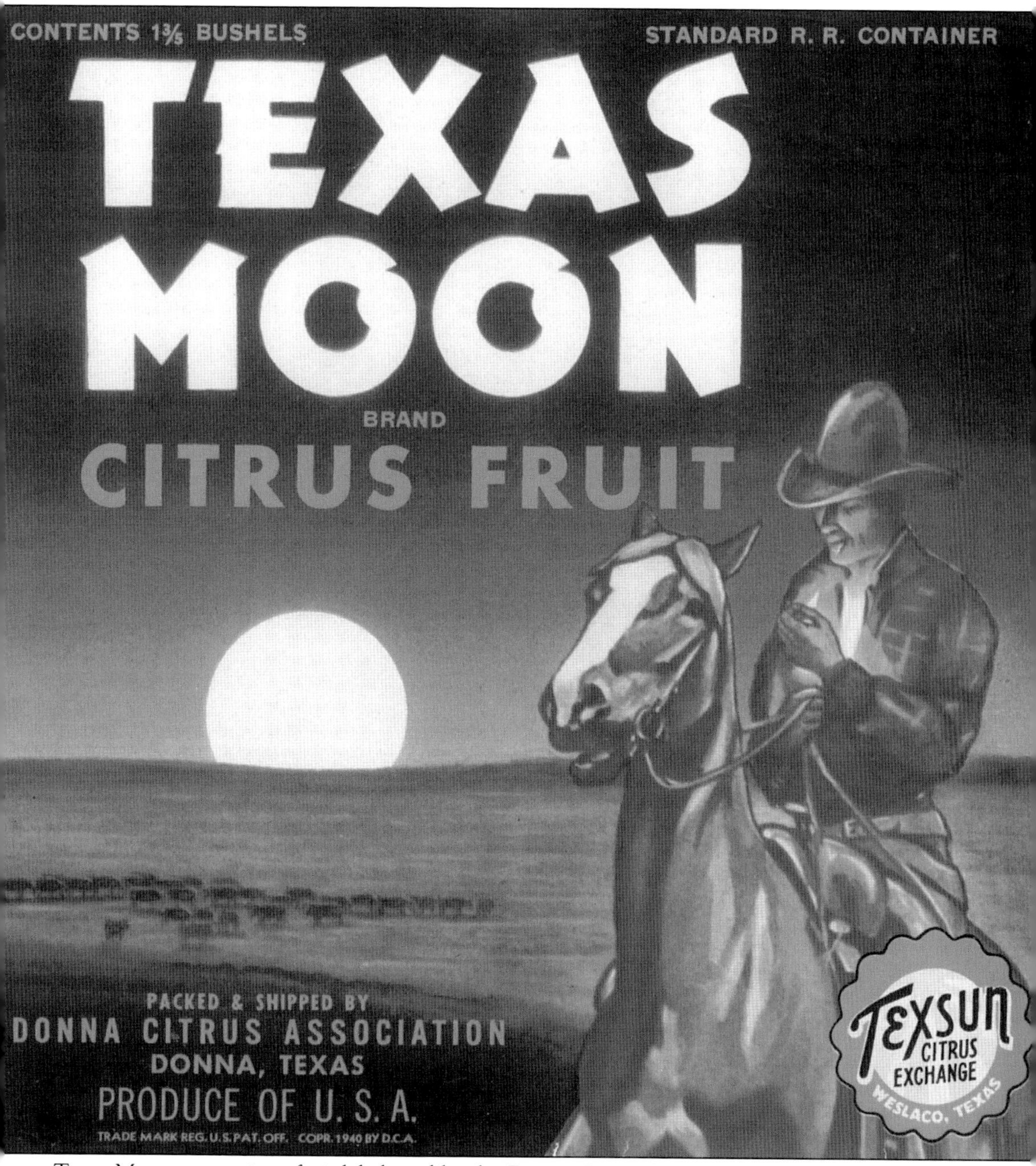

Texas Moon was a citrus fruit label used by the Donna Citrus Association, a group of growers who organized to have more influence over the marketing and sales of their produce. Graphic artists in California designed the label; today these labels are considered collectibles.

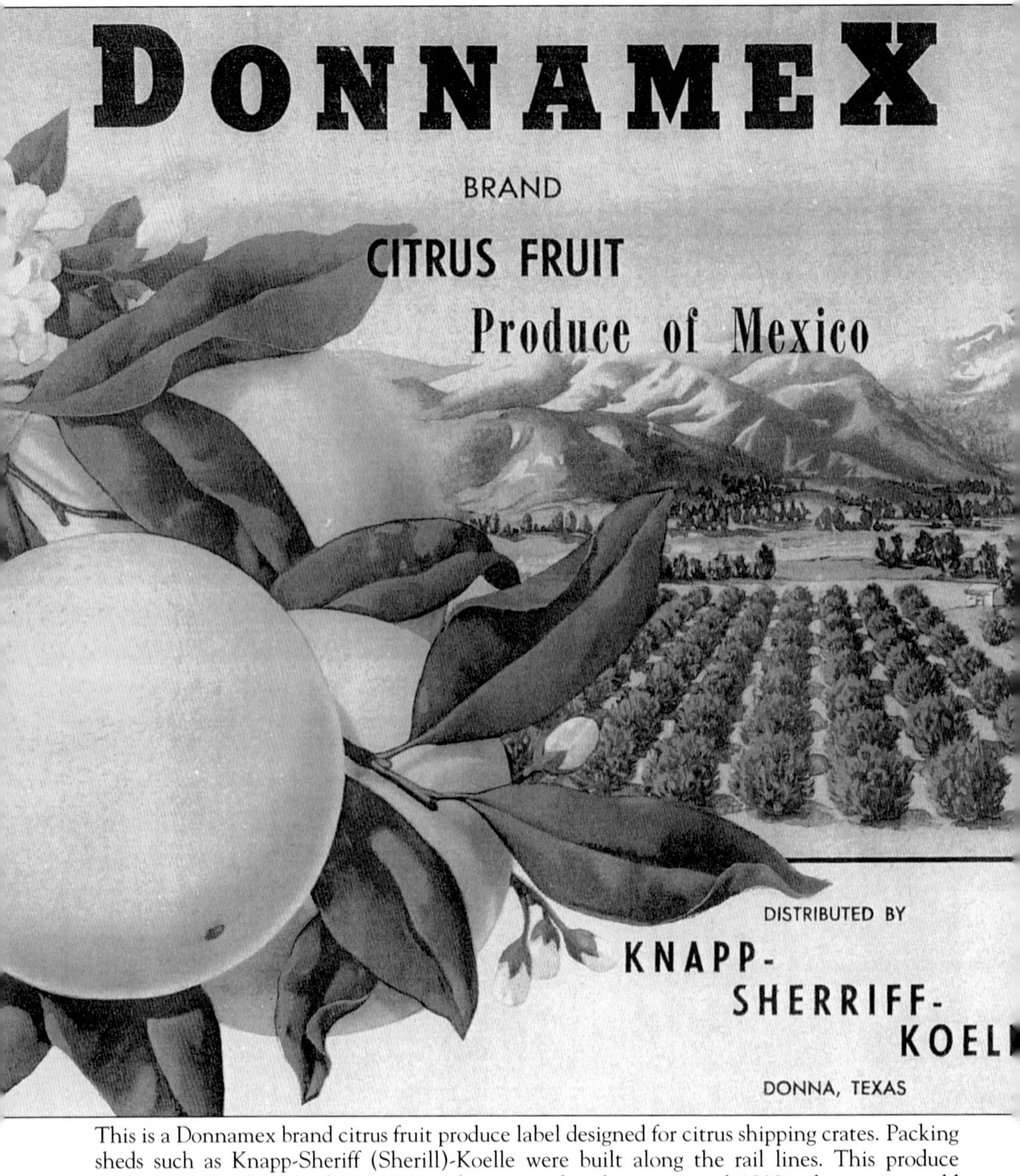

This is a Donnamex brand citrus fruit produce label designed for citrus shipping crates. Packing sheds such as Knapp-Sheriff (Sherill)-Koelle were built along the rail lines. This produce company opened in the late 1930s and continued in business until 1999, when it was sold to another company.

Eight

CELEBRATIONS

As the City of Donna grew in size and population, it began to lose its rough and ready frontier atmosphere and evolved into a settled 20th century town. Football and baseball teams, school and church activities, a variety of contests, and participation in the Citrus Fiesta added color and character to the everyday routine. The citizens of Donna worked and celebrated with equal energy, as shown in the following photographs.

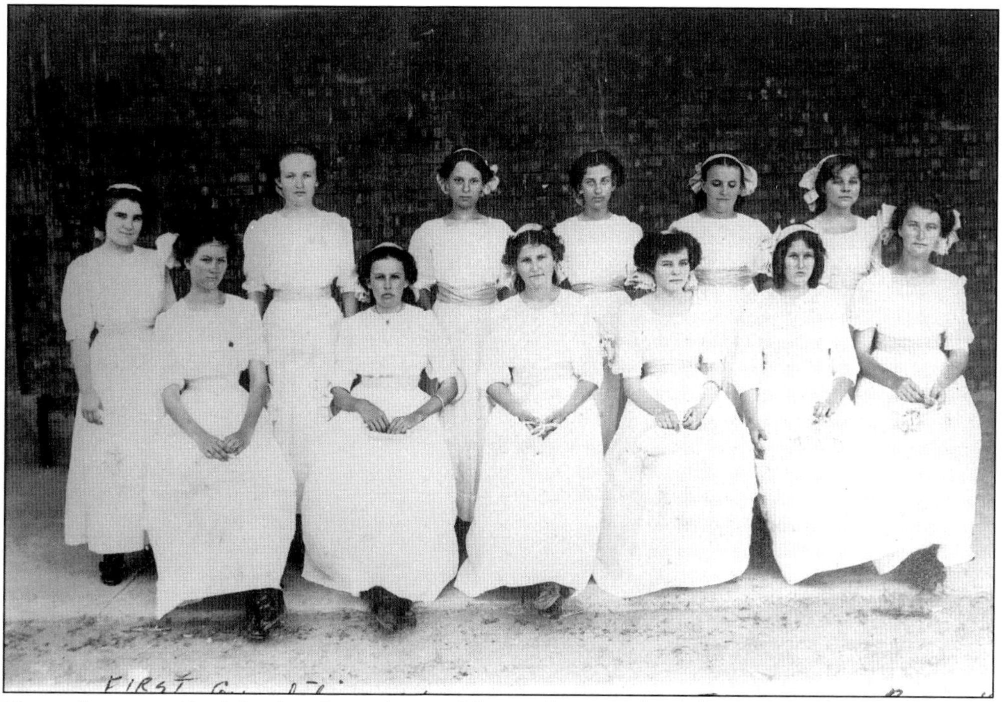

Shown here are all of the female students of the graduating class of 1913.

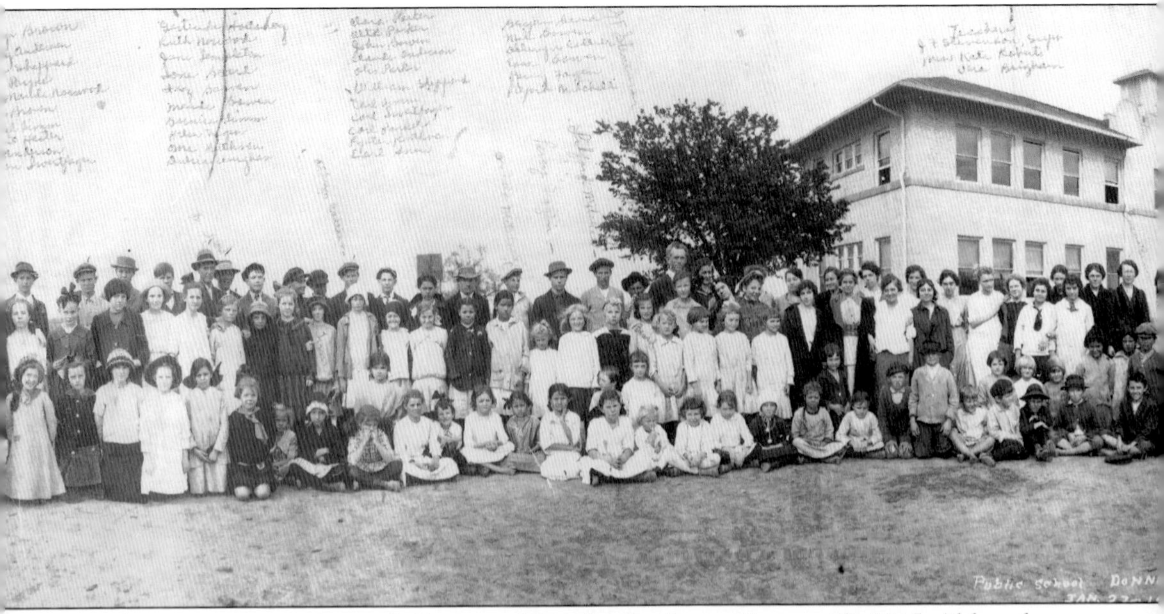

This is a panorama photo of a Donna public school, taken on January 27, 1915. Although most of the original schools in the Donna area have been razed for new structures, two remaining

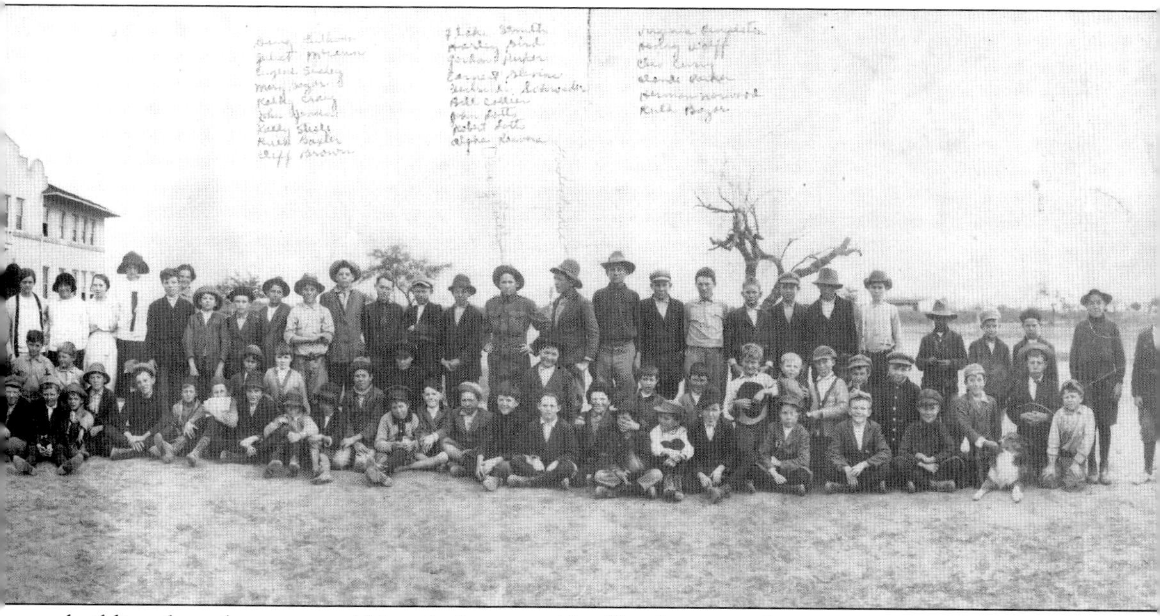

buildings have been granted historical status with official state markers.

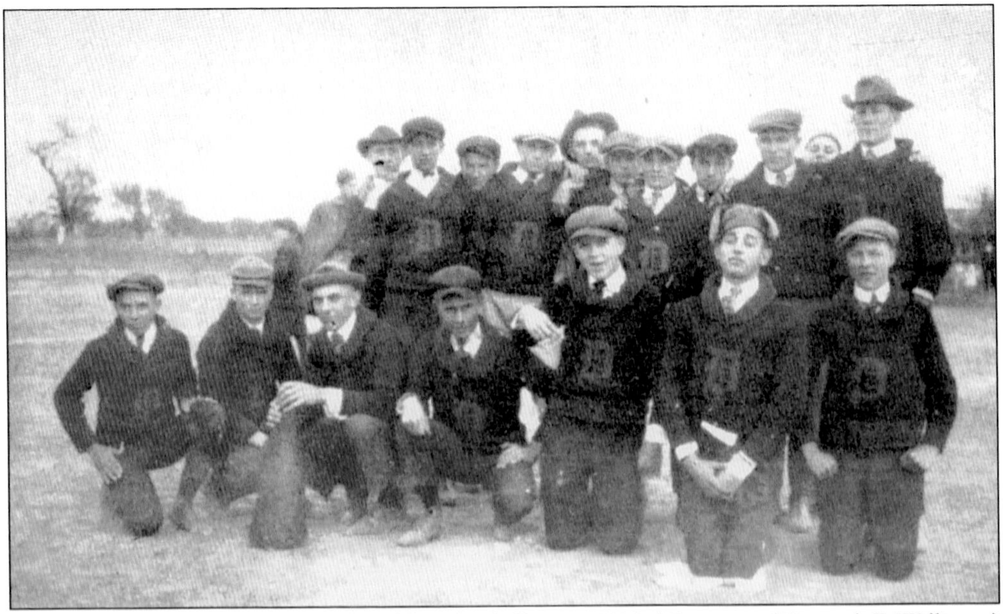

This is the first Donna High School Redskins football team, 1920. (Courtesy of Kenneth F. Williams.)

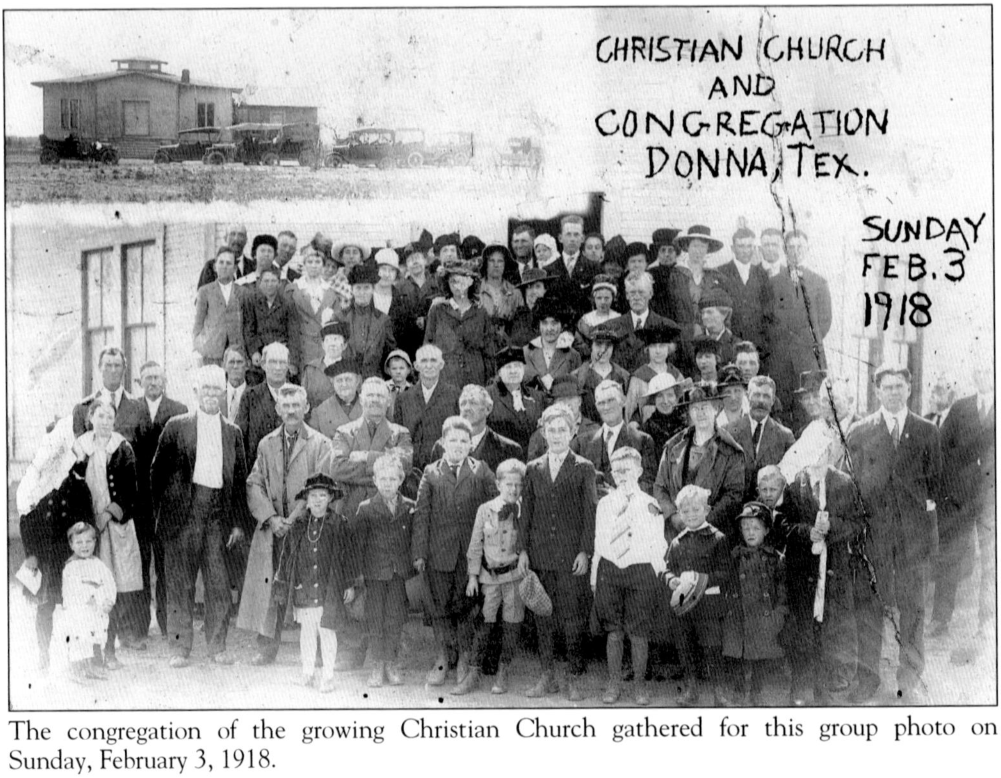

The congregation of the growing Christian Church gathered for this group photo on Sunday, February 3, 1918.

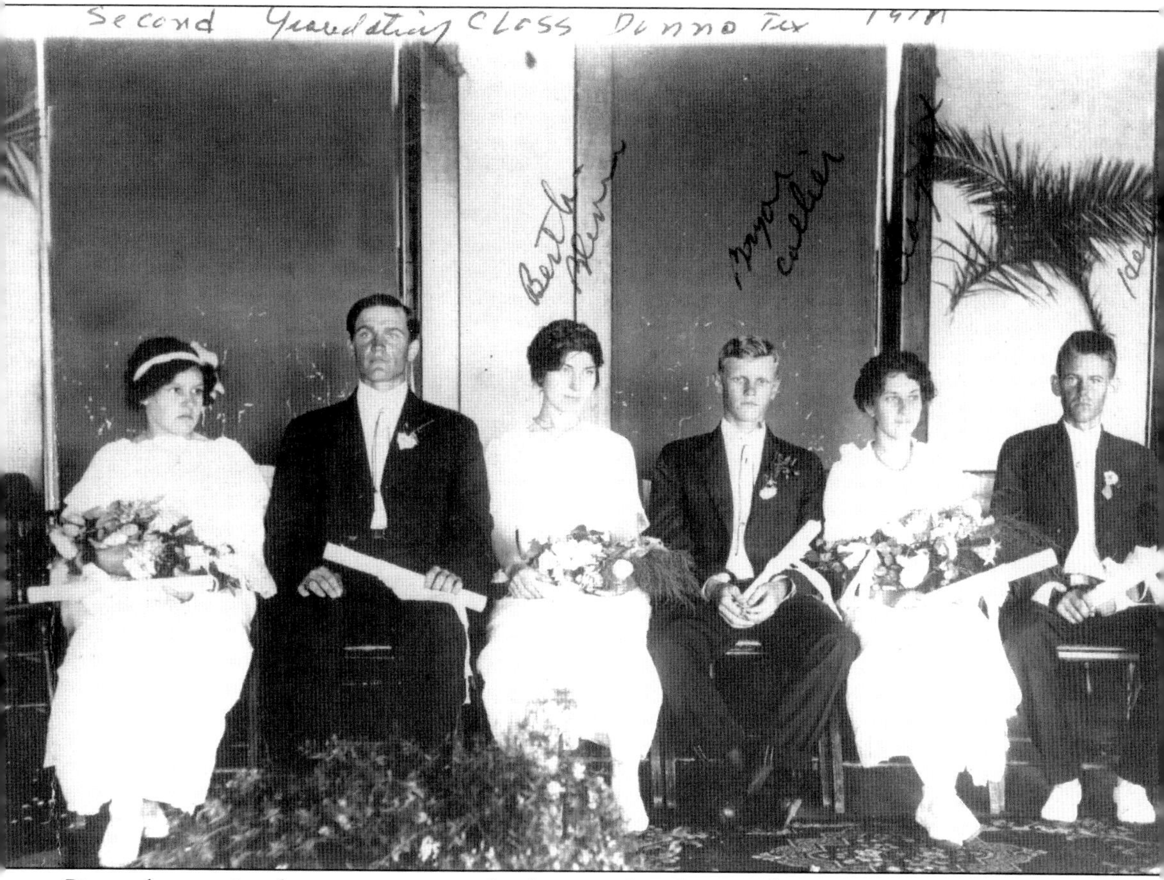

Pictured are senior class representatives for the second graduating class in 1914.

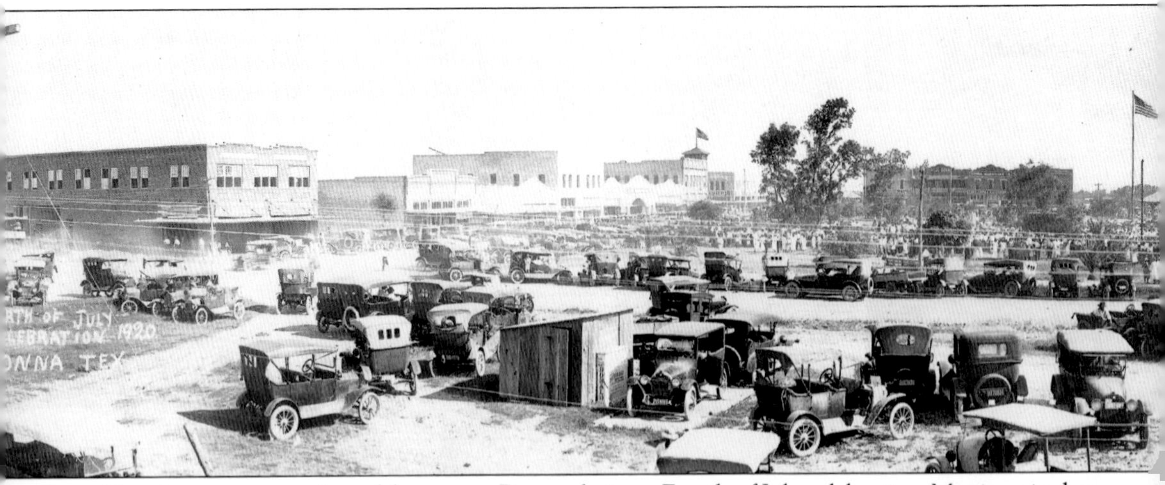

Here is a panoramic view of downtown Donna during a Fourth of July celebration. Monies raised at

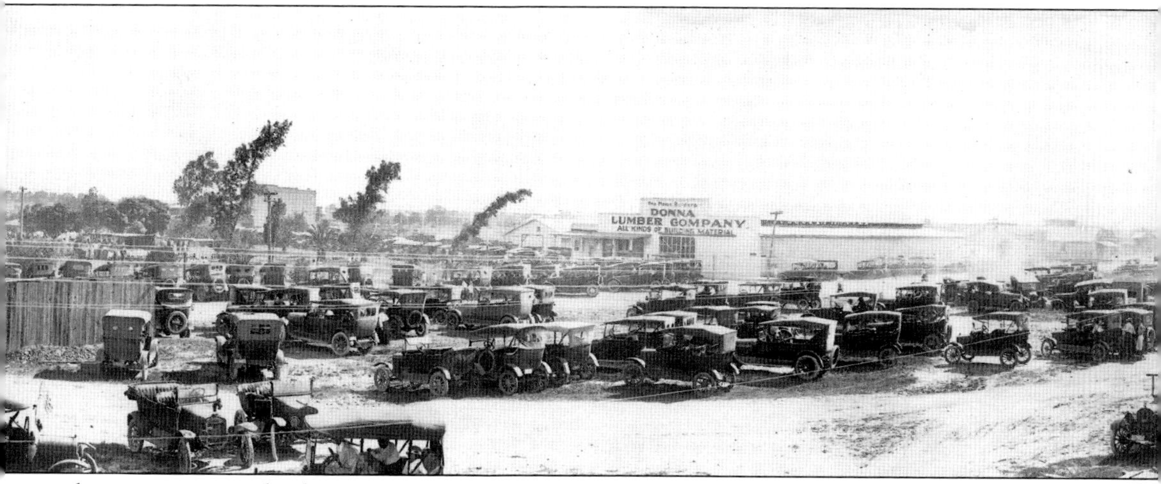

this event were used to begin construction of the world's first American Legion Building, Post 107.

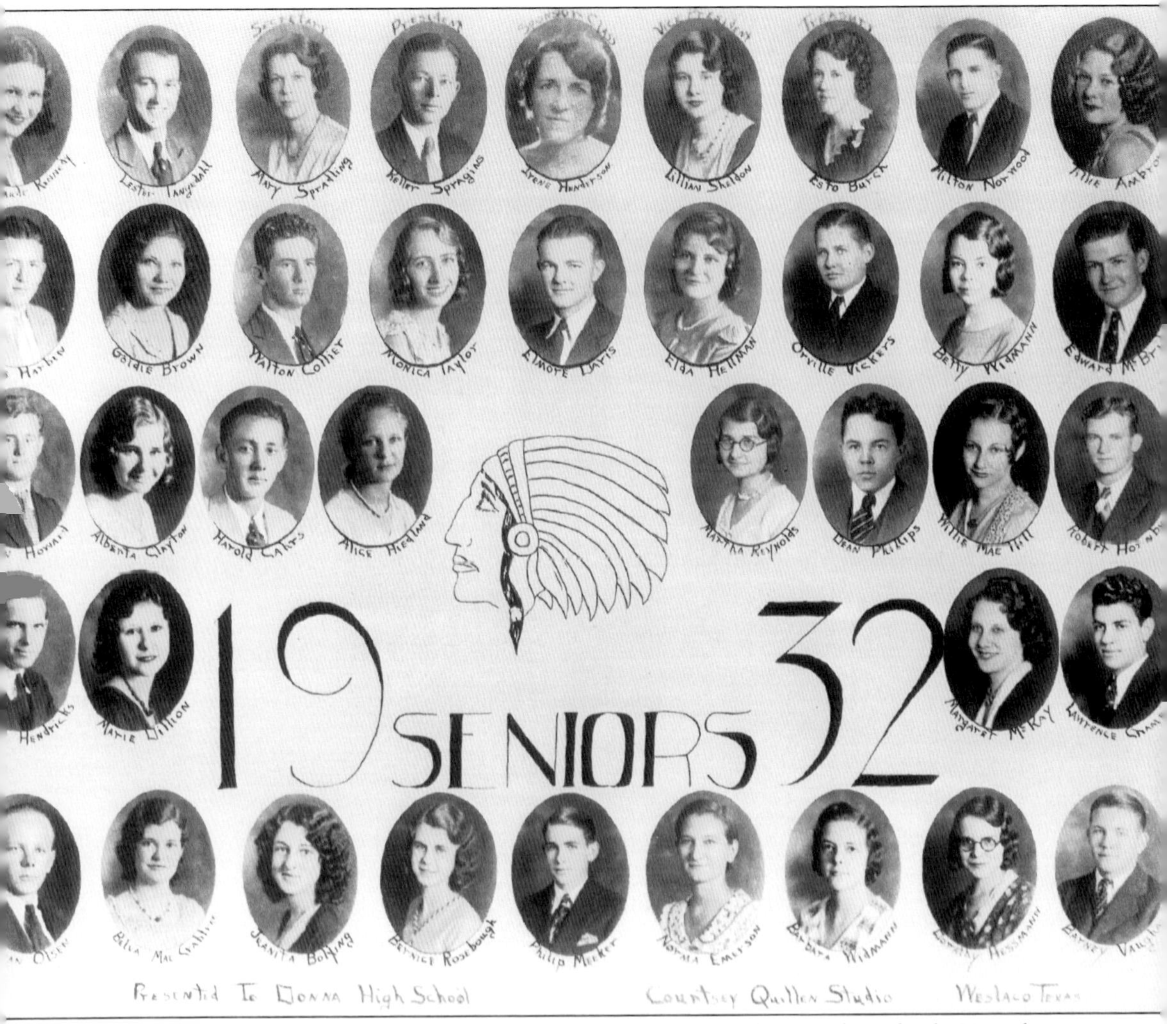

The Donna High School senior class picture of 1932 shows a graduating class of only 39 students.

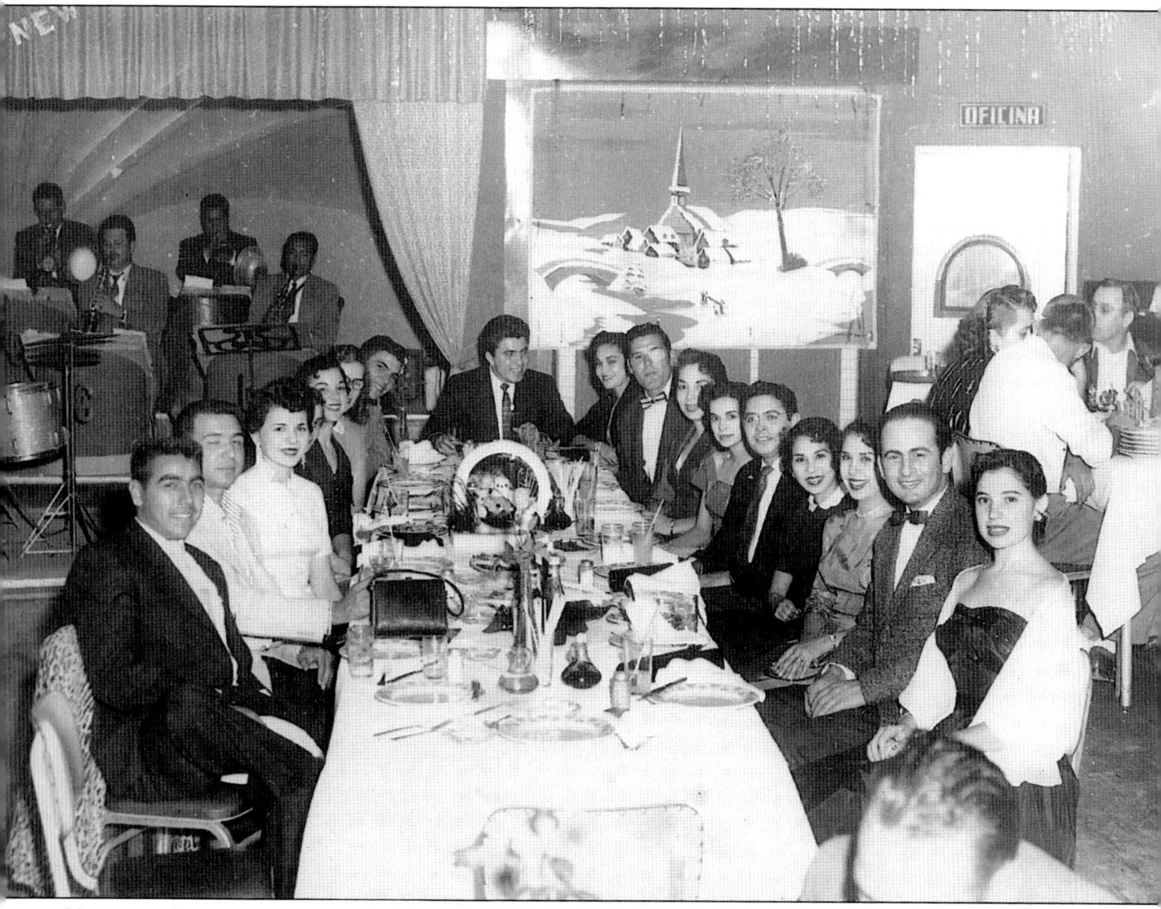

Hispanic-American young adults created the Allegro Club to encourage *amistad* (friendship) with other social organizations and to provide representation for the Hispanic community. Here the Allegro Club gathers for a formal dinner.

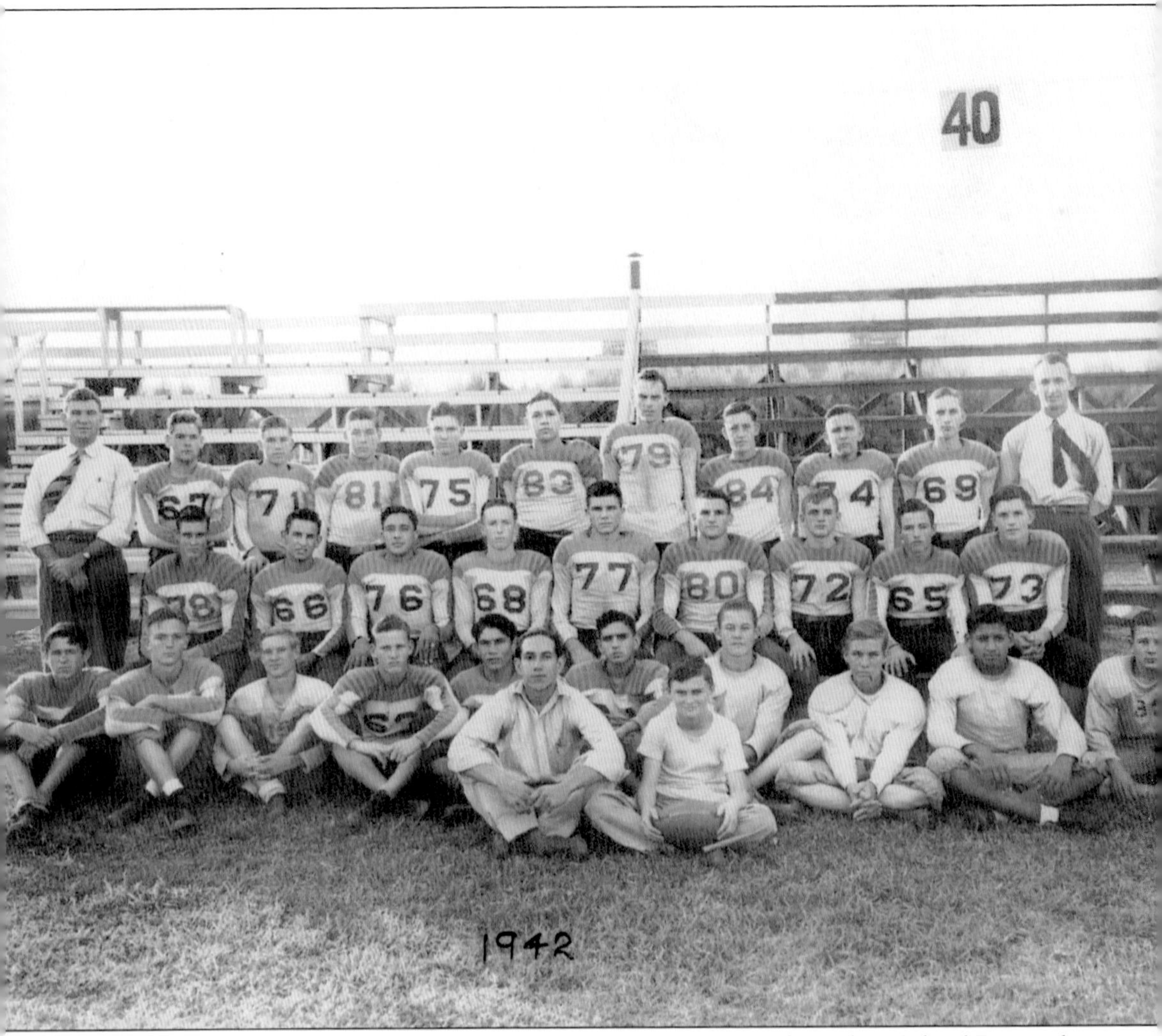

This is a team photo of the 1942 Donna Redskins. The Donna Independent School District has always had a reputation for excellent sportsmanship, particularly in football. Their tradition of football talent led to a state championship in 1961. The Donna Redskins still have a Valley-wide following of loyal fans.

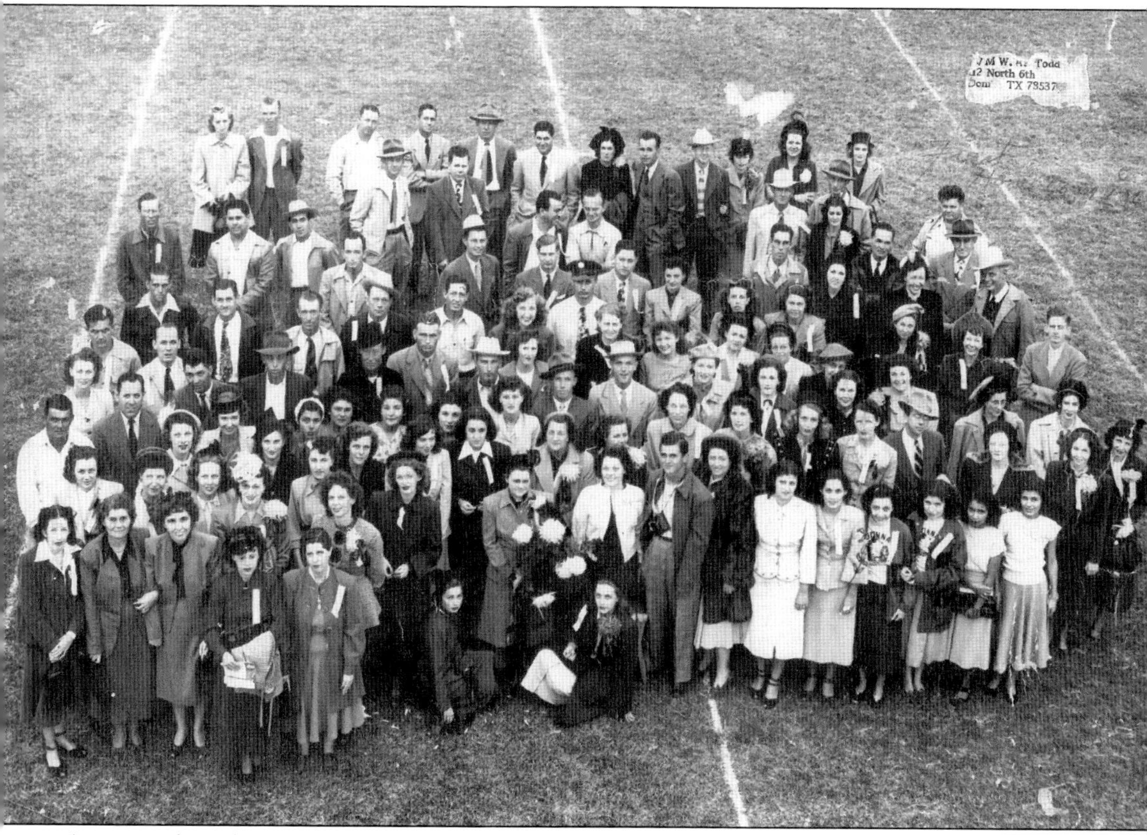

A senior class photo taken in the early 1940s shows the student body and faculty supporting their team. Students are wearing ribbons and corsages for the first homecoming celebration in Donna. Note the various hat styles worn by students.

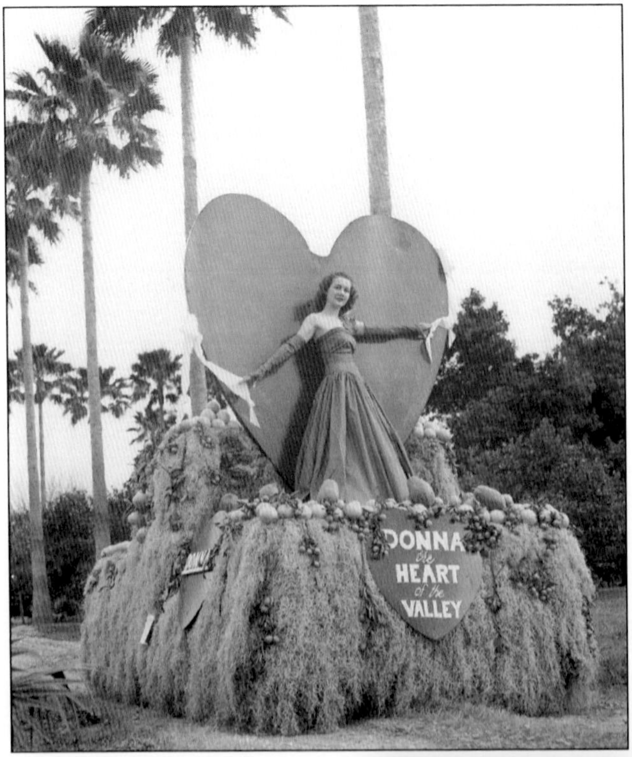

Betty Blackburn, wearing a green taffeta gown, represented Donna as the 1946 Duchess of Papaya at the Citrus Fiesta parade held in Mission.

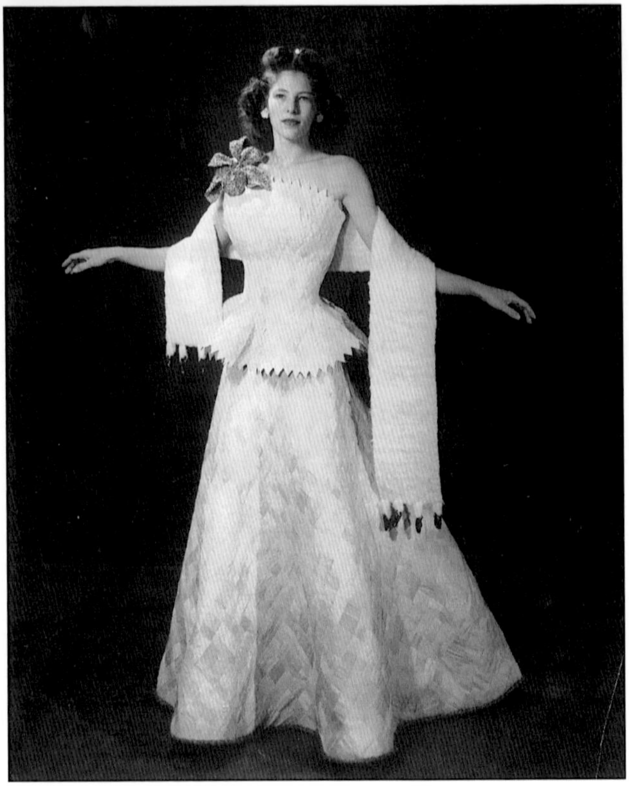

Joann Muckleroy of Donna wore a dress made of dried onionskins to compete in the Citrus Fiesta of 1944–1946.

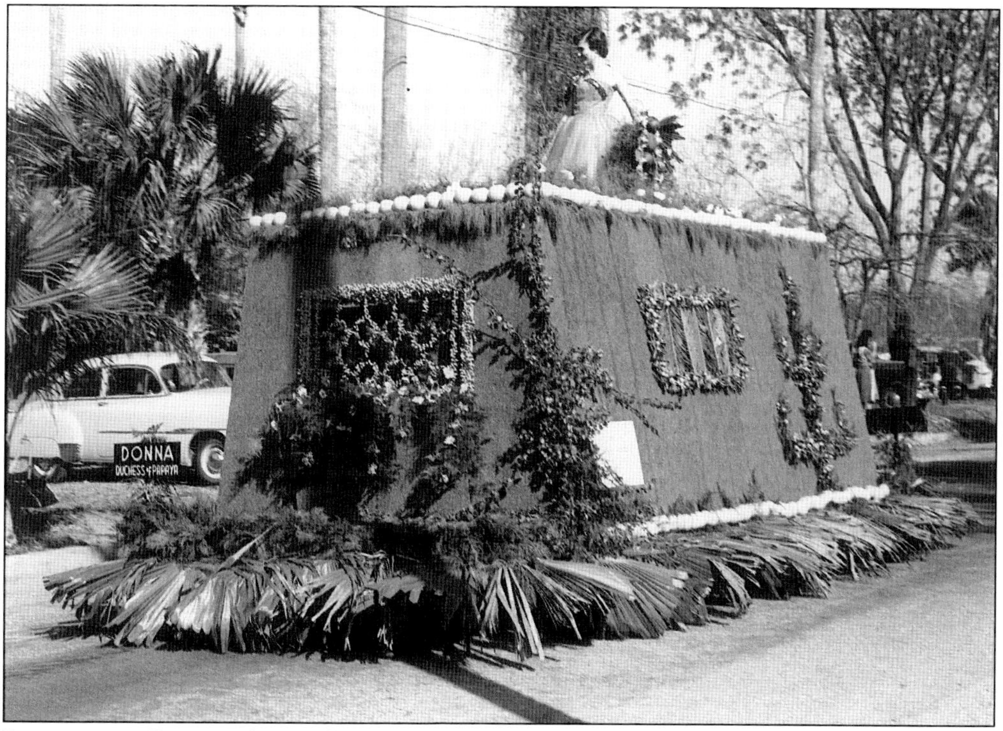

Representing Donna, the Duchess of Papaya rode on a float of raw materials in the Citrus Fiesta parade, c.1950.

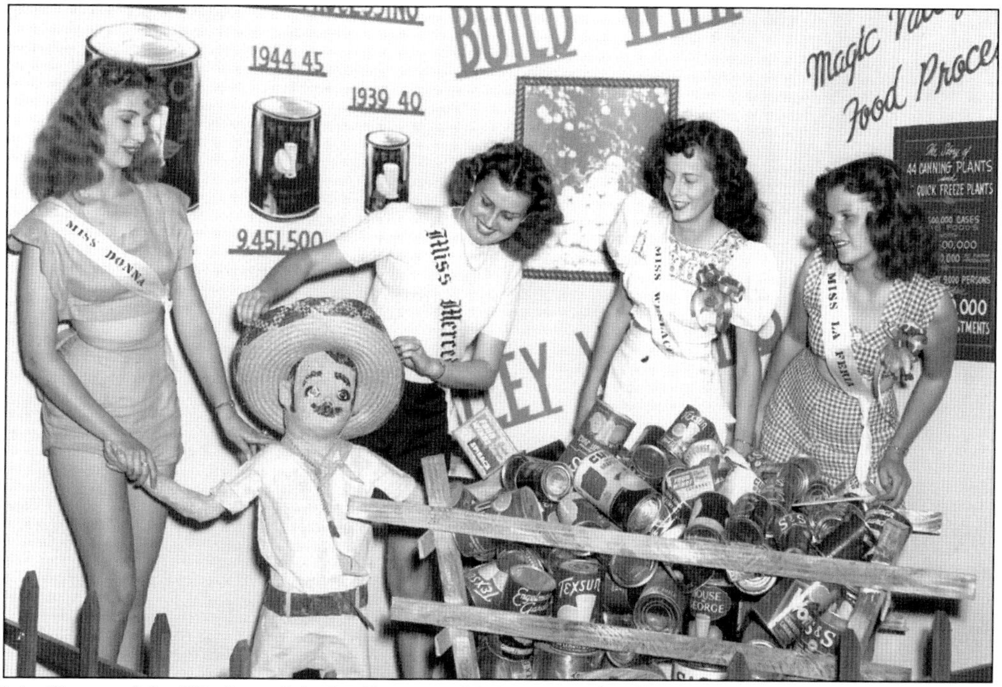

Ms. Donna, Ms. Weslaco, Ms. La Feria, and Ms. Mercedes (left to right) posed for a publicity photo advertising a canning and food processing plant located in the Valley.

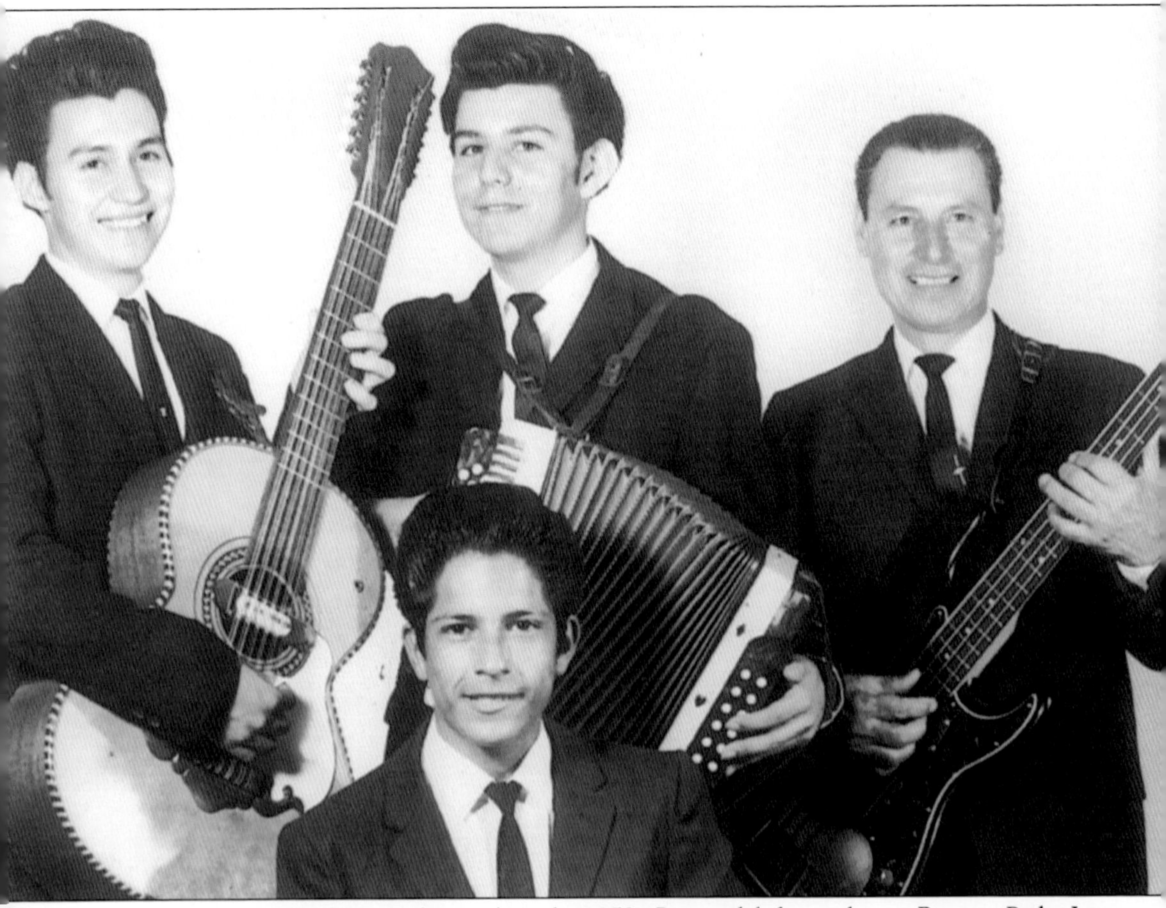

This publicity photo shows Pedro Ayala in the 1950s. Pictured, left to right, are Ramon, Pedro Jr., Pedro Sr., and Emilio, seated. Pedro Ayala Sr. was a well-known musician and accordionist throughout the Rio Grande Valley. With his sons, who accompanied him on their instruments, Mr. Ayala eventually established a nationally known *conjunto* band and an honored career. Mr. Ayala was recognized by various folk arts programs, the National Endowment for the Arts, and President Ronald Reagan, as a master traditional artist who has contributed to shaping the cultural diversity of the U.S. (Courtesy of Mrs. Pedro Ayala.)

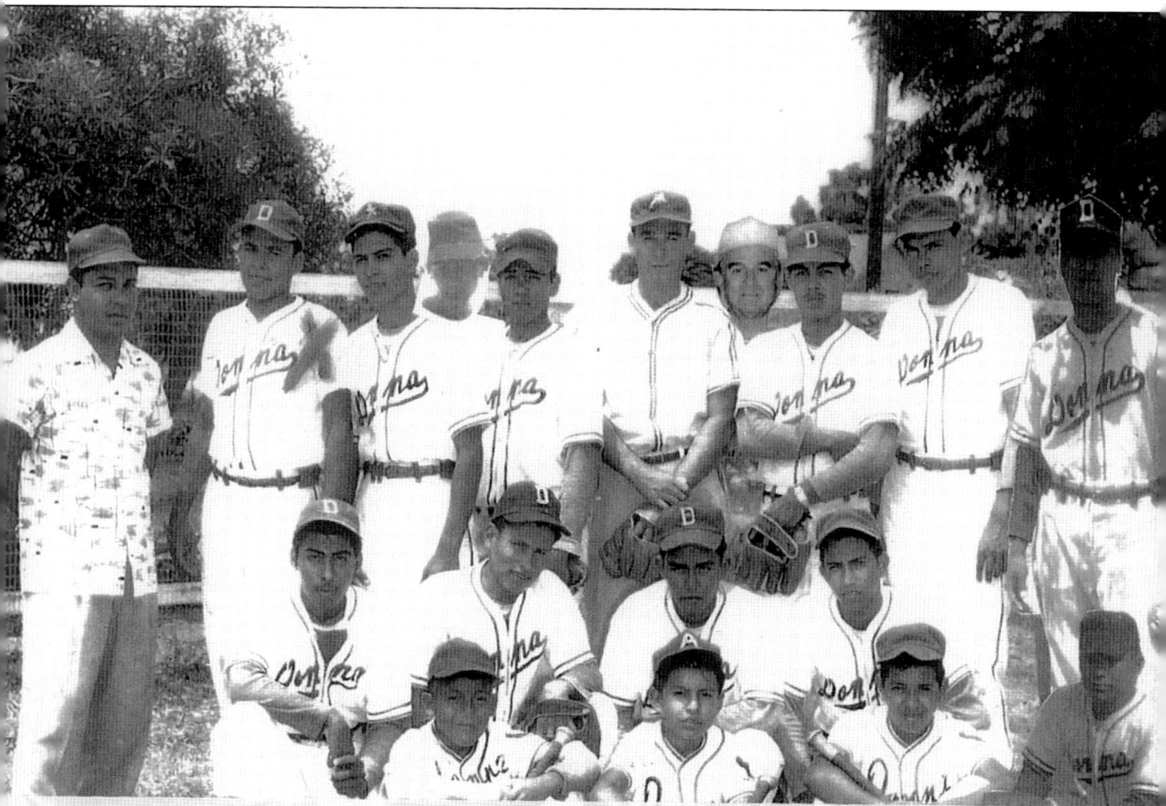

Above,Left to Right(standing)Felix Arriaga,Joaquin Guerrero,Gilberto Rocha,Gonzalo Espinoza,Jose Urrea,Valentin Guerrero,Ricardo Escobar,Lorenzo Salinas,Jose Cruz and Arturo Rodriguez

Kneeling,Left to Right Jose Gomez,Jose Ramirez,Gilberto Zamora, Ramon Rodriguez and Pete Lerma

Sitting(with bats) Ramon Guerrero,Samuel Guerrero and Santos Guerrero

Not in Picture Florencio Arriaga,Manuel Balli,Amador Guerrero, Felix Huerta and Jose Valdez

This is a team photo for the Donna Cardinals Baseball League. During the 1950s, baseball was a very popular pastime in the mid-Valley. Most towns had a team and competed against one another on Sundays. The Donna Cardinals were a favorite of fans Valley-wide. Team members first wore red and white shirts and khaki pants, while they raised money to get official team uniforms. When they won their first game, the team donated half the funds to the St. Joseph Catholic Church. (Courtesy of Pete Lerma and Arturo Rodriguez.)

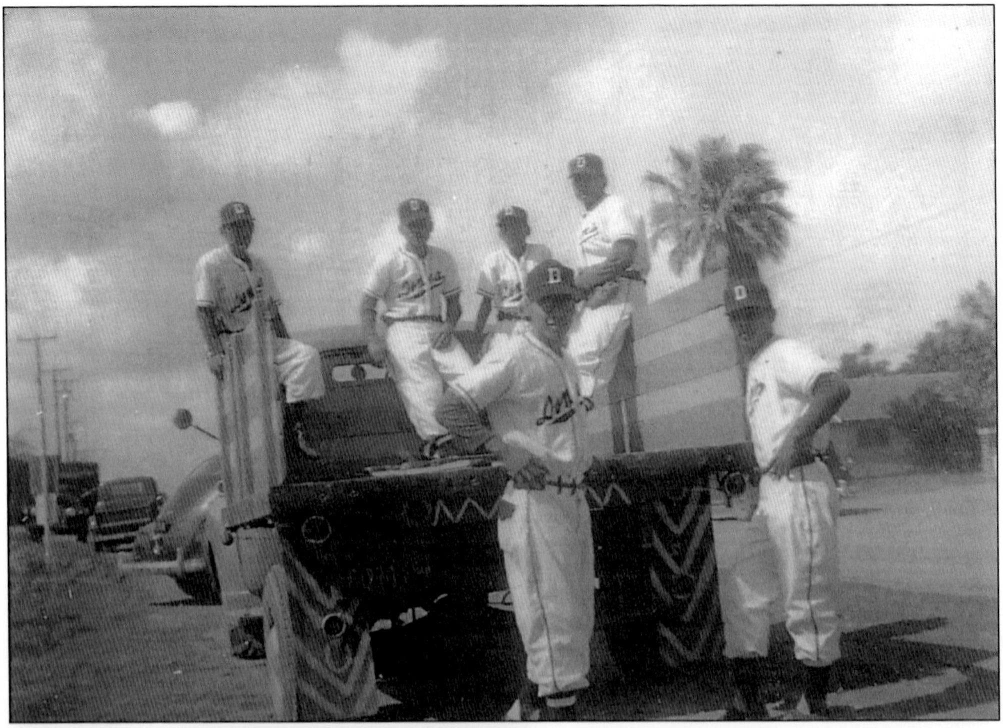

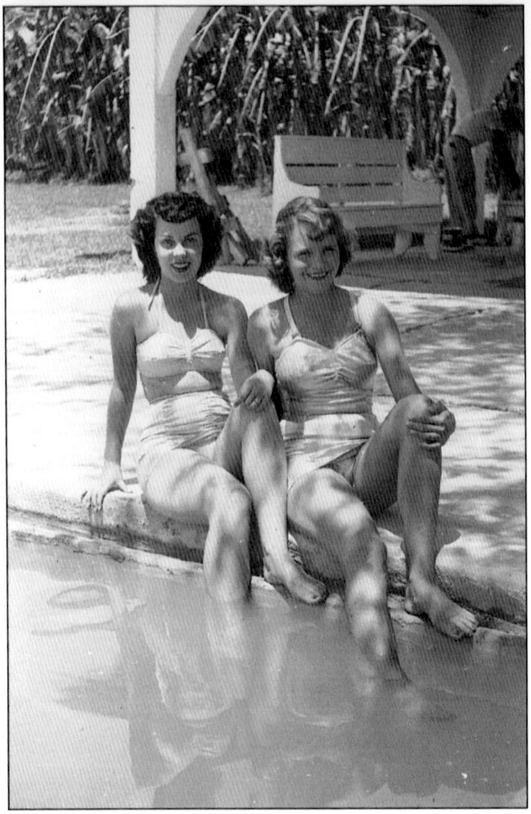

The Donna Cardinal Baseball League team members geared up to travel to an out-of-town game. They traveled in a truck owned by Mr. Marcial Gomez, an avid baseball fan and father of Jose Gomez, one of the Cardinal pitchers. (Courtesy of Pete Lerma and Arturo Rodriguez.)

These young ladies are enjoying tropical mid-Valley weather. At poolside are Pat Arrington (left) and Martha Ledbetter (right).

O'nice Johnson, a contestant for the Whitewing Fiesta Beauty Contest held in Edinburg in 1951, was sponsored by the Donna Chamber of Commerce. This is a contestant publicity photo.

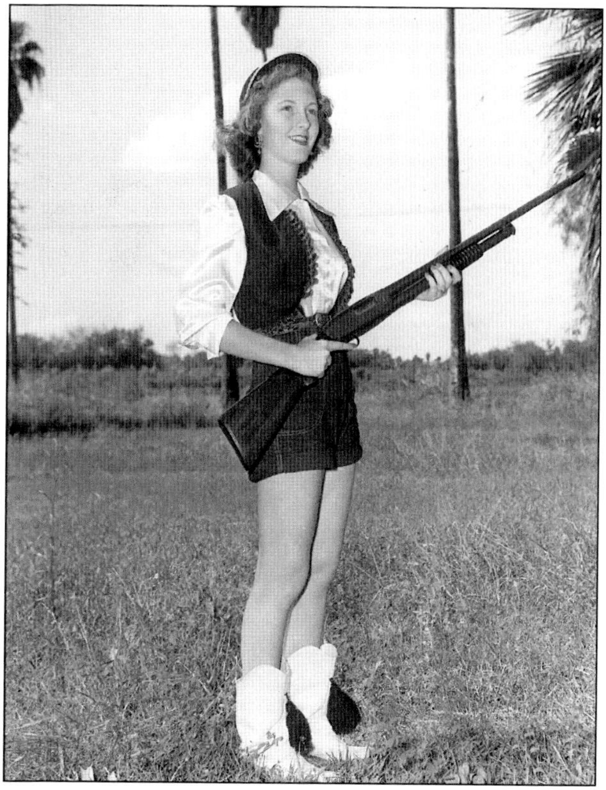

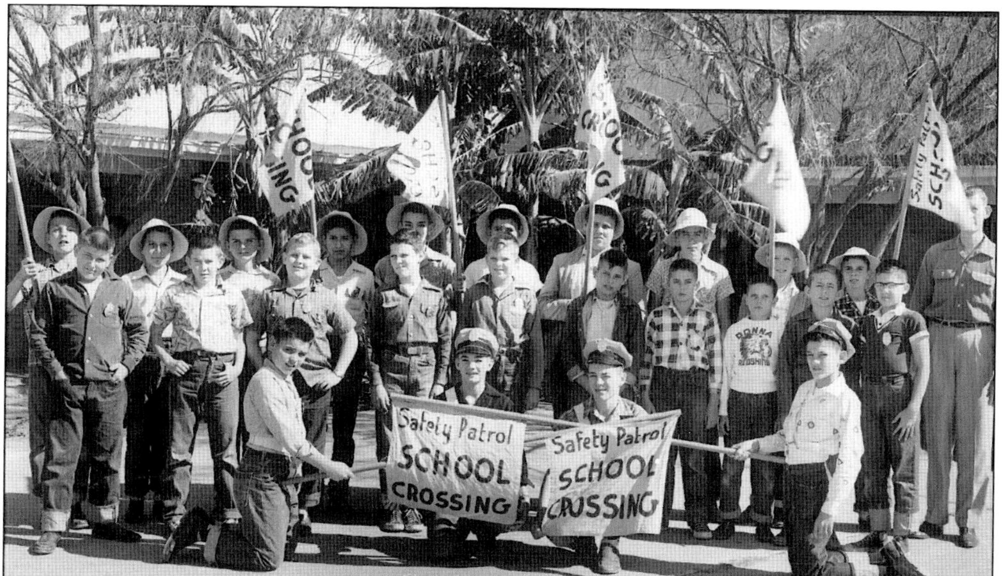

Students pose to show responsibility as Safety Patrol Crossing Guards for Donna Elementary School during the 1950s.

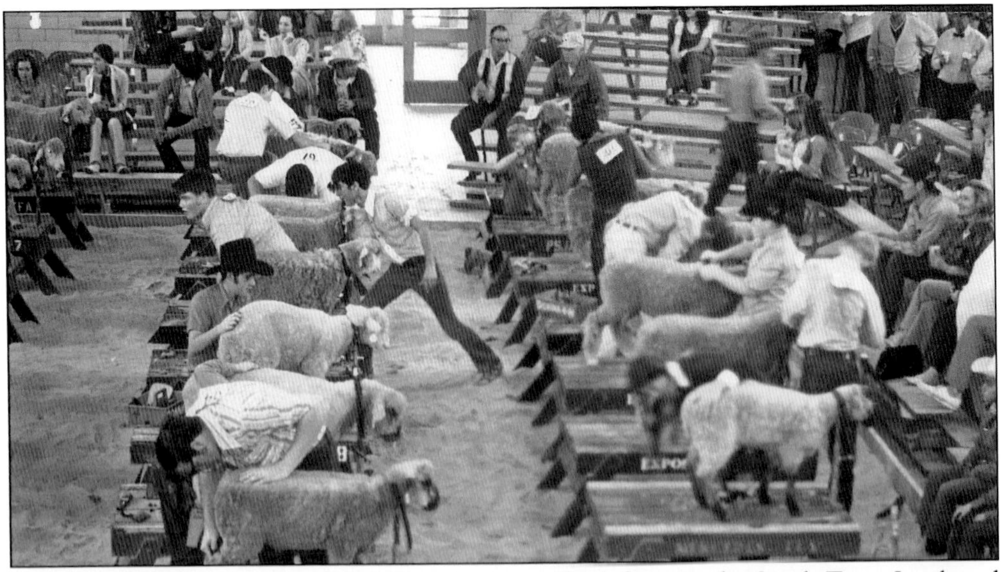

In this bird's eye view, students are preparing sheep for judging at the South Texas Lamb and Sheep Exposition, held in Donna. In 1951, James Carlton McQueen, a 4-H Club leader, founded the Exposition with the Donna Chamber of Commerce. For eight of the first nine years, the Exposition was held in the Donna City Park. In 1961, thanks to a group of citizens who had incorporated to buy land, the Exposition took place on its own grounds, used in conjunction with the National Guard Armory building. The Exposition grew from a one-day to a four-day event, an annual tradition through 1993. (Courtesy of James Carlton McQueen Jr.)

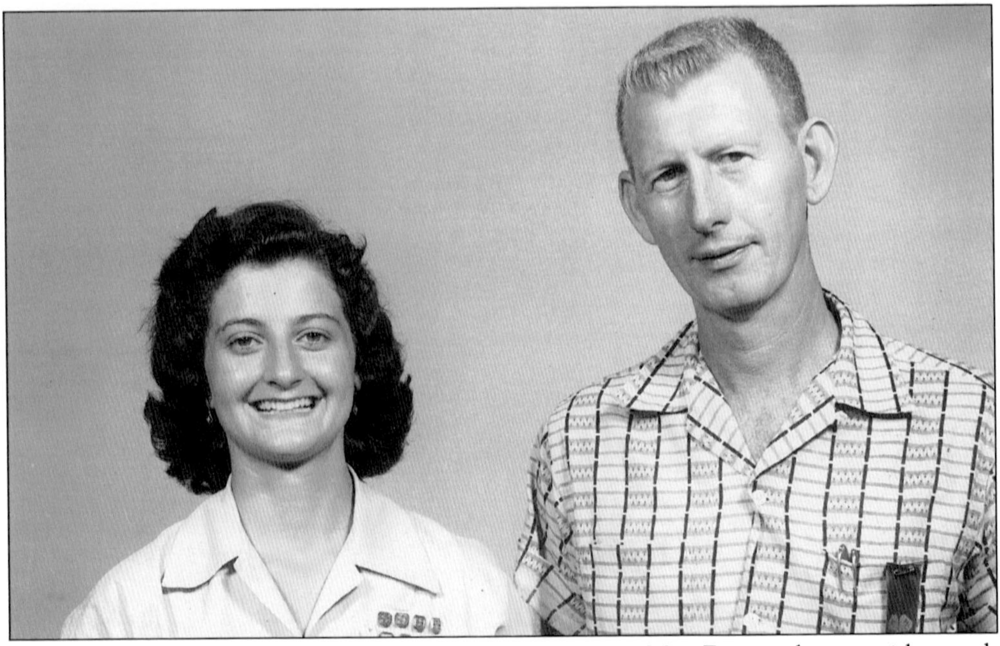

The 1959 State Public Speaking contest winner was Ms. Ennis, shown with coach James Carlton McQueen Sr. Mr. McQueen served as a coach and sponsor for many students involved in community and sports efforts, and is a legendary community servant. (Courtesy of James Carlton McQueen Jr.)

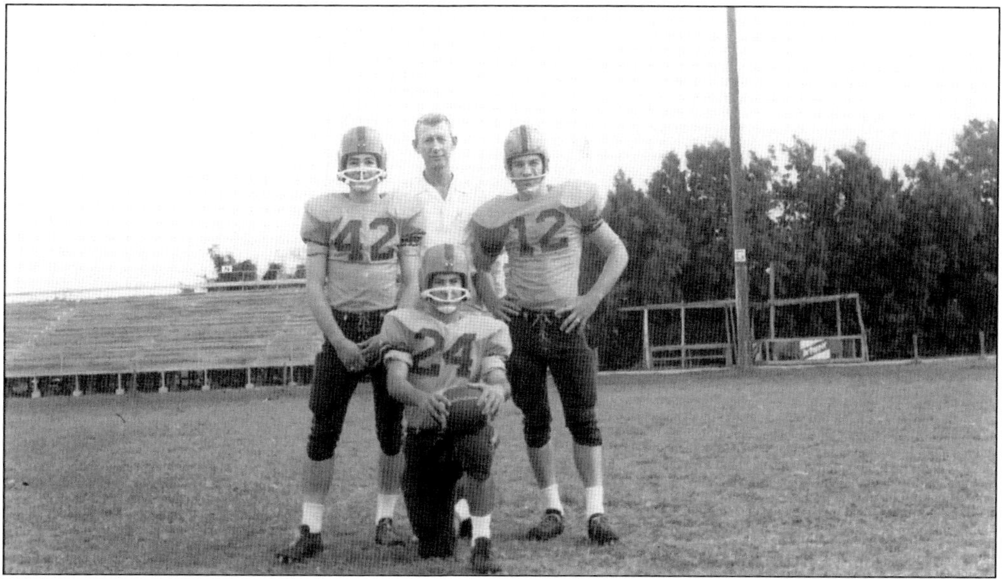

The Most Valuable Players of the Donna Redskins are shown here with coach Carlton McQueen Sr. in 1959. (Courtesy of James Carlton McQueen Jr.)

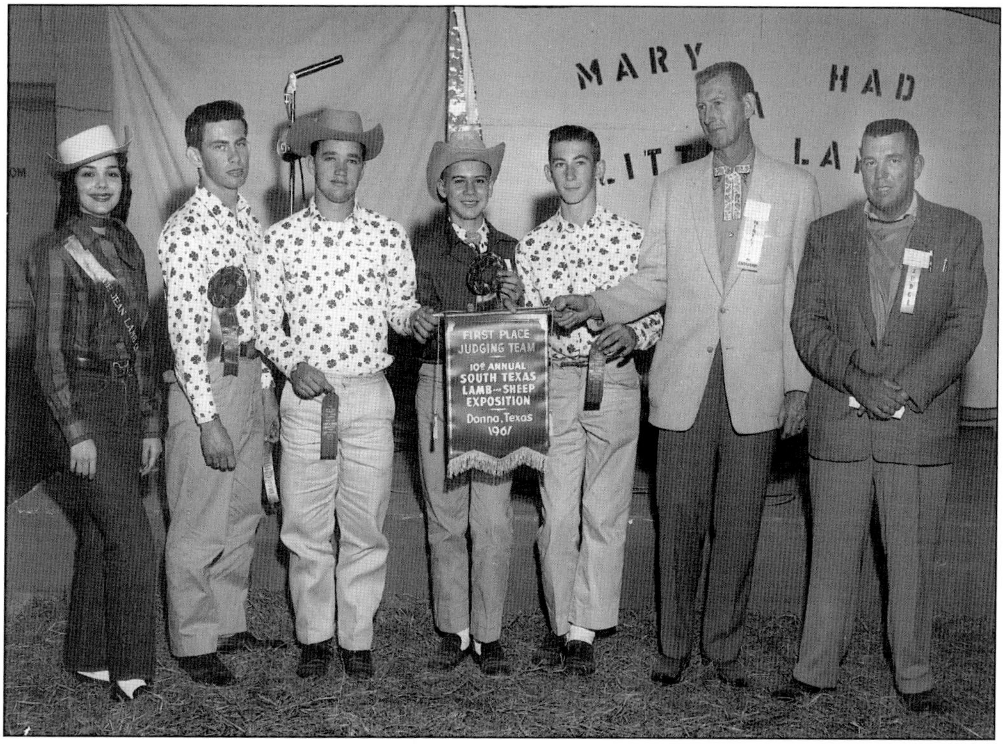

The 10th Annual South Texas Lamb and Sheep Exposition (1961) opened with the Blue Jean Lamb Queen contest on Thursday evening. The 25 contestants, wearing western shirts, blue jeans, and big smiles, competed for the title. Shown here are 4-H students, the 1961 Blue Jean Lamb Queen (far left), 4-H students, director James Carlton McQueen Sr., (second from right), and an area judge (far right). (Courtesy of James Carlton McQueen Jr.)

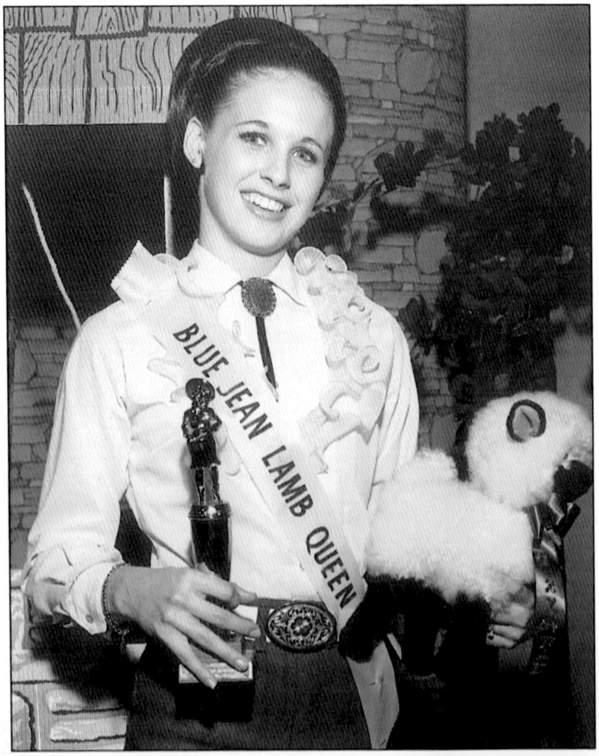

Pictured is Karen Sanders of Donna, who was crowned 1966 Blue Jean Queen at the South Texas Lamb and Sheep Exposition. (Courtesy of James Carlton McQueen Sr.)

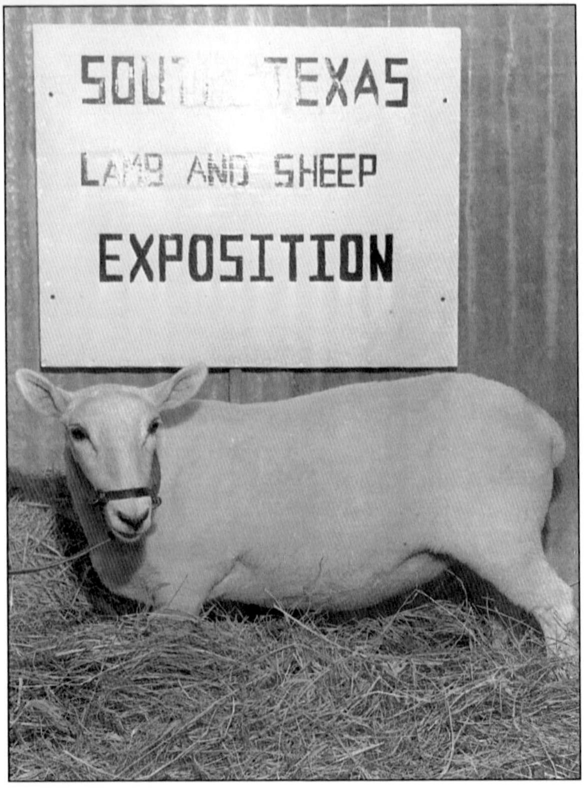

This image of a champion ewe shows how the South Texas Lamb and Sheep Exposition offered youth an excellent opportunity to raise fine quality lambs and sheep and provided a place to auction them off. (Courtesy of James Carlton McQueen Jr.)

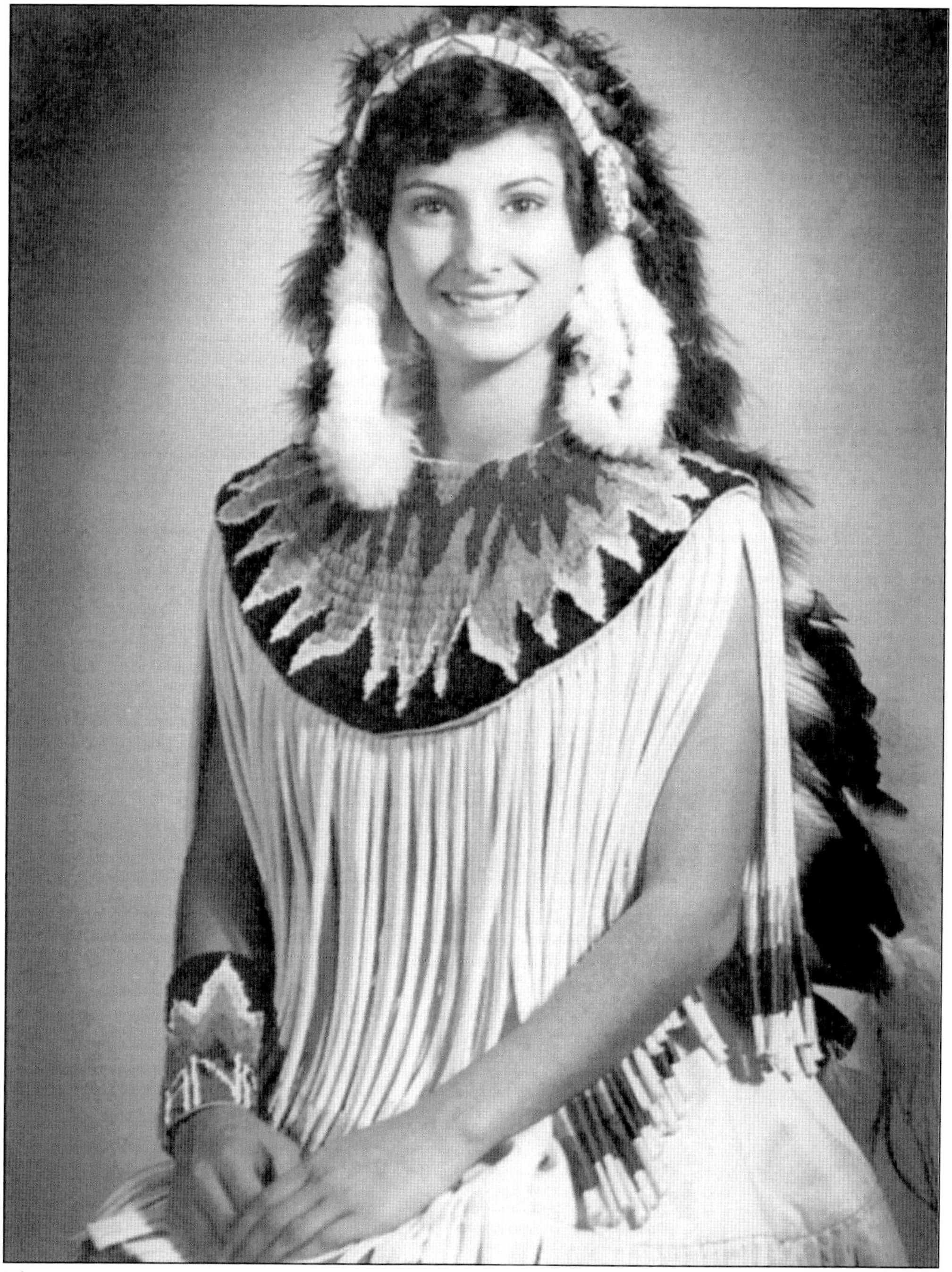

This portrait presents Ana Teresa Adame, crowned as the Indian Sweetheart of Donna for the 1974–1975 season. The tradition of Indian Sweetheart began as a fundraiser in 1934. Each class of junior students would nominate a candidate to raise pennies, and the candidate with the most pennies was then named Indian Sweetheart. The headdress was introduced in 1945. Today, the Indian Sweetheart is elected in a campaign process that takes up to six months. Design of the costume is kept secret until the coronation. The Indian Sweetheart is introduced during the annual homecoming game. (Courtesy of Eva Adame.)

TEXAS STATE CHAMPIONS

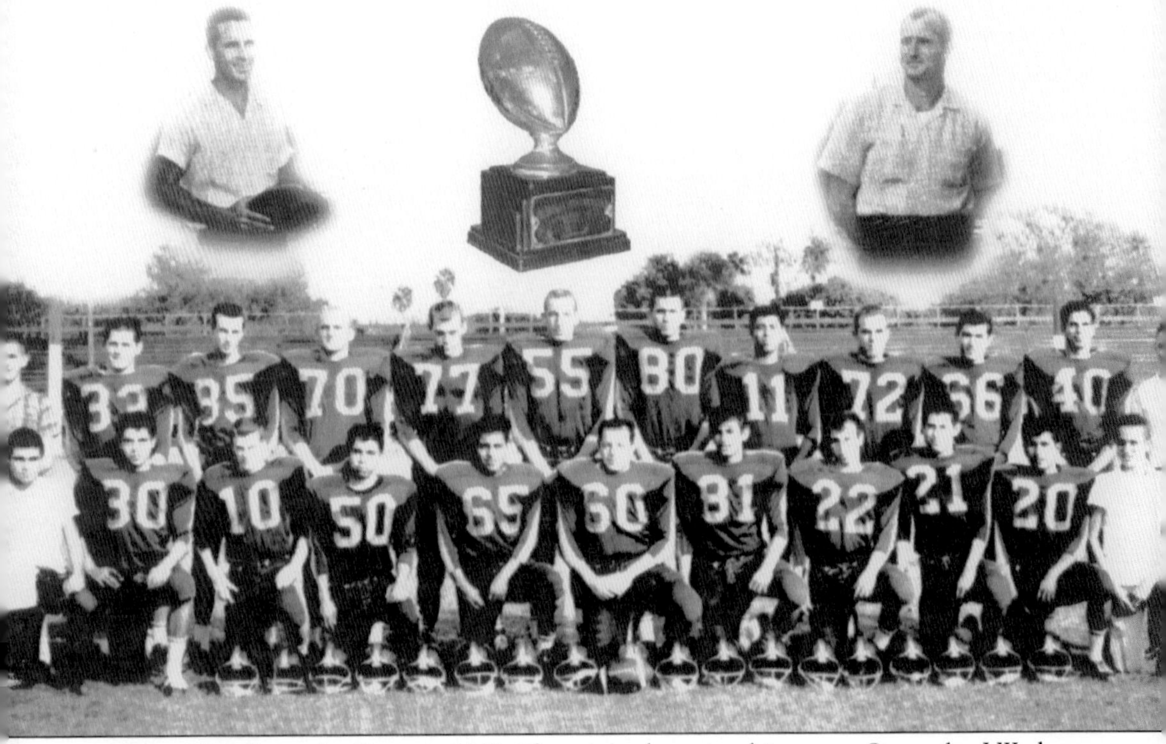

This is the photo for Donna's 1961 Class AA championship team. Since the UIL began sanctioning football titles in 1920, no other Rio Grande Valley football team has earned a state crown.